Disability, Medicine, and Healing Discourse in Early Christianity

Using contemporary theories drawn from health humanities, this volume analyses the nature and effects of disability, medicine, and health discourse in a variety of early Christian literature.

In recent years, the "medical turn" in early Christian studies has developed a robust literature around health, disability, and medicine, and the health humanities have made critical interventions in modern conversations around the aims of health and the nature of healthcare. Considering these developments, it has become clear that early Christian texts and ideas have much to offer modern conversations, and that these texts are illuminated using theoretical lenses drawn from modern medicine and public health. The chapters in this book explore different facets of early Christian engagement with medicine, either in itself or as metaphor and material for theological reflections on human impairment, restoration, and flourishing. Through its focus on late antique religious texts, the book raises questions around the social, rather than biological, aspects of illness and diminishment as a human experience, as well as the strategies by which that experience is navigated. The result is an innovative and timely intervention in the study of health and healthcare that bridges current divides between historical studies and contemporary issues.

Taken together, the book offers a prismatic conversation of perspectives on aspects of care at the heart of societal and individual "wellness" today, inviting readers to meet or revisit patristic texts as tracings across a map of embodied identity, dissonance, and corporal care. It is a fascinating resource for anyone working on ancient medicine and health, or the social worlds of early Christianity.

Susan R. Holman is John R. Eckrich Chair and Professor of Religion and the Healing Arts at Valparaiso University. Her publications include eight academic monographs, among them *Beholden: Religion, Global Health, and Human Rights* (Oxford 2015), recipient of the 2016 Grawemeyer Award in Religion.

Chris L. de Wet is Professor of New Testament and Early Christian Studies at the University of South Africa, Pretoria. His books include *Preaching Bondage: John Chrysostom and the Discourse of Slavery in Early Christianity* (2015) and *The Unbound God: Slavery and the Formation of Early Christian Thought* (2018).

Jonathan L. Zecher is Senior Research Fellow at the Australian Catholic University and Co-Director of ReMeDHe, an international working group for Religion, Medicine, Disability, and Health in Late Antiquity. His second book, *Spiritual Direction as a Medical Art in Early Christian Monasticism* (Oxford), was published in 2022.

Religion, Medicine and Health in Late Antiquity
Series editors: Mira Balberg, Andrew Crislip, Heidi Marx,
Georgia Petridou, Kristi Upson-Saia, and Jonathan Zecher

This series explores the intersections and interactions of religion, medicine, and health in late antiquity. Our aim is to give attention to the diversity of healing traditions in the late antique Mediterranean, including healing in its complex religious landscape (Greco-Roman religions, early Christianity, and Rabbinic Judaism) and the religious features of professional medicine. We welcome novel theoretical and methodological approaches that engage late ancient ideas, discourses, practices, and material remains. We invite monographs and edited collections, as well as critical editions and translations of medical and religious primary sources. This series aims to advance scholarship on religion, medicine, and health in late antiquity, while providing resources to support health humanities pedagogy and reshape contemporary conversations around health, healthcare, and disability.

For more information or to discuss a potential contribution to the series, please contact Jonathan Zecher (jonathan.zecher@acu.edu.au).

Disability, Medicine, and Healing Discourse in Early Christianity
New Conversations for Health Humanities
Edited by Susan R. Holman, Chris L. de Wet, and Jonathan L. Zecher

Disability, Medicine, and Healing Discourse in Early Christianity

New Conversations for Health Humanities

Edited by Susan R. Holman, Chris L. de Wet, Jonathan L. Zecher

First published 2024
by Routledge
4 Park Square, Milton Park, Abingdon, Oxon OX14 4RN

and by Routledge
605 Third Avenue, New York, NY 10158

Routledge is an imprint of the Taylor & Francis Group, an informa business

British Library Cataloguing-in-Publication Data
A catalogue record for this book is available from the British Library

ISBN: 978-0-367-52100-4 (hbk)
ISBN: 978-0-367-53118-8 (pbk)
ISBN: 978-1-003-08053-4 (ebk)

DOI: 10.4324/9781003080534

Typeset in Times New Roman
by Apex CoVantage, LLC

Contents

Contributors

Adam Booth is Assistant Professor of Religious Studies and Theology at Stonehill College. In 2021, he graduated with PhD from Duke University, with a dissertation entitled "Mother Jesus: The Contribution of Maternal Imagery to the Christology and Soteriology of First Peter."

Chris L. de Wet is Professor of New Testament and Early Christian Studies at the University of South Africa, Pretoria. His books include *Preaching Bondage: John Chrysostom and the Discourse of Slavery in Early Christianity* (2015) and *The Unbound God: Slavery and the Formation of Early Christian Thought* (2018).

Paul Dilley is Associate Professor of Ancient Mediterranean Religions in the Departments of Classics and Religious Studies at the University of Iowa, and the author of *Monasteries and the Care of Souls in Late Antique Christianity: Cognition and Discipline* (Cambridge, 2017).

Elisa Groff is Postdoctoral Research Assistant, Institute of the History, Philosophy and Ethics of Medicine, University of Ulm (Germany). She is also Hertha Nathorff Fellow 2023 for outstanding women in science, medical faculty, University of Ulm. Her current project is titled "The Ethics of Fetal Autopsy and Its Impact on Reproductive Medicine."

Susan R. Holman is the John R. Eckrich Chair and Professor of Religion and the Healing Arts at Valparaiso University. Her publications include eight academic monographs, among them *Beholden: Religion, Global Health, and Human Rights* (Oxford 2015), recipient of the 2016 Grawemeyer Award in Religion.

Brenda Llewellyn Ihssen teaches early and medieval Christian history at Pacific Lutheran University. Her research is focused on social ethics in late antique/early Byzantine texts era, and she has authored *John Moschos' Spiritual Meadow: Authority and Autonomy at the End of the Antique World* (2014).

Helen Rhee is Professor of Church History at Westmont College, USA. Her publications include *Illness, Pain, and Health Care in Early Christianity* (Eerdmans), *Loving the Poor, Saving the Rich: Wealth, Poverty, and Early Christian Formation* (Baker Academic), and *Early Christian Literature* (Routledge).

Anna Rebecca Solevåg is Professor of New Testament Studies at VID Specialized University. In her research she studies migration, gender, class, dis/ability, and ethnicity in early Christian texts, exploring the complexities of identity and negotiations of power taking place at these crossroads.

Jonathan L. Zecher is Senior Research Fellow at the Australian Catholic University and Co-director of ReMeDHe, an international working group for Religion, Medicine, Disability, and Health in Late Antiquity. His second book *Spiritual Direction as a Medical Art in Early Christian Monasticism* (Oxford) was published in 2022.

1 Introduction

Discourses of Health between Late Antiquity and Postmodernity

In the past decade, we have seen a significant upsurge in studies that engage with medical discourse in early Christian thought—indeed, a "medical turn" in early Christian studies. One of the most important contributions to this research is its call for a new paradigm for understanding disability, medicine, and healthcare, both in antiquity and today. This new paradigm would be one based on the complex, culturally embedded nature of illness and health rather than one reduced to the biomedical model alone.[1] Such a paradigm requires a creative and multidisciplinary approach, as is amply demonstrated by the sociality of epidemics.[2] This need should have been apparent in the early 1980s, with the first outbreak and rapid spread of the HIV and AIDS epidemic. Sadly, as time passed, HIV and AIDS came to be seen as a problem of those considered to be on the fringes of the "developed" world. On the one hand, HIV and AIDS was associated with sex workers, men who have sex with men, persons struggling with substance abuse who inject drugs, and, on the other hand, the epidemic was framed as a problem of the "developing" world, for example, an "African problem" (especially in sub-Saharan Africa). According to the UNAIDS Global HIV & AIDS Statistics Fact Sheet, 37.7 million (30.2 million–45.1 million) people around the world were living with HIV in 2020, with an average of 1.5 million new infections in that year. Since the start of the epidemic, 36.3 million (27.2 million–47.8 million) people have passed away from AIDS-related illnesses.[3] Unfortunately, it was only in the aftermath of the devastating COVID-19 pandemic that the need for a multidisciplinary approach to medicine, healthcare, and disability was more broadly recognized. COVID-19 was (and remains), indeed, a biomedical problem, but very soon the political–economic, sociocultural, and moral–religious aspects of the pandemic, and its management, became apparent. Pandemics like HIV and AIDS and COVID-19 lay bare the need for studies of disease and healthcare that go beyond biomedicine to embrace social, scientific, historical, literary, and other humanistic disciplines. But that need outlasts pandemics, and the "medical turn" in early Christianity is informed by both multidisciplinary approaches and the questions they raise and offers insights that complicate and energize those same approaches to contemporary health and healthcare.

In order to illustrate the point about this multidisciplinary approach, let us briefly turn to an example from studies on the nature, experience, and management of pain. It is widely recognized that one of the major challenges in understanding

DOI: 10.4324/9781003080534-1

and approaching pain is verbalizing and localizing it. The elusive and mysterious materiality of pain has given rise to a plethora of biological, psychological, psychosomatic, and sociocultural approaches being utilized to give it some type of form and legitimacy. The 2020 *The Oxford Handbook of the Neurobiology of Pain* introduces its collection of chapters with a history of pain research that takes into consideration the complexity of experiences and narratives of pain, including pain in ancient historical and religious contexts.[4] In a highly influential article on the history of pain, in *Nature Reviews: Neuroscience*, Edward Perl states:

> With the benefit of the past two centuries of scientific work and thought, can one define pain? Considering the evidence, it seems reasonable to propose pain to be both a specific sensation and an emotion, initiated by activity in particular peripheral and central neurons. Pain shares features with other sensations, but the strong association with disposition is special. The mechanisms of pain include specialized receptive organs, selective and convergent pathways, plasticity of responsiveness and interactive modulation. No single theory (emotion, specific, intensive, pattern or gate) fits the present evidence by itself, although a combination of ideas answers most issues. Reason suggests an integration of features is the best choice for a working hypothesis.[5]

The fact that pain is both a "specific sensation and an emotion" opens up numerous possibilities for interdisciplinary research on the topic. In its first issue of 2022, the *Journal of Early Christian History* published a collection of articles on "Contextualising Pain and Remedy in Early Judaism and Christianity" that attempt to answer certain aspects of Perl's call above for an integrative "combination of ideas."[6] This special issue aims to examine the question of pain and its management or remedy in various ancient Christian and Jewish contexts, but with a keen interest in bringing these ancient contexts into dialogue with modern issues of pain. When turning to perennial puzzles like pain, it has become clear over the last decade that theories and approaches from both anthropology and the sociology of medicine can be fruitfully applied to understanding ancient medicine and participatory connections from within the histories of religion and culture.[7]

This integrative approach, bringing antiquity into conversation with modernity, is also what characterizes the essays in this volume and the conversations that brought them together. The volume began in two sessions at the Eighteenth International Conference on Patristic Studies, held at Oxford University, 19–23 August 2019. The sessions were organized by ReMeDHe, an international working group dedicated to "Religion, Medicine, Disability, and Health in Late Antiquity."[8] Since 2013, ReMeDHe has gathered, supported, and cultivated scholars interested in these topics; its conference panels, symposia, and emerging publications have reshaped the authors' and editors' understanding of early Christian participation in the discourses and institutions of medicine and health. While ReMeDHe's scholarly focus is on late antiquity, most scholars within the ReMeDHe community also share an interest in connecting ancient healthcare issues with a multidisciplinary approach that is also mindful of modern issues and controversies.

Considered as a whole, the essays here offer soundings and entry points for much-needed conversation between early Christian studies and health humanities. In one way or another, each essay wrestles with questions, assumptions, and interests that transcend the ancient context.

The various parts of the volume further demonstrate the interaction, in ancient and modern contexts of healthcare, between individuals (bodies–patients– "performers" of health) and communities (their making, delimitation, and preservation). At the heart of the book, then, lies the *social relationality* of discourses and practices related to disability, medicine, and health—ancient and modern.

The contributions are divided into three parts, although readers will notice overlapping themes and interests, and the divisions themselves are, we realize, inevitably somewhat artificial.

Essays in Part One explore how experiences of othering and isolation can be reframed as signs of belonging. We now know that the supposed boundaries between philosophy, medicine, and religion in antiquity were more porous than modern medicalized compartmentalization and specialization would suggest, and, in some cases, were erased entirely.[9] The same is true of the boundary between what we think of as "medical science" versus "miracles," "magic," and "folk cures."[10] A special issue of *Studies in Late Antiquity* in 2018 on "Rethinking Medical Metaphors in Late Ancient Christianity," highlighted the pervasiveness and amplitude of medical metaphors in late ancient Christian discourse, along with the numerous opportunities for further research and engagement with the medical humanities.[11] It is no longer possible to explain away medical language and imagery in early Christian texts as "merely" metaphorical. Rather, these metaphors are grounded in shared cultural forms of knowledge production and bodily intervention, while their application in Christian texts serves to shape as well as express theological discourse.

Applying these ideas to one case, in Chapter 2, Anna Rebecca Solevåg explores Ignatius of Antioch's use of medical language and metaphors, showing that his theology of Christ's salvific work and the constitution of a eucharistic community are informed by Hippocratic and temple medicine alike. This, together with a frame from Disability Studies, grounds her further argument that Ignatius identifies himself as an aborted and elsewhere disabled body, as a way to construct a new community in which the stigma of disability is subverted and made the means of participating in Christ's salvific healing. Solevåg shows how Christian bodily performance, especially in the dangerous presence of "heresy," is informed and, indeed, fashioned through the discourse of disability. Her study exposes an important paradox—the disabled body (in this case, the body deaf and mute to heresy) is also a healthy body, since the real disease is, for Ignatius, heresy. By providing "positive value to non-normative bodies," the status of Christ as the divine physician is further enhanced. Thus, rather than imposing a simplistic dichotomy onto bodies disabled or healthy, Solevåg shows that such categories are not always easy to delineate and isolate.

In Chapter 3, Adam Booth examines the motivation to circumcision among converts to Judaism in the Second Temple period, as well as emphasis on circumcision among some followers of Jesus. Booth creatively applies sociological analyses of hazing rituals in contemporary American society to parse the reasons why someone would undergo a painful and irreversible bodily modification in antiquity for male bodies. Circumcision functions as shared—and repeated—trauma as well as a visible and, therefore, undeniable, mark of common identity. Booth's essay also raises questions as to the relationship between the personal and social costs of a medical (and religious) procedure and the importance of belonging to a particular social group. In this regard, we see how high-cost medical–religious procedures might serve to strengthen, on the one hand, self-worth and group solidarity and, on the other hand, "weed out," so to speak, individuals who were not willing to make the required (bodily) sacrifices to be part of a community.

In Chapter 4, Helen Rhee engages with Elaine Scarry's classic study on pain and its profound claims about the incommunicability and destructive power of pain. While agreeing with Scarry that pain is an absolutely subjective experience, Rhee shows how Augustine fostered empathy and compassion in his audiences, allowing pain to circulate, and individuals to share in its experience. Another important aspect of Rhee's analysis is its contextualization of pain within the history of emotions. This is in line with Perl's observation we have seen earlier. Pain is much more than a neurobiological phenomenon; it is exactly this social relationality of pain (even more so in the context of individuals experiencing chronic pain), which Rhee's essay also underscores, that functions in the formation of a patient's self-worth and confirmation of the legitimacy of their suffering.

Together, these essays in Part One depict bodies formed and reformed through mechanisms that inscribe on them marks of othering and belonging. At each turn, however, Christian theologians use those mechanisms in different and sometimes unexpected ways.

Part Two turns our attention to the physicians and preachers who sought to define the range, meaning, and value of illness and health for others. In Chapter 5, Elisa Groff analyses Aëtius of Amida, one of the great medical writers of late antiquity, and his often-surprising approach to infertility and sterility. Groff shows that Aëtius distinguishes these as different conditions and, while sometimes stigmatizing female patients, frequently problematizes sexual phenomena with an eye to men as well. Groff further puts Aëtius' definitions in conversation with World Health Organization statements on sexual health, revealing the long history and frequently subterranean roots of what are often imagined as purely modern ideas. Groff's analysis, like that of Solevåg, reminds us how problematic and complex the classification of bodily states of health and disease or disability could be.

In Chapter 6, Jonathan Zecher studies another late antique physician, Alexander of Tralles, whose clinical practices included amulets and incantations as well as Hippocratic recipes. Zecher shows that, although Alexander is usually presented as a Christian, there is nothing in his writing that bears this out; instead, he appears as a devotee of Galen and Hippocrates. Yet Alexander also indulges his patients' expectations for non-medical remedies and ultimately incorporates these into a more expansive conceptualization of medical arts than others might have allowed. Zecher's analysis underlines the importance of broadening the scope of medical experience, especially with his critical engagement with placebos. It also highlights some of the frustrations and tensions modern patients may experience when they hear from clinicians that their ailment or pain is "all in your head." By showing how Alexander may have accommodated various "cultures of health care" in his medical discourse and practice, we come to realize that the therapeutic endeavour is an invitation to participate in new worlds, in new *cosmoi*, so to speak, and to partake in other, often alternative, epistemologies.

In Chapter 7, Chris L. de Wet brings us back to Christian preachers and their dissemination of medical knowledge. De Wet shows that through their use of medical ideas, preachers also imposed classificatory boundaries on their congregations, subjecting them to the dominating power of discourse to divide and alienate. These boundaries are legitimized by the apparent truth—even scientific accuracy—of medical arguments. While each chapter in Part Two shows the imposition of order by those who exercise power through their claims to expertise, de Wet's chapter in particular depicts the other side of the homiletic identity-making explored in Part One: just as medical metaphors and arguments can usher people *into* community, so too they can force others *out* and police the borders between the two.

Part Three opens windows onto the lived experience of health in the context of Christian ritual, writing, and even architecture. In Chapter 8, Paul Dilley considers the emotional and psychosocial struggles layered into hagiographic accounts of monastic saints. For these, loss and renunciation are the conditions of progress in sanctity, but they are also traumas requiring mediation. Dilley shows us the means by which, for example, family is lost and reconstituted within the strictures of a hagiographic genre, in which emotional suffering is frequently downplayed.

In Chapter 9, Susan R. Holman draws on Doreen Massey's geographical theory of space and the United Nations Sustainable Development Goals (SDGs) to explore how water ethics shape religious responses to healing relevant to public health, social policy, and humanitarian relief across space and time. As a sample case, Holman considers the story of the Great Well at Shenoute of Atripe's White Monastery and Shenoute's stated concern to provide water sufficient to welcome and care for displaced refugees. She leverages archaeological evidence to suggest that Shenoute may have modelled the well on the architectural spacing around the White Monastery's church altar. Providing access to water appears as a eucharistic activity and crucial feature of the monastery's community life and relationship to the outside world.

In such an endeavour, the danger of historiographical anachronism is always a risk. Thus, Brenda Llewellyn Ihssen, in her concluding chapter (Chapter 10), offers a detailed theoretical and conceptual framing for the volume, as she explores intersections between Christian antiquity and modern healthcare. Highlighting three particular essays—those of de Wet, Holman, and Rhee—Ihssen argues that this volume showcases what Michel Foucault dubbed writing a "history of the present."[12] Writing (medical) histories of the present means we always begin our study where we are, in our own present. The topics, places, and subjects of these studies by no means exhaust the diversity of early Christian sources. Rather, they gesture to a variety of genres, locations, times, and theologies, all of which are better understood through modern medical lenses, and all of which helpfully complicate contemporary debates over the nature of health, the role of healthcare, and the experience of illness.

In each of these chapters, we can see how, behind the constraints of form and genre, considerations of health, well-being, and even medical care impinge on the daily lives of late antique Christians. They were beset by the same problems faced by many people today, the answering of which is now considered the domain of public healthcare and its various institutions, both governmental and charitable. In late antiquity, these problems received different kinds of answers, which must be uncovered from seemingly different kinds of evidence. Although different in many ways, the answers reached by early Christians are not ultimately foreign to those being sought now, especially in health humanities. For one thing, Christian theology has long been entangled in the formation of medical discourses, whether directly or indirectly, acknowledged or not. Investing physical health with spiritual significance (and vice versa) is not a thing of the past. People still pray for healing, and researchers still seek out "miracle drugs." Bodily difference still stigmatizes people as outsiders, or, if shared, creates community. Healthcare still has a healer–patient relationship at its centre, even if that relationship is now founded in systems of knowledge and money infinitely vaster than could have been imagined by early Christians. The chapters in this book show that historical difference can still be productive, and act collectively as an invitation to put historical studies to wider use in critical, interventive, and constructive conversations.

We close, therefore, with a few of the questions *not* covered in this volume, but which we hope that others will take up in similar vein. How do class, gender, and ethnic difference entwine with religious teaching and practice to produce new ideas of health? How do emotional regimes, shaped through religious participation, inflect relationships of healing? How might theologies of pain and suffering offer space to sufferers of chronic pain ill served by contemporary healthcare? What happens to healing possibilities when the limits of medical intervention are exposed, whether through miraculous healing or the rejection of biomedical approaches? What can individually focused healthcare systems learn from the embedded and porous selves of early Christian thought? What ecologies of health might be envisioned, if we take seriously the interrelatedness of humans, divinity, and the non-human world as it appears in early Christian texts? These are just a few of the many questions we hope to have hinted at or raised, and that others will take up in their turn.

This collection of collaborative chapters has been a labour of love, created during a pandemic, and constantly challenged by a seemingly endless duration of pandemic stressors. The editors are grateful to each of the contributors who stuck with the project, as well as those whose names don't appear in the Table of Contents but whose support for the vision dates equally to that first group conversation around an Oxford pub table. Thank you to Andrew Crislip and Meghan Henning for their voices in the conference sessions and affirmations as we launched the original proposal, and Amy Davis-Poynter, who saw the potential of such a study for Routledge from the start. The book simply would not exist were it not for Wendy Mayer, and for the influence that her scholarship has had on the field in shaping innovative applications of modern theory to ancient therapeutic narrative and preaching.[13] Finally, words fail in our admiration and appreciation for Heidi Marx and Kristi Upson-Saia, ReMeDHe cofounders, who welcomed this volume as the first in a new series and whose rigour, cheer, and brilliant collaborative energies have, in many ways, galvanized and energized our subfield at pivotal moments, and built a path for asking, and exploring, new questions for the health humanities.

Notes

1 See especially the comments in Stefan N. Willich and Susanna Elm, eds., *Medical Challenges for the New Millennium: An Interdisciplinary Task* (Dordrecht: Kluwer Academic, 2001). One such paradigm is the "biopsychosocial model" of health and illness, according to which biological causes interact with affect, cognition, and one's location "in the world." Disease causation maps the entanglement of bodies, minds, and environments, while the experience of illness or health refers to all of these as well. For an introduction, see Derek Bolton and Grant Gillett, *The Biopsychosocial Model of Health and Disease: New Philosophical and Scientific Developments*, Palgrave Pivot (New York: Palgrave Macmillan, 2019). See also now Helen Rhee's careful discussion of these distinctions in *Illness, Pain, and Health Care in Early Christianity* (Grand Rapids: Eerdmans, 2022).
2 For which there is now the field of "social epidemiology," which treats disease outbreaks—and the public health responses to them—as determined in large part by social conditions, requiring social–scientific methods. Increasingly, these are being paired with historical, literary, and other approaches to uncover the construction of public health events.
3 UNAIDS, "Global HIV & AIDS Statistics—Fact Sheet," 2021, www.unaids.org/en/resources/fact-sheet.
4 Fernando Cervero and John N. Wood, "A History of Pain Research," in *The Oxford Handbook of the Neurobiology of Pain*, ed. John N. Wood (Oxford: Oxford University Press, 2020), 1–28.
5 Edward R. Perl, "Ideas about Pain, a Historical View," *Nature Reviews: Neuroscience* 8.1 (2007): 78, https://doi.org/10.1038/nrn2042.
6 See several essays in Chris L. de Wet, "Contextualising Pain and Remedy in Early Judaism and Christianity," *Journal of Early Christian History* 12.1 (2022). See more generally Javier Moscoso, *Pain: A Cultural History* (Basingstoke: Palgrave Macmillan, 2012) and, for other studies in antiquity, J. R. Clarke, D. King, and H. Baltussen (eds.), *Pain Narratives in Greco-Roman Writings: Studies in the Representation of Physical and Mental Suffering*, Studies in Ancient Medicine (Leiden: Brill, Forthcoming).
7 While not directly considering Christian history or antiquity, Arthur Kleinman's work offers foundational models for this; see, for example, Arthur Kleinman, *Writing at the Margin: Discourse between Anthropology and Medicine* (Berkeley: University of California Press, 1995) and Iain Wilkinson and Arthur Kleinman, *A Passion for Society: How We Think about Human Suffering* (Berkeley: University of California Press, 2016). Byron Good, *Medicine, Rationality, and Experience: An Anthropological Perspective* (Cambridge: Cambridge University Press, 1994) remains foundational. See also Wendy Mayer, "Patristics and Postmodernity: Bridging the Gap," Plenary Lecture, Oxford Patristic Conference, 2019, forthcoming in Markus Vinzent et al. (eds.), *Studia Patristica* (Leiden: Peeters, forthcoming). Monica Green has done perhaps the most in arguing for relevant connections in public health related to pandemics; see, for example, Monica H. Green, "The Value of Historical Perspective," in *The Ashgate Research Companion to the Globalization of Health*, ed. Ted Schrecker (Farnham and Burlington: Ashgate, 2012), 17–37. For an exemplary multidisciplinary study, which marries historiography to social epidemiology, see David A. Jones, *Rationalizing Epidemics: Meanings and*

Uses of American Indian Mortality Since 1600 (Cambridge, MA: Harvard University Press, 2004).

8 See also https://remedhe.com.
9 See, for example, Philip J. Van der Eijk, *Medicine and Philosophy in Classical Antiquity: Doctors and Philosophers on Nature, Soul, Health and Disease* (Cambridge: Cambridge University Press, 2005).
10 The literature on this is vast; see, for example, Vivian Nutton, "Medicine and the Religions of the Roman Empire," in *Ancient Medicine*, ed. Vivian Nutton (London: Routledge, 2004), 273–91; and Megan Nutzman, *Contested Cures: Identity and Ritual Healing in Roman and Late Antique Palestine* (Edinburgh: University of Edinburgh Press, 2022).
11 See especially the special issue's introductory framework essay, Wendy Mayer, "Medicine and Metaphor in Late Antiquity: How Some Recent Shifts Are Changing the Field," *Studies in Late Antiquity* 2.4 (2018): 440–63.
12 Michel Foucault, *Discipline & Punish: The Birth of the Prison*, trans. Alan Sheridan (New York: Vintage, 1977), 30–1. See also David Garland, "What Is a 'History of the Present'? On Foucault's Genealogies and Their Critical Preconditions," *Punishment & Society* 16.4 (2014): 365–84.
13 See especially Wendy Mayer, "The Persistence in Late Antiquity of Medico-Philosophic Psychic Therapy," *Journal of Late Antiquity* 8.2 (2015): 337–51.

Bibliography

Bolton, Derek and Grant Gillett, *The Biopsychosocial Model of Health and Disease: New Philosophical and Scientific Developments*, Palgrave Pivot (New York: Palgrave Macmillan, 2019).

Cervero, Fernando and John N. Wood, "A History of Pain Research," in *The Oxford Handbook of the Neurobiology of Pain*, ed. John N. Wood (Oxford: Oxford University Press, 2020), 1–28.

Clarke, J. R., D. King and H. Baltussen (eds.), *Pain Narratives in Greco-Roman Writings: Studies in the Representation of Physical and Mental Suffering*, Studies in Ancient Medicine (Leiden: Brill, forthcoming).

Foucault, Michel, *Discipline & Punish: The Birth of the Prison*, trans. Alan Sheridan (New York: Vintage, 1977).

Garland, David, "What Is a 'History of the Present'? On Foucault's Genealogies and Their Critical Preconditions," *Punishment & Society* 16.4 (2014): 365–84.

Good, Byron, *Medicine, Rationality, and Experience: An Anthropological Perspective* (Cambridge: Cambridge University Press, 1994).

Green, Monica H., "The Value of Historical Perspective," in *The Ashgate Research Companion to the Globalization of Health*, ed. Ted Schrecker (Farnham and Burlington: Ashgate, 2012), 17–37.

Jones, David A., *Rationalizing Epidemics: Meanings and Uses of American Indian Mortality Since 1600* (Cambridge, MA: Harvard University Press, 2004).

Kleinman, Arthur, *Writing at the Margin: Discourse Between Anthropology and Medicine* (Berkeley: University of California Press, 1995).

Mayer, Wendy, "Medicine and Metaphor in Late Antiquity: How Some Recent Shifts Are Changing the Field," *Studies in Late Antiquity* 2.4 (2018): 440–63.

———, "Patristics and Postmodernity: Bridging the Gap," Plenary Lecture, Oxford Patristic Conference, 2019, forthcoming in Markus Vinzent et al. (eds.), *Studia Patristica* (Leiden: Peeters, forthcoming).

Moscoso, Javier, *Pain: A Cultural History* (Basingstoke: Palgrave Macmillan, 2012).

Nutton, Vivian, *Ancient Medicine*, 2nd ed. (London: Routledge, 2014).

Nutzman, Megan, *Contested Cures: Identity and Ritual Healing in Roman and Late Antique Palestine* (Edinburgh: University of Edinburgh Press, 2022).

Perl, Edward R., "Ideas About Pain, a Historical View," *Nature Reviews: Neuroscience* 8.1 (2007): 78, https://doi.org/10.1038/nrn2042.

Rhee, Helen, *Illness, Pain, and Health Care in Early Christianity* (Grand Rapids, MI: Eerdmans, 2022).

UNAIDS, "Global HIV & AIDS Statistics—Fact Sheet," 2021, www.unaids.org/en/resources/fact-sheet.

Van der Eijk, Philip J., *Medicine and Philosophy in Classical Antiquity: Doctors and Philosophers on Nature, Soul, Health and Disease* (Cambridge: Cambridge University Press, 2005).

Wilkinson, Iain and Arthur Kleinman, *A Passion for Society: How We Think About Human Suffering* (Berkeley: University of California Press, 2016).

Willich, Stefan N. and Susanna Elm (eds.), *Medical Challenges for the New Millennium: An Interdisciplinary Task* (Dordrecht: Kluwer Academic, 2001).

Part One

Marking Bodies, Making Communities

2 Christ, the Physician, and His Deaf Followers

Medical Metaphors in the Letters of Ignatius of Antioch

Anna Rebecca Solevåg

Introduction

Metaphorical tropes drawn from the field of medicine shaped early Christian think-ing, as recent studies have shown.[1] This chapter explores the use of medical meta-phors in the letters of Ignatius. I show how he not only uses established medical metaphors and paradigms, but also creates new and creative imagery related to the body and health. These metaphors, I argue, are specifically chosen to fit a particular rhetorical strategy, where he aligns heresy with disease and orthodoxy with good health. Moreover, his medical imagery also underscores important theological themes in Ignatius' letters, such as his anti-docetic stance, his concerns about the unity of the church under the authority of the bishop, and his "theology of silence."

Ignatius was a Christian church leader, probably the Bishop of Antioch, in the first half of the second century.[2] He is known to us through his letters, written to various churches, *en route* from Antioch through Asia Minor to Rome, where he is expecting to be martyred. There are hardly any other sources to Ignatius' life and death, save a few mentions in Polycarp's letters. Ignatius' letters testify to the ideol-ogy of martyrdom that developed at this time,[3] as well as the rhetorical context of the Second Sophistic.[4] This chapter is a study of the so-called Middle Recension of Ignatius' letters.[5] Recently, the scholarly consensus on the authenticity of the middle recension has been challenged.[6] James G. Givens argues that the accepted textual history does not account for the full range of evidence, and that it delimits attention to the complex textual fluidity of the Ignatian corpus.[7] For a study of early Christian uses of medical metaphors, it could be just as interesting to look at other texts within the Ignatian tradition. Since my study is limited, I have chosen to work with the traditional collection of texts.

The chapter has two main parts. In Part I, I dissect how Ignatius uses and expands on the New Testament notion of Christ as the true physician. This meta-phorical blend asserts an analogy between good bodily health and right faith. In Part II, I show how Ignatius also uses metaphors that subvert the normative alliance between sense perception and good health on the one side and superior moral quali-ties, salvation, and right faith on the other.

DOI: 10.4324/9781003080534-3

A Disability Perspective on Metaphor Theory

The theoretical framework for this presentation is twofold. Firstly, I draw on a number of conceptual approaches to metaphor within what is known as cognitive theory. In their seminal book, *Metaphors We Live By*, George Lakoff and Mark Johnson argue that metaphors are among our principal vehicles of meaning and suggest that they play a central role in the construction of social and political reality.[8] More than rhetorical flourish or poetic creativity, metaphors are integral to the way we think.[9] Building and expanding on Lakoff and Johnson, the theoretical field of cognitive theory has developed, enabling a better understanding of how the human mind is shaped by bodily, affective, and material structures. In this chapter, I will use Conceptual Metaphor Theory and blending theory, which theorize the role of mental images and imagistic thinking for human cognition.[10] I use the simple but foundational theoretical terms, *source domain* and *target domain*. Simply put, the target is the concept that one tries to understand, while the source is the concept used to explain it.[11] I also use the terms *mapping*, which refers to the basic conceptual correspondences between source and target, and *blends*, which refers to the fusion of two or more mental spaces, creating emergent meaning.[12]

Cognitive theories have been fruitfully applied to late ancient and medieval texts.[13] In early Christian literature, conceptual metaphors functioned as powerful cognitive tools that enabled readers or listeners to think about abstract and difficult theological concepts in terms of more concrete and familiar ideas and imagery.[14] Conceptual metaphors are shaped by the social context and particular experiences of the writer. As Line Cecilie Engh and Mark Turner point out, mapping and conceptual blending are imaginative and creative operations, yet they do not work randomly: "They are constrained by culturally contingent background knowledge and grounded in embodied experience."[15]

In a special issue of *Studies in Late Antiquity* devoted to early Christian use of medical metaphors, several articles contribute to a substantial rethinking of the discursive interconnections between early Christian writings and medical texts. In the introduction to volume, Kristi Upson-Saia pinpoints three changes in how scholars think about medical metaphors in early Christian texts.[16] Firstly, scholars are increasingly resisting a rigid divide between the domains of religion and medicine. We should not assume a neat division between literal and metaphorical language, where medicine related to the literal body, while religion borrowed medical concepts to speak metaphorically about the health of the soul. Rather, both domains were concerned with the health of both body *and* soul. Secondly, she points out the complexity and nuance that characterize the Christian usage of medical metaphors, often showing highly specific and technical knowledge of anatomy, physiology, diagnosis, and treatment. Finally, she argues that medical metaphors are not just a conceptual framework for Christian authors, but that they borrowed medical ideas to think about material bodies as well.

Wendy Mayer, likewise, gives an important contribution to thinking about this topic in more nuanced and complex ways.[17] She points to "the persistence in

Late Antiquity of permeability and slippage between literal and metaphorical" as an aspect of early Christian discourse that needs further scrutiny. These insights underscore the social and cultural contingency of metaphor; it is only meaningful within a certain cultural context, but can, in turn, become tremendously forceful in shaping discourse as well as social structures.[18] Mayer argues that medical metaphors became forceful enough to influence social norms when they were integrated into religious systems. She points to concepts of pollution and the notion of illness as punishment from the gods as examples.[19]

Within Disability Studies, the insight that medical metaphors and other discursive practices framing the disabled body can be extremely influential in shaping culture is foundational. Studies from this interdisciplinary field have shown that metaphorical constructions drawing on illness and disability permeate cultural discourse in ways that exclude, demonize, or otherwise "other" people with disabilities. One example, which I will draw on in this chapter, is David Mitchell and Sharon Snyder's concept of *narrative prosthesis*. They argue that literary uses of disability, from antiquity until the present, show some recurring traits. One of these is the reliance on physiognomic reasoning in the way metaphors are used. Going back to the ancient quasi-science of physiognomy, disability has been interpreted as an external symptom of an inner, moral deviance, according to Mitchell and Snyder. Disability has thus been used by writers to allow a metaphorical play between macro- and micro-registers of meaning.[20] In their words, "either the deviant body deforms subjectivity or deviant subjectivity violently erupts upon the surface of its bodily container."[21]

In my opinion, perspectives from Disability Studies complement insights on metaphor from cognitive science, by forefronting medical metaphors' effect on society. Ignatius' medical metaphors are not only powerful tools to think with but had real social repercussions, not only in their immediate context, but also as they were received and transmitted, shaping an emerging Christian discourse about health and disability in Late Antiquity.

Part 1: Jesus the Physician—A Productive Metaphor

Jesus as the True Physician

I start by looking at a key metaphorical blend in Ignatius' letters: his construction of Jesus as physician. In several places, Ignatius uses and develops the Jesus logion found in both Matthew and Mark: "Those who are well have no need for a physician [ἰατροῦ], but those who are sick; I have come to call not the righteous but sinners" (Mark 2:17 // Matt 9:12–13).

In the *Letter to the Ephesians*, Ignatius draws on this tradition, saying:

> For there is one physician (ἰατρός), both fleshly and spiritual, born and unborn, God come in the flesh, true life in death, from both Mary and God, first subject to suffering and beyond suffering, Jesus Christ our Lord.
>
> (Ign. *Eph* 7.2 [LCL, Ehrman])

Here Ignatius introduces the metaphor of Christ as physician. As the first attribute in a long list of titles and attributes, Ignatius forefronts Jesus' role as doctor. A closer look at the context surrounding this often quoted passage reveals that Ignatius draws on several concepts from the source domain of medicine to construct a metaphorical blend that not only has a Christological component, but also very much relates to ecclesiology:

> For some are accustomed to bear the name in wicked deceit, while acting in ways that are unworthy of God. You must shun them as wild animals. For they are raving dogs [κύνες λυσσῶντες] who bite when no one is looking [λαθροδῆκται]. You must guard against them, for they are hard to tame [δυσθεραπεύτους].
>
> (Ign. *Eph* 7.1 [LCL, Ehrman])

Ignatius likens those who "bear the name in wicked deceit," by which he means heretics, to raving dogs who bite when no one is looking. The verb λυσσάω (to rave, or be mad) when used about dogs usually refers to rabid dogs.[22] These dogs are also called δυσθεραπεύτους, which LSJ translates as "hard to cure."[23] Several ancient sources reflect the notion that rabies was hard to cure.[24] William Schoedel translates κύνες λυσσῶντες as "rabid dogs" and δυσθεραπεύτους as "almost incurable."[25] In Ehrman's translation, the medical aspect of the dog references in this verse is lost. His translation simply states that they are raving and "hard to tame." But the metaphorical blend of "rabid dogs" that are hard to cure and Jesus as the "one physician" reveals a notion of heretics as somehow sick and in need of healing. Heresy, in this understanding, is as infectious as a bite from a rabid dog.

The phrasing also dehumanizes the heretics, reducing them to raving dogs biting indiscriminately. Here we may also see a connection to physiognomic reasoning, where zoological markers denoted certain moral traits. Negative characteristics associated with dogs included, according to Polemon's *Physiognomy*, that they were "covetous, miserly, stubborn, prattling, gluttonous, dirty, bad-natured, lacking in modesty; and mundane."[26] Mitchell and Snyder's concept of narrative prosthesis underscores how such reasoning projects a sick—in this case even infectious—body onto what is perceived to be a sick mind.

The medical imagery is expanded in another passage in the same letter. Here, the Eucharist is referred to as a medicine, when taken in unity under one bishop:

> [B]reaking one bread, which is a medicine that brings immortality [φάρμακον ἀθανασίας], an antidote [ἀντίδοτος] that allows us not to die but to live at all times in Jesus Christ.
>
> (Ign. *Eph* 20.2)

This famous quotation is part of the ending of the letter, and thus particularly forceful. According to Schoedel, he is here urging his listeners to an appropriate response.[27] The Eucharist is described through two metaphors from the source domain of medicine. It is φάρμακον as well as ἀντίδοτος. The Greek term φάρμακον refers to a drug, whether it is healing or noxious.[28] In other words, it can mean both medicine and poison. Its use is widespread from Homer onwards, and its usage is not limited to medical sources, but well attested also there. The meaning of φάρμακον here is clearly positive. The Eucharist is understood as a healing agent providing immortality. The phrase "medicine of immortality" (φάρμακον ἀθανασίας) is not Ignatius' invention. It occurs in a comedy by Antiphanes (*Frag.* 86.6) and a historical work by Diodorus Siculus (*Bibliotheca historica* 1.25.6). Similar constructions also occur elsewhere in the Greek and Latin corpus of antiquity. Seneca refers to the hemlock drunk by Socrates as *medicamentum immortalitatis* (*De prov.* 3.2). *Athanasia*, "Immortality," was the name of a drug supposedly discovered by Isis and used to raise Horus from the dead. A medicine by this name was also attributed to king Mithridates VI and was used against poisonous venomous bites, and problems with internal organs.[29]

Ἀντίδοτος, meaning antidote or remedy,[30] is mainly used in medical literature, and we find the term particularly often in Galen. The notion of an antidote, as well as the "medicine of immortality" may point back to the "hard to cure" heretics and their infectious bites in 7.1–2. The medical imagery of medicine and drugs expands upon the metaphorical blend introduced there. Not only is Jesus a physician, and heresy the almost incurable bite of a rabid dog. Here comes the solution: the Eucharist *is* the cure, the antidote, which gives healing in the form of eternal life. In particular, it may refer back to the image of rabid dogs biting and suggest that (rightly regulated) communion is the particular medicine that needs to be taken in order to heal damages caused by exposure to heretics. Thus, Ignatius constructs the Eucharist as space for healing.

Ignatius continues to run the blend (i.e. elaborate on the metaphorical construction) also in his other letters. In the *Letter to the Trallians*, he refers to heresy as a bad plant and a poisonous drug:

> Therefore I am urging you—not I, but the love of Jesus Christ—make use of Christian food (χριστιανῇ τροφῇ) and abstain from a foreign plant (ἀλλοτρίας δὲ βοτάνης), which is heresy. Even though such persons seem to be trustworthy, they mingle Jesus Christ with themselves, as if giving a deadly drug [θανάσιμον φάρμακον] mixed with honeyed wine, which the unsuspecting gladly takes with evil pleasure but then dies.
>
> (Ign. *Trall* 6.2)

In this passage, we see that Ignatius plays with the double meaning of φάρμακον. Here, Ignatius draws out heresy as a deadly poison, θανάσιμον φάρμακον. Heresy, then, represents the complete opposite of communion, which he called medicine of immortality, φάρμακον ἀθανασίας. He also expands on the blend by bringing in the term βοτάνη, meaning herb or plant. The term can have medical connotations and is, for example, used by Galen to speak of healing herbs and medicinal plants.[31]

Also in the *Letter to the Philippians* does Ignatius use the imagery of heresy as a bad plant: "Abstain from the evil plants [κακῶν βοτανῶν] which Jesus Christ does not cultivate, since they are not a planting of the father" (Ign. *Phil* 3.1). In both these passages, Ignatius uses the plant imagery (now part of a complex "Jesus as physician" blend) to create a distinction between true believers and heretics that has xenophobic overtones. By calling the heretics alien and evil, and originating from a different garden, heresy is understood in terms of ethnic and geographical categories. The blend contributes to an othering and excluding of certain elements or groups in the Christ-believing community as strangers and not Christian. By expanding the blend of Christ as physician with a notion of Christ as gardener, he also introduces the possibility of "rooting out" heresy, that is to engage various exclusionary practices, such as excommunication or banishment.

The Bishop as Medical Expert

A final example of the expanded "Christ as physician" imagery is from the *Letter to Polycarp*. Here, the bishop is drawn into this complex metaphorical blend in two different passages. In the first chapter of his letter, Ignatius urges Polycarp to "bear the illnesses of all [πάντων τὰς νόσους] as a perfect athlete" (Ign. *Polycarp* 1.3). He continues the medical language in the following chapter:

> It is nothing special for you to love good disciples; instead, gently bring those who are more pestiforous [λοιμοτέρους] into subjection. Not every wound [τραῦμα] is cured [θεραπεύεται] with the same plaster [ἐμπλάστρῳ]. Soothe paroxysms of fever [παροξυσμοὺς] with cold compresses [ἐμβρωχαῖς]. Be wise as a serpent in all things, and always pure as a dove. You are fleshly and spiritual for this reason, that you may deal gently with what is visible before you. But ask that what is unseen may be made visible to you.
>
> (Ign. *Polycarp* 2.1–2)

In both these passages, the bishop is given a healing role, but he is not called a doctor. He is constructed as an athlete, and his role seems to be to alleviate pain by carrying his flock's illnesses vicariously. Yet, in the second quotation, the practice of the ancient doctor is quite clearly mapped onto the practice of the bishop. As a doctor might, he has a variety of remedies in his medical kit, in order to heal and soothe his patients. Ignatius mentions some disciples that are called pestiferous, or pestilentious (λοιμοτέρους).[32] Λοιμός is the Greek term for plague, and the term Λοιμότης connects these disciples to notions of contagion and plague.[33] We can assume that these "bad" disciples are the heretics. This is the group that has been branded with the negative medical imagery of disease and infection throughout Ignatius' letters, as I have shown earlier.

Ancient medical writers believed that disease could be transmitted to a person from its surroundings, but there were various medical theories about how this happened. Some doctors thought that the air could contain bad elements, "seeds," that emanated from the stars, from the earth (in particular from marshes), or decomposing cadavers. Other medical writers dismissed this theory and argued that it was the climate itself and climatic changes in the seasons that caused epidemics and other diseases that somehow seemed to spread in a population.[34] The various remedies that are mentioned show the range of options that the bishop must weigh to bring heretics "into subjection," as Ignatius says. In fact, these remedies fit the symptoms associated with various plagues and epidemics, as they are described in medical literature, such as sores, pustules, and fever.[35] Ignatius here quotes a medical maxim from Galen that "one drug cannot suit all bodies," and uses terminology similar to Galen about healing wounds with plasters.[36] Metaphorical use of such medical advice was common in ancient rhetoric as an advice to adopt remedies fit for the occasion.[37] Ignatius' point is that each case must be considered and handled separately, according to the bishop's judgement of which approach would be most wise.

There may even be a medical connotation in reference to what is visible and what is unseen. Schoedel argues that Ignatius here draws on the diagnostic method of the dogmatic and rationalist schools to infer from the visible to the invisible.[38] Perhaps even the injunction to be "wise as a serpent" can be understood as medical. The serpent was the symbol of Asclepius, the healing god, and (dreaming about) serpents were an element in the healing rituals of the Asclepian temples.[39] The medical language here also blends with biblical language, drawing on Jesus' advice to the apostles for the coming persecution, to "be wise as serpents and innocent as doves" (Matt 10:16).

The Rhetorical Purpose of the Christ as Physician Blend

In the aforementioned examples, Ignatius draws on various medical themes and insights, including nosology, diagnostics, pharmacology, and ideals about the doctor as therapist. He also shows knowledge of various medical schools, and the Asclepian healing tradition. This deep medical knowledge is put to use as he builds a complex blend of metaphors around the notion of Christ as physician. Ignatius maps various aspects of the field of medicine onto nascent Christian theology and community life. Jesus, and the bishops functioning as his deputies, are the healers; the heretics are the sick—they are rabid dogs and infected by plague; heresy is a deadly drug and an evil, foreign plant. Finally, the Eucharist is prescribed as the antidote and medicine for the plague of heresy that is infecting the church, and bishops are trusted to use their discretion to choose the right remedy in each instance. As Jared Secord puts it: "Christ is presented here almost as a panacea, and Christianity itself as a religion of the healthy."[40]

Ignatius' medical metaphors are not mere ornamentation in his letters. They are rhetorical tools chosen to get his message across. Mayer suggests that the usage of medical metaphors in early Christian writings is quite diverse and that the choices individual authors made should be closely considered because they "function as a window into their personal theological thought world and provide important clues as to how those thought worlds intersect with and differ from" other Christian thinkers.[41] In the case of Ignatius, the metaphorical blend of Christ as physician may have been prompted by his anti-docetic stance. He strongly argues for the incarnation, the physicality of the body of Christ, and his true suffering and death. References to his birth by Mary (e.g. *Eph.* 7.2; 18.2; *Trall.* 9.1), his bloodline with David (*Eph* 7.2; *Trall* 9.1), and the insistence on a physical body even after the resurrection (e.g. *Sm*. 1–2) underscore this concern. The reference to Christ as physician appears as part of a Christological statement in which the duality of Christ as both God and man is a major point. He has a concern for the physical body, not only of Christ, but also of the bishops. He uses the same word pair, "fleshly" (σαρκικός) and "spiritual" (πνεθματικός) to describe both (*Eph* 7.2; *Poly.* 2.2). Ignatius does not see flesh and spirit as incompatible, going against both Hellenistic and Pauline traditions.[42] Ignatius also shows concern for the physicality of the elements of the Eucharist, which he insists are the flesh and blood of Christ (e.g. *Sm.* 7.1; *Rom* 7.3). This attention to the physical body, driven by his anti-docetic stance, may then lie behind his use of these particular medical metaphors, which also forefront the materiality of the body.

The Christ as physician blend is a rhetorical device used to argue two major themes in Ignatius' letters: his concerns about heresy and his advocacy for the authority of the bishop. The imagery Ignatius uses establishes a link between Christianity and sound health, while heresy connects with the unorderly world of illness, but also of untamed nature, with wild beasts and poisonous plants. Mayer points out that such commonplace social–medical concepts as "evil is a disease" or the notion of a social entity being sick if it is not in harmony played a powerful role in Christian discourse in late antiquity.[43] One of the main points in her article is that "scholars have been slow to acknowledge the slippage between the literal and the metaphorical" in early Christian texts.[44] She argues that a number of culturally normative ideas nurtured this slippage, such as the understanding of philosophy and medicine as sibling therapies; the common use of ascetic practice as regimen for both body and soul; and the notion of rhetoric as therapy.[45]

Applying these insights to Ignatius, we may ask: what is metaphorical and what is literal in Ignatius' rhetoric? Does he conceive of the Eucharist as an actual medicine that physically gives eternal life when a congregant ingests wine and bread? And likewise, is heresy understood as literally lethal? I think that particularly in this aspect of the blend, concerning the right and wrong use of the Eucharist, a slippage between the metaphorical and literal is quite plausible. To Ignatius mind, partaking in a heretical sacrament, for example, a Eucharist that is not sanctioned by a bishop, would be harmful for the physical bodies of the congregants. The notion that such a mingling of Christ's body with the body of an officiating heretic is harmful even for the unsuspecting believer (Ign. *Trall* 6.2) seems to suggest that he is thinking in terms of the physical bodies of those participating in such rituals.

Susan Sontag's insights on the use of illness imagery in modern political polemic may be useful here. In *Illness as Metaphor* and *AIDS and Its Metaphors*, she shows how different illnesses invoke different metaphorical associations. She warns against the dangers of such politicized illness discourse, pointing out that the concept of disease is never innocent when drawn on for polemical purposes. In her study, she found that the use of cancer talk in political discourse encouraged fatalism and justified severe measures against the group targeted with this kind of speech.[46] Concerning HIV, she found that AIDS was described as a plague invading both the individual body and global society, and that the rhetoric clearly encompassed racist, xenophobic, and homophobic fears.[47] In Ignatius' case, the medical metaphors underscore the severity of the situation and points to episcopal authority as the solution: the bishops are the healers who can rightfully administer the medicine of the Eucharist and thus restore the health of the church. Ignatius' metaphorical blend creates a notion of severity and urgency. He posits that the church as a communal body is sick. This illness in the community calls for a variety of remedies and justifies severe measures. The metaphorical construction also authorizes the bishop as medical expert to put the needed measures in place. A fear of contagion may underlie some of these medical metaphors, such as the references to rabies and pestilence, and the bad plants that need to be rooted out.

Part II: Subverting an Ableist Narrative

Be Deaf to Heresy

However, it is not possible to put Ignatius use of medical metaphors on a simple formula. While the "Christ as physician" blend draws on the normative correlation between healthy body and correct faith, he also subverts this correlation in other cases. As noted in the introduction, disability scholars have pointed out a literary dependency on disability in order to speak about moral character, what Mitchell and Snyder call *narrative prosthesis*. In antiquity, physiognomic reasoning was quite commonplace, and, as a result, people with disabilities were easy targets as symbols of moral deviation. In early Christian discourse, this logic often worked in tandem with another one, namely the notion of disability as a punishment for sin. One example is John 9, where the disciples asks Jesus, "Rabbi, who sinned, this man or his parents, that he was born blind" (9:2). Another example is the church father Papias' description of the suffering and death of Judas (*Frag.* 4).[48] In this text, disability invective is used to reveal Judas's depraved soul. His painful illness and suffering in death function as divine punishment for his betrayal of Jesus.[49] Ignatius subverts this commonplace alignment of disability with sin, as I will show in the following.

In Ignatius' *Letter to the Trallians*, Ignatius uses an interesting metaphor from a disability perspective: "Be deaf [κωφώθητε] when someone speaks to you apart from Jesus Christ" (Ign. *Trall* 9.1). The verb κωφόω means to be numb, to put to silence, or to become deaf,[50] and the adjective κωφός usually refers to being mute, deaf, or both.[51] Christian Laes has argued that in an oral culture like the ancient Mediterranean, speech and hearing were closely connected to each other, and were extremely important in order to take part in society.[52] Muteness and deafness were often understood in terms of mental incapacity or demon possession.[53] Whereas blindness could sometimes be understood in positive terms, such as in the trope of the blind seer,[54] this was not the case with deafness. In this passage, however, deafness is turned into a positive attribute. It is something the recipients of the letter should strive for.

Ignatius uses similar imagery connected to lack of hearing also elsewhere in his letters. He commends the Ephesians for not listening to heresy (*Eph.* 6.2): "On the contrary, you no longer listen [ὀυδὲ ἀκούετέ] to anyone, except one who speaks truthfully about Jesus Christ" (Ign. *Eph.* 6.2). Later in the same letter, he goes on to use the imagery of plugging one's ears (*Eph.* 9.1) to avoid the bad seeds of heresy taking root: "But you did not permit them to sow any seeds among you, plugging your ears [βύσαντες τὰ ὦτα] so as not to receive anything sown by them" (Ign. *Eph.* 9.1). Note that Ignatius here draws on the metaphor of heresy as a bad plant, discussed earlier. The imagery of sowing seeds comes very close to the notion of contagion, which, as noted earlier, could be understood as a seed. Ignatius argues that heresy can be sown in the soul, like a seed, if it is not closed off.

A Theology of Silence

The positive valence that Ignatius gives to deafness is not limited to the case of false preaching. The references to deafness and closed ears also connect with another theme in Ignatius' letters, namely that of silence. According to Ignatius, the ability to remain silent is an attribute of Christ and should also be found in his followers:

> It is better to be silent [σιοπᾶν] and to exist than to speak and not to exist. It is good to teach, if the one who speaks also acts. For there was one teacher who also spoke and it happened. And the things that he has done while remaining silent [ἃ σιγῶν] are worthy of the father. The one who truly possesses the words of Jesus is able to hear his silence [τῆς ἡσυχίας αὐτοῦ] as well. He will, as a result, be perfect, acting through what he says and being understood through what he does not say [δι' ὧν σιγᾷ γινώσκηται].
>
> (Ign. *Eph.* 15.1–2)

Jesus, who was "the one teacher," nonetheless also sometimes acted in silence. Ignatius may be thinking here in particular of Jesus' silence in front of Pilate (Mark 15:5).[55] Later in the same letter, Ignatius speaks about silence as an attribute of God. The triple mystery of the incarnation (Mary's virginity, the birth, and the death of Christ) are described thus: "Three mysteries of a cry which were accomplished in the silence of God [ἐν ἡσυχίᾳ θεοῦ]" (Ign. *Eph.* 19.1). For Ignatius, the most perfect Christian is the one who can live up to the divine ability to know when to speak and when to keep silent. Unsurprisingly, silence is thus also an ideal for the bishop. They are able to accomplish more through silence than those who vainly talk (*Phd.* 1.1), and they should be revered for their silence (*Eph.* 6.1).

Another aspect of Ignatius' theology of silence is its connection to martyrdom. Ignatius encourages the Romans to remain silent about him and "grant him this act of self-sacrifice" (*Rom.* 2.2). He admonishes them to not speak on his behalf to the authorities to save him from martyrdom, because he truly wants to be martyred. Here, too, we may hear echoes of Jesus' silence in his suffering. Ignatius seems to want to emulate Christ's silence as he willingly approaches death.

When we take into consideration that κωφόω can refer to muteness as well as deafness, the correlation is quite clear: to be mute as well as to be deaf can be attributes of the true Christ follower. Thus, deafness and muteness seem to be positive attributes of the communal body of Christ, and the particular markers of a good bishop. These attributes are grounded in a Christology which likewise imprints supposed markers of disability onto Christ and connect them to the mystery of the incarnation.

In this metaphorical construction, an intact body is not the ideal. There is no dependency on disability as a negative contrast. To the contrary, there is a *subversion* of ableist narrative patterns.[56] The imagery has a similar logic to the following Jesus logion:

> If your right eye causes you to sin, tear it out and throw it away; it is better for you to lose one of your members than for your whole body to be thrown into hell. And if your right hand causes you to sin, cut it off and throw it away; it is better for you to lose one of your members than for your whole body to go into hell.
>
> (Matt 5:29–30)

In this saying, disability is aligned with salvation and a healthy, able body is aligned with the potentiality to sin and thus go to hell. Candida Moss has pointed out that this Jesus saying stands in contrast to healing stories that strive towards bodily perfection, and the more common biblical alignment of disability with sin.[57] Similarly, Ignatius' statements about deafness and silence open up a space for thinking about sensory impairment as positive bodily traits, aligned with good discipleship and Christlikeness.

Ignatius' Own Disabled Body

Ignatius also uses the imagery of non-normative bodies with a positive valour in his self-description. In the letter to the Romans, he draws on Paul's self-description from 1 Cor 15, and calls himself a miscarriage: "But I am ashamed to be called one of them; for I am not at all worthy, as the least of them and a miscarriage [ἔκτρωμα]" (Ign. *Rom* 9.2). The term ἔκτρωμα was used as a term of contempt,[58] and aligns his body with that which is monstrous and deformed. By drawing this similarity between his own body and that of Paul, he points to their similar positions as co-sufferers in the faith. Like Paul boasts of a beaten body, so does Ignatius. This imagery also corresponds with the admonition to the bishops to carry the illnesses of others as good athletes. To be an athlete was to be an ascetic. Jared Secord argues that the athletic imagery in Ignatius draws on notions of bodily discipline closely associated with athletes, such as a strict diet and sexual abstinence.[59]

These examples, where Ignatius gives a positive valence to less than ideal bodies, disabled and marked by persecution and violence, may also point us towards his theology. In particular, they support his anti-docetic stance and his positive view of martyrdom. In the letter to the Romans, Ignatius claims to long for the total destruction of his body. In a disturbingly descriptive passage, he imagines his own flesh ground into complete annihilation by the beasts in the arena: "I am the wheat of God and am ground by the teeth of wild beasts, that I may be found to be the pure bread of Christ" (Ign. *Rom.* 4.1). In this passage, Ignatius claims that his own body, devoured by the beasts, will become a sacrament. His martyred body is transformed into the wheat of God, a eucharistic element. In this imagery as well, the metaphorical seems to slip into the literal. In what way does he understand that his body will become a sacrament in martyrdom? The significance that the physical body has for him, and his understanding of the Eucharist as a medicine of immortality, suggests that he envisions some kind of physical transformation taking place in martyrdom, in which he himself becomes the medicine that will grant him eternal life.

Conclusion: The Malleability of Metaphor

Ignatius uses medical metaphors freely and extensively. I have shown that he draws on medical knowledge, although the metaphors he uses are shaped to serve his rhetorical purposes. The "Jesus as true physician" blend underscores his main focus of fight against heresy and unity under one bishop. The metaphor makes purging of heretics a logical next step. It becomes a matter of necessity for the church in order to remain sound and healthy. The injunction to "be deaf" is likewise designed to fit his fight against heresy. Moreover, it also connects with the Ignatian theme of silence as a marker of true Christian discipleship. Both these metaphorical constructions support Ignatius's anti-docetic theology, in which the full humanity of Christ is paramount.

Whereas the Christ as physician blend follows the normative alliance between good health and superior moral quality, the other metaphors I have discussed subvert it. His encouragement to the believers to "be deaf," his theology of silence, and his self-description as a miscarriage give positive valence to non-normative bodies. We thus have something of a paradox in Ignatius' use of medical metaphors. Although healing, and a healthy, able body is an ideal for the metaphorical blend of Christ as physician, it is not an ideal for the body of the believer, who should be deaf and mute; nor for the body of Ignatius, who is described as a miscarriage, and whose body is willingly given up for destruction in martyrdom.

This diversity in Ignatius usage of medical and disability metaphors underscores the malleability of metaphor. Imagery gives room for the playful and open-ended, and can be used in a variety of ways to serve the writer's purposes. From a disability perspective, the examples of metaphorical discourse that uses disability as a positive trait are particularly important to point out and unpack, since they go against the main trend of narrative prosthesis in the physiognomic tradition. In fact, there are aspects of Ignatius' theology that may have served as positive, inclusive imagery for people with disabilities among the readers of his letters.

These examples from Ignatius' letters show that early Christian medical discourse was wider and more complex than just a simple adoption of common tropes. Rather, as Mayer also has pointed out, the interchange of medical and theological ideas varied from writer to writer. Ignatius drew on medical discourse and medical insights in order to express his theological views. In turn, his letters became part of a religious–medical conversation that continued to develop in the centuries that followed.

Notes

1 See, for example, Kristi Upson-Saia, "Rethinking Medical Metaphors in Late Ancient Christianity," *Studies in Late Antiquity* 2, no. 4 (2018); Wendy Mayer, "Medicine and Metaphor in Late Antiquity: How Some Recent Shifts Are Changing the Field," *Studies in Late Antiquity* 2, no. 4 (2018).
2 Bart D. Ehrman, "Introduction: Letters of Ignatius," in *The Apostolic Fathers: I Clement, II Clement, Ignatius, Polycarp, Didache*, LCL (Cambridge: Harvard University Press, 2003), 203–5.
3 Candida R. Moss, *The Other Christs: Imitating Jesus in Ancient Christian Ideologies of Martyrdom* (Oxford: Oxford University Press, 2010).
4 Allen Brent, *Ignatius of Antioch and the Second Sophistic: A Study of an Early Christian Transformation of Pagan Culture*, Studien und Texte zu Antike und Christentum, vol. 36 (Tübingen: Mohr Siebeck, 2006); Allen Brent, *Ignatius of Antioch: A Martyr Bishop and the Origin of Episcopacy* (London: T&T Clark, 2009).
5 Ignatius, *Letters of Ignatius*, trans. Bart D. Ehrman, LCL (Cambridge, MA: Harvard University Press, 2003). On the middle recension, see Ehrman, "Introduction," 212–13; Paul Foster, "The Epistles of Ignatius of Antioch (Part 1)," *Expository Times* 117, no. 12 (2006): 488–9.
6 See, for example, James Gregory Given, *Ignatius of Antioch and the Historiography of Early Christianity* (Cambridge, MA: Harvard University, 2019); Paul R. Gilliam, *Ignatius of Antioch and the Arian Controversy* (Leiden: Brill, 2017).
7 Given, *Ignatius of Antioch*.
8 George Lakoff and Mark Johnson, *Metaphors We Live By* (Chicago: University of Chicago Press, 1980), 159.
9 Lakoff and Johnson, *Metaphors We Live By*, 3–4.
10 Line Cecilie Engh and Mark Turner, "Introduction: A Case of Symbolic Cognition," in *The Symbolism of Marriage in Early Christianity and the Latin Middle Ages: Images, Impact, Cognition*, ed. Line Cecilie Engh (Amsterdam: Amsterdam University Press, 2019), 16.
11 Mark J. Landau, Michael D. Robinson, and Brian P. Meier, eds., "Introduction," in *The Power of Metaphor: Examining Its Influence on Social Life* (Washington, DC: American Psychological Association, 2014), 5.
12 Zoltán Kövecses, *Metaphor in Culture: Universality and Variation* (Cambridge: Cambridge University Press, 2005), 6–7.
13 See, for example, Hugo Lundhaug, *Images of Rebirth: Cognitive Poetics and Transformational Soteriology in the Gospel of Philip and the Exegesis on the Soul* (Leiden: Brill, 2010); Mayer, "Medicine and Metaphor in Late Antiquity"; Anna Rebecca Solevåg, "Marriage Symbolism and Social Reality in the New Testament: Husbands and Wives, Christ and the Church," in *The Symbolism of Marriage in Early Christianity and the Latin Middle Ages: Images, Impact, Cognition*, ed. Line Cecilie Engh (Amsterdam: Amsterdam University Press, 2019). See also the introduction to this volume, Engh and Turner, "Introduction."
14 Lundhaug, *Images of Rebirth*, 27.
15 Engh and Turner, "Introduction," 17.
16 Upson-Saia, "Rethinking Medical Metaphors," 437–8.
17 Mayer, "Medicine and Metaphor in Late Antiquity."
18 See Marianne Bjelland Kartzow, *The Slave Metaphor and Gendered Enslavement in Early Christian Discourse: Double Trouble Embodied*, Routledge Studies in the Early Christian World (London: Routledge, 2018), 8–10.
19 Mayer, "Medicine and Metaphor in Late Antiquity," 450–7.
20 David T. Mitchell and Sharon L. Snyder, *Narrative Prosthesis: Disability and the Dependencies of Discourse* (Ann Arbor: University of Michigan Press, 2001), 60–2.

21 Mitchell and Snyder, *Narrative Prosthesis*, 58.
22 S.v., LSJ.
23 S.v., LSJ. For medical usage, see, for example, Hippocrates, *De Medico* (Leiden: Brill, 1978), 10.
24 See, for example, W. H. S. Jones, trans., *Pliny: Natural History*, vol. 8. Loeb Classical Library (Cambridge: Harvard University Press, 1963), 25.6.17; 28.43.153; Galen Sect. 8.
25 William R. Schoedel, *Ignatius of Antioch: A Commentary on the Letters of Ignatius of Antioch*, Hermeneia (Philadelphia: Fortress Press, 1985), 59.
26 Simon Swain, ed. *Seeing the Face, Seeing the Soul: Polemon's Physiognomy from Classical Antiquity to Medieval Islam* (Oxford: Oxford University Press, 2007), 385. See also my reading of the dog metaphor in the story of the Syro-Phoenecian woman (Mark 7:24–30). Anna Rebecca Solevåg, *Negotiating the Disabled Body: Representations of Disability in Early Christian Texts*, ed. David G. Horrell, Early Christianity and Its Literature (Atlanta, GA: SBL Press, 2018), 41–9.
27 Schoedel, *Ignatius of Antioch*, 96.
28 S.v., LSJ.
29 Schoedel, *Ignatius of Antioch*, 97.
30 S.v., LSJ.
31 See, for example, Galen of Pergamon, "De Antidotis," in *Claudii Galeni Opera Omnia*, ed. Carl Gottlob Kühn (Leipzig: Libraria Karl Knobloch, 1821–33), 1.3, 1.11 (Kühn 14:18, 55); Claudii Galeni, "De Simplicium Medicamentorum [Temperamentis Ac] Facultatibus," in *Claudii Galeni Opera Omnia*, ed. Carl Gottlob Kühn (Leipzig: Libraria Karl Knobloch, 1821–33), 9.15, 11.1 (Kühn: 12:92, 361).
32 LSJ, s.v. λοιμότης, "pestilent condition."
33 LSJ, s.v. λοιμός: "plague, pest"; BDAG, s.v.: "pestilence, plagues, diseases."
34 Jacques Jouanna, "Air, Miasma and Contagion in the Time of Hippocrates and the Survival of Miasmas in Post-Hippocratic Medicine (Rufus of Ephesus, Galen and Palladius)," in *Greek Medicine from Hippocrates to Galen*, ed. Philip J. van der Eijk (Leuven: Brill, 2012), 125.
35 Vivian Nutton, *Ancient Medicine* (London: Routledge, 2004), 26.
36 Galen, Comp. Med. Gen. 2.1 (Kühn, CGO 13.468–9).
37 Schoedel, *Ignatius of Antioch*, 262.
38 Schoedel, *Ignatius of Antioch*, 263.
39 Emma J. Edelstein and Ludwig Edelstein, *Asclepius: Collection and Interpretation of the Testimonies*, vol. 2 (Baltimore: Johns Hopkins University Press, 1998), 153.
40 Jared Secord, "The Celibate Athlete: Athletic Metaphors, Medical Thought, and Sexual Abstinence in the Second and Third Centuries CE," *Studies in Late Antiquity* 2, no. 4 (2018): 478.
41 Mayer, "Medicine and Metaphor in Late Antiquity," 462.
42 According to Schoedel, flesh does not represent the sphere of sin to Ignatius, but rather the sphere of corruptibility. Schoedel, *Ignatius of Antioch*, 23.
43 Mayer, "Medicine and Metaphor in Late Antiquity," 445–7.
44 Mayer, "Medicine and Metaphor in Late Antiquity," 444.
45 Mayer, "Medicine and Metaphor in Late Antiquity," 460.
46 Susan Sontag, *Illness as Metaphor and Aids and Its Metaphors* (London: Penguin Books, 2002), 84.
47 Sontag, *Illness as Metaphor*, 151.
48 Papias, Frag. 4. Bart D. Ehrman, trans., *The Apostolic Fathers: Epistle of Barnabas, Papias and Quadratus, Epistle to Diognetus, the Shepherd of Hermas*, vol. 2, LCL (Cambridge: Harvard University Press, 2003).
49 Solevåg, *Negotiating the Disabled Body*, 117.
50 S.v. LSJ.
51 BDAG and LSJ, s.v. "κωφός."

52 Christian Laes, "Silent History? Speech Impairment in Roman Antiquity," in *Disabilities in Roman Antiquity: Disparate Bodies a Capite ad Calcem*, eds. Christian Laes, C. F. Goodey, and M. Lynn Rose (Leiden: Brill, 2013), 153–5.
53 Martha L. Rose, *The Staff of Oedipus: Transforming Disability in Ancient Greece* (Ann Arbor: University of Michigan Press, 2003), 72, 76–7.
54 On metaphorical uses of blindness in the ancient Mediterranean people, see, for example, Chad Hartsock, *Sight and Blindness in Luke-Acts: The Use of Physical Features in Characterization*, BINS (Leiden: Brill, 2008); Lisa Trentin, "Exploring Visual Impairment in Roman Antiquity," in *Disabilities in Roman Antiquity: Disparate Bodies a Capite ad Calcem*, eds. Christian Laes, C. F. Goodey, and M. Lynn Rose (Leiden: Brill, 2013); Jennifer L. Koosed and Darla Schumm, "Out of the Darkness: Examining the Rhetoric of Blindness in the Gospel of John," in *Disability in Judaism, Christianity, and Islam: Sacred Texts, Historical Traditions, and Social Analysis*, eds. Darla Schumm and Michael Stoltzfus (New York: Palgrave Macmillan, 2011).
55 Another biblical passage which links silence to the figure of Christ is Acts 8:32. Luke quotes Is 53:7, referring to the "suffering servant" as ἄφωνος.
56 Mitchell and Snyder, *Narrative Prosthesis*.
57 Cf. Moss' reading of this parable. Candida R. Moss, "Mark and Matthew," in *The Bible and Disability. A Commentary*, eds. Sarah J. Melcher, Mikeal C. Parsons, and Amos Yong (Waco, TX: Baylor University Press, 2017).
58 "Untimely birth," s.v., LSJ.
59 Secord, "The Celibate Athlete," 480.

Bibliography

Ancient Sources

Edelstein, Emma J., and Ludwig Edelstein. *Asclepius: Collection and Interpretation of the Testimonies*. Vol. 2. Baltimore: Johns Hopkins University Press, 1998.
Ehrman, Bart D., trans. *The Apostolic Fathers: Epistle of Barnabas, Papias and Quadratus, Epistle to Diognetus, the Shepherd of Hermas*. LCL. Vol. 2. Cambridge: Harvard University Press, 2003.
Galen, Claudii. "De Simplicium Medicamentorum [Temperamentis Ac] Facultatibus." In *Claudii Galeni Opera Omnia*, edited by Carl Gottlob Kühn. Vol. 20, 11:369–12:377. Leipzig: Libraria Karl Knobloch, 1821–33.
Galen of Pergamon. "De Antidotis." In *Claudii Galeni Opera Omnia*, edited by Carl Gottlob Kühn. Vol. 20. Leipzig: Libraria Karl Knobloch, 1821–33, 14:1–209.
Ignatius. *Letters of Ignatius*. Translated by Bart D. Ehrman. LCL. Cambridge, MA: Harvard University Press, 2003.

Modern Sources

Brent, Allen. *Ignatius of Antioch and the Second Sophistic: A Study of an Early Christian Transformation of Pagan Culture*. Studien Und Texte Zu Antike Und Christentum. Vol. 36. Tübingen: Mohr Siebeck, 2006.
———. *Ignatius of Antioch: A Martyr Bishop and the Origin of Episcopacy*. London: T&T Clark, 2009.
Ehrman, Bart D. "Introduction: Letters of Ignatius." In *The Apostolic Fathers: I Clement, Ii Clement, Ignatius, Polycarp, Didache*. LCL, 203–17. Cambridge: Harvard University Press, 2003.

Engh, Line Cecilie, and Mark Turner. "Introduction: A Case of Symbolic Cognition." In *The Symbolism of Marriage in Early Christianity and the Latin Middle Ages: Images, Impact, Cognition*, edited by Line Cecilie Engh, 13–35. Amsterdam: Amsterdam University Press, 2019.

Foster, Paul. "The Epistles of Ignatius of Antioch (Part 1)." *Expository Times* 117, no. 12 (2006): 487–95.

Gilliam, Paul R. *Ignatius of Antioch and the Arian Controversy*. Leiden: Brill, 2017.

Given, James Gregory. *Ignatius of Antioch and the Historiography of Early Christianity*. Cambridge: Harvard University Press, 2019.

Hartsock, Chad. *Sight and Blindness in Luke-Acts: The Use of Physical Features in Characterization*. Bins. Leiden: Brill, 2008.

Jouanna, Jacques. "Air, Miasma and Contagion in the Time of Hippocrates and the Survival of Miasmas in Post-Hippocratic Medicine (Rufus of Ephesus, Galen and Palladius)." In *Greek Medicine from Hippocrates to Galen*, edited by Philip J. van der Eijk, 121–36. Leuven: Brill, 2012.

Kartzow, Marianne Bjelland. *The Slave Metaphor and Gendered Enslavement in Early Christian Discourse: Double Trouble Embodied*. Routledge Studies in the Early Christian World. London: Routledge, 2018.

Koosed, Jennifer L., and Darla Schumm. "Out of the Darkness: Examining the Rhetoric of Blindness in the Gospel of John." In *Disability in Judaism, Christianity, and Islam: Sacred Texts, Historical Traditions, and Social Analysis*, edited by Darla Schumm and Michael Stoltzfus, 77–91. New York: Palgrave Macmillan, 2011.

Laes, Christian. "Silent History? Speech Impairment in Roman Antiquity." In *Disabilities in Roman Antiquity: Disparate Bodies a Capite Ad Calcem*, edited by Christian Laes, C. F. Goodey, and M. Lynn Rose, 145–80. Leiden: Brill, 2013.

Lakoff, George, and Mark Johnson. *Metaphors We Live By*. Chicago: University of Chicago Press, 1980.

Lundhaug, Hugo. *Images of Rebirth: Cognitive Poetics and Transformational Soteriology in the Gospel of Philip and the Exegesis on the Soul*. Leiden: Brill, 2010.

Mayer, Wendy. "Medicine and Metaphor in Late Antiquity: How Some Recent Shifts Are Changing the Field." *Studies in Late Antiquity* 2, no. 4 (2018): 440–63.

Mitchell, David T., and Sharon L. Snyder. *Narrative Prosthesis: Disability and the Dependencies of Discourse*. Ann Arbor: University of Michigan Press, 2001.

Moss, Candida R. *The Other Christs: Imitating Jesus in Ancient Christian Ideologies of Martyrdom*. Oxford: Oxford University Press, 2010.

———. "Mark and Matthew." In *The Bible and Disability: A Commentary*, edited by Sarah J. Melcher, Mikeal C. Parsons, and Amos Yong, 275–302. Waco, TX: Baylor University Press, 2017.

Nutton, Vivian. *Ancient Medicine*. London: Routledge, 2004.

Rose, Martha L. *The Staff of Oedipus: Transforming Disability in Ancient Greece*. Ann Arbor: University of Michigan Press, 2003.

Schoedel, William R. *Ignatius of Antioch: A Commentary on the Letters of Ignatius of Antioch*. Hermeneia. Philadelphia: Fortress Press, 1985.

Secord, Jared. "The Celibate Athlete: Athletic Metaphors, Medical Thought, and Sexual Abstinence in the Second and Third Centuries Ce." *Studies in Late Antiquity* 2, no. 4 (2018): 464–90.

Solevåg, Anna Rebecca. *Negotiating the Disabled Body: Representations of Disability in Early Christian Texts*. Early Christianity and Its Literature. Edited by David G. Horrell. Atlanta, GA: SBL Press, 2018.

―――. "Marriage Symbolism and Social Reality in the New Testament: Husbands and Wives, Christ and the Church." In *The Symbolism of Marriage in Early Christianity and the Latin Middle Ages: Images, Impact, Cognition*, edited by Line Cecilie Engh. Amsterdam: Amsterdam University Press, 2019.

Sontag, Susan. *Illness as Metaphor and Aids and Its Metaphors*. London: Penguin Books, 2002.

Swain, Simon, ed. *Seeing the Face, Seeing the Soul: Polemon's Physiognomy from Classical Antiquity to Medieval Islam*. Oxford: Oxford University Press, 2007.

Trentin, Lisa. "Exploring Visual Impairment in Roman Antiquity." In *Disabilities in Roman Antiquity. Disparate Bodies a Capite Ad Calcem*, edited by Christian Laes, C. F. Goodey, and M. Lynn Rose, 89–114. Leiden: Brill, 2013.

Upson-Saia, Kristi. "Rethinking Medical Metaphors in Late Ancient Christianity." *Studies in Late Antiquity* 2, no. 4 (2018): 437–9.

3 A Circumcising Mission to the Gentiles and Hazing Culture

Adam Booth

Introduction

Alexander and Ben have much in common. They both are incredibly nervous, standing disrobed and somewhat intoxicated, experiencing shame and fear of impending pain, yet fully convinced that what is about to happen is right, necessary, what they need to do to be fully united with the men standing around them, and what they need to do to have a real future. While Alexander and Ben have much in common, they are separated by almost 2,000 years. Ben is a first-year undergraduate at State U, awaiting the paddling that will constitute the final stage of his initiation into his fraternity of choice.[1] Alexander is a first-century follower of Christ and a member of a Pauline church somewhere in Galatia. At least, he had considered himself a member, but recently, after Paul's departure, a second wave of teachers had arrived, and they had convinced him that he had to be circumcised to really belong, to really be "in Christ."[2] How might Alexander and Ben have been convinced to accept such a high-cost initiation? The thesis of this chapter is that modern psychological research on Ben's situation, hazing, may help us understand the motivations of both Alexander and the second-wave teachers.[3]

Recent scholarship on the movement that Paul opposes in Galatians has concentrated on attempting to reconstruct what kind of arguments the second-wave teachers may have used to persuade gentile men like Alexander to be circumcised.[4] For instance, Matthew Thiessen argues that these teachers

> preached that just as Abraham, who was of gentile origin, heard God's call . . . and underwent circumcision, so too should gentiles in Galatia . . . [and] that they also argued for the virtue-inducing power of circumcision . . . by pointing to the connection that Gen 17:1 makes between wholeness and circumcision.[5]

The results have been impressive, but an assumption that drives much of this research is that people are primarily persuaded to do apparently costly things by intellectually clever (in this case, exegetical) arguments.[6] However, both anecdotally and empirically, we know that people are more inclined to accept or produce intellectual justifications for a course of action that is already appealing to them.[7]

DOI: 10.4324/9781003080534-4

Modern psychological research on hazing provides insights as to why organizations with high-cost initiations are attractive to people. Such insights cannot be automatically assumed to map directly onto the motivations of people operating in a very different culture. However, they provide one possible avenue of escape from a narrowly intellectual conception of why people in a first-century Galatian context found demands to engage in this form of body modification so compelling. These more "gut-level" motivations can then be tested against the available textual evidence to determine how well they may have corresponded to the lives of people in these Pauline communities.

In the first section of the chapter, I show that a modern psychological definition of hazing describes well how gentile church members would likely have regarded circumcision. In the second section, I present two psychological accounts of hazing motivations and compare these to what we can reconstruct of life in the Pauline churches from Galatians and other Pauline letters.

The costs of circumcision

Psychologist Ando Cimino defines hazing as follows: "the generation of induction costs (i.e. part of the experiences necessary to be acknowledged as a 'legitimate' group member) that appear unattributable to group-relevant assessments, preparations, or chance."[8] I begin this section by outlining some of the social and bodily costs that circumcision would generate for a gentile male church member, organized under the headings of pain and shame. I then show that, while the second-wave teachers may have believed these costs were group-relevant, gentile church members would have initially viewed such a claim with suspicion. That is, they would have understood the second-wave teachers to be offering to haze them.

Pain

Any surgical procedure in antiquity would be painful and dangerous. Vivian Nutton posits the risk of operative trauma and wound infection as the reason why Galen and other contemporary medical authors regarded "surgical intervention [as] the treatment of last resort."[9] Circumcision was no exception, and at least some ancient Jewish authors acknowledged this. Even in the context of a defence of circumcision, Philo still acknowledges that the procedure involves "severe pains" (χαλεπῶν ἀλγηδόνων; *On the Special Laws* 1.3).[10] We find mention of the dangers of circumcision also in certain rabbinic texts, such as m. Šabb. 19.5, which recommends delaying circumcision if a child is sick, and t. Šabb. 25:8, in which R. Nathan tells a woman to stop circumcising her sons, as they are dying from haemophilia. There is also a reference in b. Me'il. 17a to the difficult nature of post-operative recovery following adult circumcision.

Modern studies of circumcisions performed outside of clinical settings confirm the danger and also show that men expect the procedure to be painful. In a literature review, Kate Bonner collects the following data: of patients referred to hospitals in Kenya and Nigeria with complications following a circumcision performed by an "unqualified traditional surgeon," 16% had serious or fatal injuries (including death from septicaemia or haemorrhage and complete loss of the penis from gangrene); in Pakistan, an increased incidence of tetanus can be detected in boys shortly after their circumcision, leading to death in 1.6% of cases.[11] Another study shows that adverse effects are more common in adult men than in boys or infants.[12] In a study of reasons why men in Tanzania are reluctant to become circumcised as adults, even with access to modern pain management, "the first fear mentioned was the fear of the pain involved in the operation and in the healing process."[13] Interviewees also believed the pain would be worse in adult men than in children.[14]

Few ancient sources give detailed accounts of the pain or physical danger associated with circumcision. However, especially given the public performative nature of much medical practice at the time,[15] members of the Pauline churches in Galatia would likely expect such a procedure to be both traumatic and dangerous. If the second-wave teachers are gentiles,[16] relatively inexperienced in performing circumcisions, this would augment the risks.

Shame

In his wide-ranging study of ancient Greco-Roman attitudes to the foreskin, Frederick Hodges demonstrates that its removal would, for a typical gentile male, constitute a "desexualization, disinvigoration, and uglification of the body."[17] Similarly, Andreas Blaschke shows that, among a wide range of pagan authors who comment on the practice, "Circumcision appears in conceptual proximity to, and as an intensification of, other forms of bodily mutilation."[18] According to Daniel Boyarin's analysis, "pre-modern Jewish males frequently perceived themselves as femminized (sic.), in part because of their circumcision."[19]

A sampling of the evidence suffices for illustrative purposes. In a wide variety of Greek artistic depictions of idealized males, the prepuce is substantially longer relative to the shaft than is naturally observed.[20] Lucian confirms that a long prepuce was perceived as attractive (*Lexiphanes* 12.3.62). The reasonably common use of prepuce (πόσθων) as a synecdoche for penis helps explain a cultural conflation between circumcision and castration, a highly taboo practice.[21] For instance, in a common Greek myth, attested by Philo of Byblos, Kronos circumcised himself as atonement for castrating his father Ouranos.[22] While the relevant Roman legislation is slightly later than Paul's period, certain prohibitions of castration included explicit exceptions allowing Jews to circumcise their children (e.g. *Digest* 48.1.11.1). The exceptive clauses only make sense if the legislator would have assumed that at least some readers of the laws have understood a ban on castration to also disallow circumcision.[23]

Hodges discusses the methods men would use for avoiding "unseemly externalization of the glans"[24] while exercising nude, something that would be impossible for a circumcised man. That exposing the glans was taboo even in contexts when a complete lack of clothing was expected is reflected in the fact that both the Greek term ψωλός and the Latin *verpus* do double-duty, meaning both circumcised and erect.[25] The best evidence that lack of foreskin brought shame may be the fact that some men who considered themselves to lack sufficient foreskin sought out surgery to modify their bodies, despite the risks of surgical interventions described previously.[26]

Jews in the Hellenistic world were well aware of these attitudes. In Josephus' account of King Izates' conversion to Judaism, he states that the king was reluctant to be circumcised not because of the pain or danger, but because his mother warned him that it would cause his subjects to despise him (*Ant.* 20.39). Josephus and Philo both report that circumcision is mocked and derided (Josephus, *Ag. Ap.* 2.137; Philo, *Spec.* 1.1.1–2). Philo also describes circumcision as a way of "checking [a man's] pride" (*QG* 3.47). Andrew Jacobs analyses Talmudic ceremonies for a man's conversion to Judaism (arguing they reflect earlier traditions) and finds that they associate and highlight the man's circumcision and his adoption of Israel's "pained, oppress, harassed, and torn" status.[27]

The study of men's resistance to adult circumcision in Tanzania referenced earlier suggests one additional dimension of shame: the experience of being circumcised by someone younger. One interviewee said to a student researcher, "Those who circumcise should also be elders. You know if you bring a grown-up man to a young man like you, and you start touching him and circumcise him, he won't agree."[28] For many of the men surveyed, this shame was strong enough to outweigh any social pressure to be circumcised that may be generated by belief in public health benefits in the form of reduced community HIV/AIDS incidence.[29] Of course, it is impossible to know the relative ages of the second-wave teachers and the gentile church-members in Galatia they are trying to reach, but in a society that associates hierarchy with age, an age-based status mismatch might have provided additional shame-related cost to becoming circumcised.

Group relevance

In the previous two sections, I have shown that, evaluated within the relevant cultural encyclopaedia, circumcision would have constituted a high-cost initiation. That alone is not enough, though, for it to count as hazing under Cimino's definition; it must also "appear unattributable to group-relevant assessments, preparations, or chance."[30] For instance, Cimino gives the example that being required to sing solo would not be hazing if it was part of a choir's initiation ceremony, but likely would be if it formed part of the lacrosse team's. The word "appears" in Cimino's definition suggests that two different observers could come to different conclusions as to whether or not a certain activity constituted hazing based upon their particular conceptions of what is relevant to the group.

There are many reasons the second-wave teachers may have thought (and proposed to others) that circumcision was group-relevant. They may have seen it as a legal obligation.[31] They may also, like Philo, have understood circumcision to both symbolize and help to effect "the excision of pleasure and all passions and the putting away of impious conceit."[32] The belief that the removal of part of the body would help someone avoid sin and enter into the kingdom of God is also attested in Mark 9:43–48.[33]

At some point, gentile church members in Galatia may have become convinced by these arguments. The focus of this chapter, though, is on how they could have found the invitation to be circumcised to be compelling before they became intellectually convinced. There is good reason to think that they would not have been instantly convinced by either of these arguments.

They would have been disinclined to believe that circumcision was a divine mandate for the simple reason that Paul had not told them it was, even though he had taught other culturally surprising obligations.[34] Possibly, he had even taught them that by remaining uncircumcised, they served as "eschatological gentiles . . . [with an] exclusive commitment to the god of Israel," fulfilling prophecy and guaranteeing that the day of the Lord was at hand.[35] Josephus' narrative of the conversion of King Izates (*Ant.* 20.17–19) features a Jewish missionary, Ananias, who promotes gentile observance of the entire law except circumcision. Blaschke argues that Ananias is here describing two different paths of salvation (for men): circumcised and not.[36] While Josephus seems to disagree with Ananias's position, it must have had some defenders to be worth polemicizing against and shows that the necessity of circumcision for those who desire to be allied with the Deity of the Torah was not the only conceptually available reading of this law.

As for the argument that circumcision would aid the male gentile church members eliminate their passions, Hodges explains well why "the Greeks would have found incomprehensible, ludicrous, and chilling the alien ideological milieu in which Philo could formulate [such] a rationalization."[37] *Inter alia*, he points out:

> [While] the Greeks did value modesty, moderation, and restraint, . . . the idea of cutting off part of the genitals to achieve these moral objectives would have appeared to be counterproductive, to say the very least, for by permanently and artificially externalizing the glans, the remnant penis and its possessor would be cast into a permanent state of lewdness.[38]

While the gentile church members in Galatia may at some point have come to see circumcision as group-relevant preparation, they would not have initially viewed it that way. Insights from recent psychological studies of hazing suggest that such a group-irrelevant high-cost initiation might nevertheless have been attractive to them. These studies can help us understand previously overlooked elements of the motivations of both the Galatians and the second-wave teachers.

Two Psychological Accounts of Hazing

In the following two sections, I discuss two complementary understandings of hazing that have recently been proposed by psychologists. The first understands hazing as reinforcing the dominant status of group veterans over group newcomers; the second instead looks at the ways in which hazing is perceived to increase solidarity amongst group members. Both of these types of theories aim to account for both why groups haze and why people are attracted to groups that haze. After describing in more detail these theories and the reasons why psychologists propose them, I consider how these motivations might be reflected in Paul's letters.

2.1 Dominance Theories

When Émile Durkheim studied religious rites of passage from childhood to adulthood, he compared some of them to hazing, claiming that both reinscribed the superiority of the elders.[39] Caroline Keating and her collaborators describe a psychological mechanism whereby discomforting initiations may stimulate social dependency of newcomers on hazers:

> Harsh conditions trigger goal-directed responses in organisms seeking refuge from the duress. . . . Hence the infant seeks out a caregiver when hungry, fearful, tired, or in pain. Under mundane circumstances, manifesting such social dependency would be adaptive. . . . However, the response can be elicited even when the caregiver is the source of the discomfort; that is social dependency may be directed toward the very agent of the mistreatment.[40]

An extreme example of this would be Stockholm syndrome, whereby hostages develop affection for their captors.[41]

Keating's research group has found evidence of this phenomenon in both survey-based field studies and laboratory experiments. Surveying undergraduates who were members of single-sex organizations, Keating's group found that "initiations characterized as involving social deviance were linked to perceptions of the relative power of leaders over new members and to elaborated power structures."[42] In a follow-up study with a larger, all-male, sample group, Gentry McCreary and Joshua Schutts found similar correlations. In particular, a respondent's toleration for hazing was highly predictive of their likelihood to explain the function of their group's initiation process in terms of social dominance.[43]

The same effects were observed in the laboratory. In one experiment carried out by Keating's research team, young men were inducted into a group by performing either innocuous or embarrassing charades. Once inducted, they joined with veteran group members in evaluating the performance of non-group members in various tasks. Participants who had performed the embarrassing charades as opposed to the innocuous ones rated the veteran members as more powerful and were less likely to give evaluations that contradicted those of the veterans.[44]

As we saw earlier, for a first-century Galatian gentile to become circumcised would be highly socially deviant. The comparative data from Tanzania also show that at least some Tanzanian men attribute additional shame to being circumcised by someone inferior in status. The social dominance theory of hazing suggests that a group with this kind of hazing is likely to be one in which leaders have high levels of power. This does not mean that participants (veteran or initiate) would necessarily explain this initiation as one that creates or reinforces such power relationships. Rather, the initiation has its own power to strengthen the authority of the circumciser (possibly via the psychological mechanism Keating describes), and people searching for stronger leadership structures are attracted to join the group. This could occur because they simply observe the power these leaders have, because those who desire strong leaders are also predisposed to have a high tolerance for hazing, or because of some intuitive sense that such initiations create and maintain powerful leaders.

This explanation is more likely to explain the Galatians' motivations if there is other evidence that they were dissatisfied with Paul as a leader, especially if they perceived him as weak. Paul's letter to the Galatians, read in the context of other letters of Paul's, confirms that this was likely true of at least some of the Galatian church members. For instance, on the basis of Paul's extended self-justification in Gal 1–2, Barclay rates as "certain or virtually certain" the claim that the second-wave teachers "brought into question the adequacy of Paul's gospel and his credentials as an apostle."[45] Paul also tells us that he was physically weak when the Galatians first met him (Gal 4:13).[46]

Evidence from the broader Pauline corpus confirms that some people in many of the churches Paul founded saw him as a weak leader. Beverly Gaventa describes Paul as "an authority who does not conform to standard norms of authority"[47]; in her study of Galatians, Susan Eastman reads him as "vulnerable yet authoritative."[48] These two modern scholars give both appreciative and nuanced readings of Paul who "when weak, is strong" (cp. 2 Cor 12:10). Certain of his contemporaries, though, were considerably less impressed and perceived in Paul not an evangelical tension between vulnerability and authority, but weakness *simpliciter*.

Some of the Corinthians, for instance, complained that Paul's "bodily presence [was] weak, and his speech contemptible" (2 Cor 10:10). In 1 Cor 2:1–5, Paul admits to a lack of skill in public speaking, offering instead "weakness and trembling, traits that depicted a shameful, cowardly, and incompetent person in his speech."[49] As Albert Harrill argues, "to accuse a person of weak bodily presence and deficient speech is to call that person unfit for public office or otherwise to dominate others."[50]

Paul also used metaphors to describe himself that characterized him as weak and dependent. For instance, in First Thessalonians, Paul describes himself as an infant (2:7)[51] and as orphaned when separated from the church at Thessalonica, as if the church members were his parents (2:17).[52] Speaking of these images, Reidar Aasgard comments that "Paul is putting himself at their [the Thessalonians'] mercy."[53] Of course, Paul also presents himself as powerful in several places (e.g. 1 Cor 4:21), but if one were looking for reasons to reject Paul as too weak to be a good leader, there would be no lack of data available to support such a judgement.

In his letter to the Galatians, Paul responds to a desire for more straightforwardly authoritarian leadership in two main ways. The first is to recharacterize his weakness as revelatory of Christ. Paul makes clear in 1 Cor 11:1 that he believes that imitation of him constitutes imitation of Christ. Similarly, he tells the Galatians that he has died and it is Christ who lives in him (2:20). When the Galatians first met him, they had welcomed him as Christ (4:14). Louis Martyn spells out the connection:

> The odiously sick ... figure [Paul] was seen, then, to be in fact an angel sent from God, just as the legally executed criminal was seen to be in fact God's own Son. That correspondence caused the Galatians to welcome Paul, and that correspondence caused their attachment to Paul to be an attachment to Christ.[54]

Paul also portrays his ongoing suffering as something fruitful and life-giving for them: he is giving birth to them (4:19). As Eastman has persuasively argued, "Paul's 'labor' represents God's 'labor,' both as intense anguish on behalf of God's people and as a creative power bringing the new creation to birth."[55] Paul seeks to persuade the Galatians that they should prefer his "weak" form of leadership to the second-wave teachers' more domineering form, as it is his form that faithfully reproduces the Passion of Christ and of God.

Paul's second response to a desire for dominant leaders focuses less on his own leadership style, and more on the ways he hopes for the Galatians to participate in their church community. In Gal 4:1–9, Paul characterizes the church members as children in distinction to slaves. While his rejection of the pedagogue (3:24–25) is primarily about the role of the Mosaic law in the church's common life, it also presents a certain form of leadership as belonging to a former age for which they should no longer yearn. In 5:13–15, he calls them to mutual submission, excluding the existence of a class demanding special one-sided submission. In 6:13, he suggests that the second-wave teachers wish to treat those they persuade to become circumcised as objects of boasting, not as equal partners in the gospel. Paul rejects the kind of leadership that hazing might engender or sustain.

2.2 Solidarity Theories

In a study of female genital mutilation/cutting in Senegambia, Bettina Shell-Duncan and her collaborators found that one social function of FGM/C is to "signal to other circumcised women that a girl or woman has been trained to respect the authority of her circumcised elders and is therefore worthy of inclusion in their social network."[56] This is an explanation of a body modification in terms of promoting group solidarity by reassuring veterans that newcomers can be trusted, and is paralleled by various studies of collegiate hazing. In addition to the connection between hazing tolerance and social dominance, the McCreary and Schutts survey of members of all-male collegiate organizations also found that toleration of hazing was significantly predictive of a desire to create group solidarity.[57] Keating's survey data found a connection between how important an individual rated a group to which they belonged and how physically severe its initiation was.[58] These field studies are consistent with previous experimental work carried out by Cimino. Cimino hypothesized that hazing would be most severe when organizations need to guard themselves against newcomers exploiting the automatic benefits of membership.[59] Automatic benefits are distinguished from benefits with slow or costly accrual processes. For instance, membership in the basket-weaving club may afford the benefit of increased skill in the weaving of baskets, but only if a member commits time and effort to the training and mentorship available in the club. Membership in an elite fraternity, though, provides access to status, group protection, and common property automatically upon admission. There would be greater need to guard oneself against exploitation of such benefits if maintaining the availability of these benefits requires costly cooperative action on the part of veteran members.

Cimino tested this theory using vignette experiments (wherein undergraduate participants answered questions about what type of initiation they would devise if they were members of various types of groups, as described by materials created and supplied by the experimenter). He found that participants expected to haze more severely in groups that strongly require cooperation and have high automatic benefits, and that the level of non-automatic benefits did not impact the desired level of hazing activity.[60]

Cimino classes this as a solidarity theory, as hazing thus motivated serves to reassure veteran members that free-riding by newcomers is effectively impossible.[61] On this theory, hazing creates trust. Given previous work demonstrating that the perception of the presence of freeloaders leads other participants to lower their contributions to a collective action, Cimino further suggests that hazing ensures continued commitment from veterans as a cooperative group incorporates new members.[62]

Cimino's characterization of groups that are likely to haze corresponds rather well to the Pauline church in Galatia. Paul has sought to form a community in which members "bear one another's burdens" (6:2). Material poverty is one of the types of burdens that must be shared (2:10). While the community was instructed to "do good" for all, they were to concentrate their euergetism on insiders (6:10). This provides automatic benefits to members and demands costly cooperative activity. In addition to the social and material benefits directly provided by the community, Paul told his followers in Corinth that when they exclude someone from the group, that person is especially subject to Satan's malevolent activity (1 Cor 5:1–13). As Paul would write to Christ followers in Rome, gentiles who are part of this community are "grafted in" to the fruitful tree of Israel, the recipients of God's promises (Rom 11:17). These are valuable automatic benefits, given graciously, not slowly accrued (compare 2 Cor 5:17). It would then be reasonable for veteran church members to be concerned that newcomers may be freeloaders. Cimino's theory does not assume that veterans would consciously put a costly initiation in place in order to discourage such freeloaders, or that newcomers consciously seek out such an initiation for similar reasons. Rather, Cimino's work suggests that groups with these kinds of concerns are naturally predisposed to favour costly initiations.

Paul does little to deny that the community might be "taken for a ride" by freeloaders. Paul's primary response mirrors his explicit statement to the church members in Corinth: "Why not rather be wronged?" (1 Cor 6:4). If veteran church members in Galatia are concerned that they will suffer loss because of freeloading newcomers, Paul's main response is to point to his own suffering (4:13–14, 19) as both a model for them (4:12) and modelled upon Christ's suffering (6:17).[63] For Paul, even if a low-cost initiation would lead to harm for veterans, this is no reason to prefer a high-cost initiation, for suffering is a necessary part of the call of his gospel until one has "departed to be with Christ" (cp. Phil 1:23). As Eastman puts it, "Christ will be formed in the Galatians when they 'become like' Paul by exchanging the marker of circumcision for the brand marks of Jesus—that is, when they join the apostle in suffering for the sake of the gospel."[64] Paul also uses metaphors to reframe how the community thinks about the admission of new members. Veterans are still children in God's family, and it is God who adopts (e.g. 4:5). Children do not get to pick their adopted siblings. That is rather the exclusive domain of *patresfamiliae*.

Paul does some work to discourage freeloading behaviour. He states that those who do not live up to certain demanding moral standards should not expect to receive automatic eschatological benefits (5:18–21). He encourages all to participate in group euergetism (6:10) and asserts the right of teachers to expect support (6:6). He devotes somewhat more attention to counsel that would tend to mitigate the potential for veterans to reduce their group input out of concern for the presence of freeloaders. He warns against envy and conceit (5:26) and instructs people to concern themselves with their own work without paying attention to that of others (6:4). People who refrain from comparing their input to the group with others' are less likely to classify another group member as a freeloader. When correcting erring church members, Paul cautions them to do so gently, "lest you also be tempted" (6:1).[65] Paul does not state what particular temptation should be avoided but one, when faced with the perception of freeloaders, is to reduce one's effort.

Conclusion

Insights from modern psychological research on hazing draw our attention to two features of Pauline communities that are predictive of a tendency to haze: the perceived need for stronger authority figures and to guard against group-resource exploitation by freeloading newcomers. This helps explain the motivations of the second-wave teachers in promoting circumcision of gentile male group members, and the motivations of those who are attracted to them. None of this is to deny that their intellectual (exegetical) arguments were important to them. Likely, those who were convinced of the need to circumcise male church members would have articulated that need in those terms. This research however gets at something prior to the articulation of the convinced: the psychological reasons why some would have been motivated to construct and accept these arguments.

Similarly, Paul certainly responds to exegetical arguments with exegetical arguments, and his rebuttal constitutes a large portion of the text of his letter to the Galatians. But wittingly or not, Paul is also attempting to build a community and form people in ways that would make hazing less likely. He redefines what leadership should look like and encourages members of his churches not to act out of fear of potential suffering or loss. His program for rebuilding social and personal identity undercuts the factors that motivate hazing. By looking at the struggles of the nascent church in Galatia in terms of hazing, we can see how debates about modification of male bodies do not begin or end with intellectual or textual argumentation but are deeply interwoven with basic psychological motivations related to how people live together in communities.

Notes

1 For documentation that such experiences can be part of such initiations, see the litera-ture review in Elizabeth J. Allan et al., "College Student Hazing Experiences, Attitudes, and Perceptions: Implications for Prevention," *Journal of Student Affairs Research and Practice* 56 (2019): 32–48, 34–5.
2 It is hard to reconstruct many of details of precisely how such an adult circumcision might have taken place. On the possibility that Alexander would have consumed alco-hol prior to his circumcision, which is merely evocative and upon which the following argument does not rest, see the discussion on the use of wine to diminish sensitivity to pain before surgery in Valentine Belfiglio, "Perioperative Anesthesia in Ancient Rome: 27 B.C.–A.D. 476," *Neurology and Neuroscience Reports* 1 (2018): 1–3. Paul's letter presupposes that many church members in Galatia had accepted circumcision at the urging of these teachers (3:1; future more vivid conditional in 5:2). See also John M. G. Barclay, "Mirror-Reading a Polemical Letter: Galatians as a Test-Case," *Journal for the Study of the New Testament* 31 (1987): 73–93, 88.
3 These teachers are often referred to as Paul's "rivals" or "opponents." However, as Peder Borgen has argued, they may well have presented themselves as bringing (nearer) to completion the good work begun through Paul: as his successors, not rivals. In order to describe their relationship to the initial Pauline mission without taking a stance on this question, I describe them as "second-wave teachers." See discussion in Peder Bor-gen, "Observations on the Theme 'Paul and Philo': Paul's Preaching of Circumcision in Galatia (Gal 5:11) and Debates on Circumcision in Philo," in *Die paulinische Literatur und Theologie*, ed. Sigfred Pedersen, Teologiske Studier 7 (Aarhus: Aarhus University Press, 1980), 85–102, 91; Barclay, "Mirror-Reading a Polemical Letter," 80; J. Louis Martyn, *Galatians*, vol. 33a, AB (New York: Doubleday, 1997), 117. The scholarship cited above counsels against assuming these second-wave teachers were Jewish. Isaac Soon has recently argued that one text often adduced in support of the proposition that some Jews forcibly circumcised adults, 1 Macc 2:46, shows no such thing. Isaac T. Soon, "'In Strength' Not 'by Force': Re-Reading the Circumcision of the Uncircumcised ἐν ἰσχύι in 1 Macc 2:46." *Journal for the Study of the Pseudepigrapha* 29 (2020): 149–67.
4 Presumably, these teachers would also have wanted to persuade female church mem-bers who were mothers of young boys to have their sons circumcised. The focus of this chapter (like that of Paul in his epistle responding to this development), though, is on their appeal to men to accept circumcision in their own bodies (and not their sons' either). For discussion of how the gendered nature of circumcision as a sign was later weaponized in anti-Jewish Christian polemic, see M. Adrael Tong, "'Given as a Sign': Circumcision and Bodily Discourse in Late Antique Judaism and Christianity" (PhD dissertation, Fordham University, New York, 2019). When I refer to male gentile mem-bers of a Pauline church in Galatia, I also assume that such people were uncircumcised prior to their encounter with the second-wave teachers. For texts from Jewish and gen-tile authors (respectively) referring to circumcision as an exclusive *nota Judaica* in this period, see the summaries in Andreas Blaschke, *Beschneidung: Zeugnisse der Bibel und verwandter Texte*, Texte und Arbeiten zum neutestamentlichen Zeitalter 28 (Tübingen: Francke, 1998), 320, 360. To be circumcised was to "cross the border" into Judaism, to borrow a phrase from Nissan Rubin, *"Brit Milah*: A Study of Change in Custom," in *The Covenant of Circumcision: New Perspectives on an Ancient Jewish Rite*, ed. Elizabeth W. Mark (Hanover, NH: Brandeis University Press, 2003), 87–97, 88.
5 Matthew Thiessen, *Paul and the Gentile Problem* (Oxford: Oxford University Press, 2018), 76, 31. For further reconstruction of these teachers' arguments, see J. Louis Mar-tyn, *Theological Issues in the Letters of Paul* (Edinburgh: T&T Clark, 1997), 7–24. For an alternative approach, which understands Paul's aversion to gentile circumci-sion as resistance to Roman power, see Andrew Jacobs, *Christ Circumcised: A Study in Early Christian History and Difference* (Philadelphia: University of Pennsylvania

Press, 2012). For evidence that debates on circumcision of Christ followers became more exegetically elaborate into the second century, see Soon, "Satan and Circumcision: The Devil as the ἄγγελος πονηρός in Barn 9:4," *VC* 76 (2022), 60–72.

6 For instance, John Barclay states that the second-wave teachers "clearly presented their argument with some persuasion," citing Gal 3:1, which in fact presents the Galatians not as persuaded, but as "bewitched" (τίς ὑμᾶς ἐβάσκανεν). Barclay, "Mirror-Reading a Polemical Letter," 86. All translations of ancient texts are my own unless otherwise stated.

7 See, for instance, Jonathan Haidt et al., *Moral Dumbfounding: When Intuition Finds No Reason*, 2000, available from http://theskepticalzone.com/wp/wp-content/uploads/2018/03/haidt.bjorklund.working-paper.when-intuition-finds-no-reason.pub603.pdf; Fredrik Björklund, "Intuition and Ex-Post Facto Reasoning in Moral Judgment: Some Experimental Findings," *Lund Philosophy Reports* 2 (2004): 36–50.

8 Aldo Cimino, "The Evolution of Hazing: Motivational Mechanisms and the Abuse of Newcomers," *Journal of Cognition and Culture* 11 (2011): 241–67, 242.

9 Vivian Nutton, *Ancient Medicine*, 2nd ed. (London: Routledge, 2013), 246. For further data on adverse outcomes, including fatalities, from surgical procedures, see Ibid., 188–9.

10 Andrew Rillera uses this along with other evidence to argue that Philo is referring to *periah* rather than *milah* circumcision, the former of which involves the removal of far more skin. See Andrew Rillera, "Paul's Philonic Opponent: Unveiling the One Who Calls Himself a Jew in Romans 2:17" (PhD dissertation, Duke University, Durham, 2021). For more recent Samaritan opposition to Jewish *periah* circumcision on the grounds that it is more painful ("a superfluous cruelty") than Samaritan *milah* circumcision, see John Mills, *Three Months' Residence at Nablus, and an Account of the Modern Samaritans* (London: John Murray, 1864), 190.

11 Kate Bonner, "Male Circumcision as an HIV Control Strategy: Not a 'Natural Condom'," *Reproductive Health Matters* 9 (2001): 143–55, 147.

12 Vera Frajzyngier et al., "Safety of Adult Medical Male Circumcision Performed by Non Physician Clinicians in Kenya: A Prospective Cohort Study," *Global Health Science Practice* 9 (2014): 93–102.

13 Deanna Kerrigan et al., *Strategic Assessment to Define a Comprehensive Response to HIV in Iringa, Tanzania: Voluntary Medical Male Circumcision* (John Hopkins Center for Global Health, 2014), 13, available from www.jhsph.edu/research/centers-and-institutes/research-to-prevention/publications/iringa/vmmc-brief-final.pdf.

14 Ibid., 15.

15 See discussion in Nutton, *Ancient Medicine*, 4.

16 See Johannes Munck, *Paulus und die Heilsgeschichte* (Aarhus: Aarhus University Press, 1954), 79–81; Thiessen, *Paul and the Gentile Problem*, 26.

17 Frederick Mansfield Hodges, "The Ideal Prepuce in Ancient Greece and Rome: Male Genital Aesthetics and Their Relation to Lipodermos, Circumcision, Foreskin Restoration, and the Kynodesme," *Bulletin of the History of Medicine* 75 (2001): 375–405, 387–8.

18 Blaschke, *Beschneidung*, 330.

19 Daniel Boyarin, *Unheroic Conduct: The Rise of Heterosexuality and the Invention of the Jewish Man* (Berkeley: University of California Press, 1997), 240. "Feminized" is a *terminus technicus* that Boyarin uses to mean culturally constructed as feminine. For another argument for the same conclusion, see Jacobs, *Christ Circumcised*, 21.

20 Hodges, "Ideal Prepuce," 376.

21 On the synecdoche, see Ibid., 379. The strength of negative attitudes among Latin authors towards the castrated can be seen from Jennifer Blackwell's comment after exhaustive study of the sources that "one is hard pressed to find a favorable reference to a eunuch anywhere at all." Jennifer Blackwell, "*Spadones et Castrati*: Two Types of Eunuchs in Roman Literature and Law" (MA thesis, University of Florida, Gainesville, FL, 2003), 32. For instance, she cites Juvenal who blames them for "the sexual depravity that has

taken over [Rome]," Rufus' rejection of them as "oriental" and un-Roman. Ibid., 20, 29. For more Roman stereotypes of eunuchs, as feminized and greedy, see Sean Tougher, *The Eunuch in Byzantine History and Society* (London: Routledge, 2002), 35.

22 See discussion in Ra'anan Abusch, "Circumcision and Castration under Roman Law in the Early Empire," in *The Covenant of Circumcision*, ed. Elizabeth W. Mark (Lebanon, NH: Brandeis Press, 2003), 75–86, 82.

23 Ibid., 85.

24 Hodges, "Ideal Prepuce," 383.

25 See discussion in Blaschke, *Beschneidung*, 347; Hodges, "Ideal Prepuce," 392, 405.

26 For surgical intervention on those who suffer from "natural *lipodermos*" (i.e. those with insufficient foreskin who have not been circumcised), see Celsus, De medicina 7.25.1, cited and commented on in Blaschke, *Beschneidung*, 350–3; Hodges, "Ideal Prepuce," 398–9.

27 Jacobs, *Christ Circumcised*, 21.

28 Kerrigan et al., *Strategic Assessment*, 16.

29 UNAIDS, *Making Decisions on Male Circumcision for HIV Risk Reduction: Modelling the Impact and Costs*, 2007, available from www.unaids.org/sites/default/files/media_asset/jc1630_stellenbosch_report_en_2.

30 Cimino, "Evolution of Hazing," 242.

31 On the necessity of circumcision for Jewish proselytes, see Philo, *QE*, 92; b. Šabb. 31. See also discussion in Borgen, "Paul and Philo," 88.

32 Ibid., 86. See Philo, *Migration*, 92; *QG* 3.46–52; *Spec.* 1.8–9. In other words, "morality could be surgically engineered." Hodges, "Ideal Prepuce," 388. For the claim that the second-wave teachers taught this Philonic position, see also Thiessen, *Paul and the Gentile Problem*, 31. Paul says that the Galatians wish to "perfect themselves in the flesh" (Gal 3:3).

33 See discussion in Candida R. Moss, *Divine Bodies: Resurrecting Perfection in the New Testament and Early Christianity* (New Haven: Yale University Press, 2019), 41–65.

34 On the counter-cultural status of Paul's command to "remember the poor" (Gal 2:10), for instance, see Bruce W. Longenecker, *Remember the Poor: Paul, Poverty, and the Greco-Roman World* (Grand Rapids: Eerdmans, 2010).

35 Paula Fredriksen, "Why Should a 'Law-Free' Mission Mean a 'Law-Free' Apostle?" *Journal of Biblical Literature* 134 (2015): 637–50, 650.

36 Blaschke, *Beschneidung*, 240.

37 Hodges, "Ideal Prepuce," 387.

38 Ibid., 388.

39 Émile Durkheim, *The Elementary Forms of Religious Life*, trans. Karen E. Fields (New York: Free Press, 1995), 318n74.

40 Caroline F. Keating et al., "Going to College and Unpacking Hazing: A Functional Approach to Decrypting Initiation Practices among Undergraduates," *Group Dynamics: Theory, Research, and Practice* 9 (2005): 104–26, 107.

41 Louis J. West, "A Psychiatric Overview of Cult-Related Phenomena," *Journal of the American Academy of Psychoanalysis* 21 (1993): 1–19.

42 Keating et al., "Going to College and Unpacking Hazing," 116.

43 Gentry R. McCreary and Joshua W. Schutts, "Why Hazing? Measure the Motivational Mechanisms of Newcomer Induction in College Fraternities," *Journal of Cognition and Culture* 19 (2019): 343–65, 354. For details on their measures of hazing toleration and social dominance, see Ibid., 349, 351, respectively.

44 Keating et al., "Going to College," 119.

45 Barclay, "Mirror-reading a Polemical Letter," 88. This can be true even if these teachers do not present themselves as Paul's rivals. It is possible they presented Paul as having made an important beginning in the work of initial evangelization, while still being inadequate to lead them into the fullness of the truth.

46 For discussion of this passage, and an argument that this "weakness" refers to the physi-cal effects of persecution, see A. J. Goddard and S. A. Cummins, "Ill or Ill-Treated? Conflict and Persecution as the Context of Paul's Original Ministry in Galatia (Galatians 4:12–20)," *Journal for the Study of the New Testament* 52 (1993): 93–126.

47 Beverly R. Gaventa, *Our Mother Saint Paul* (Louisville: Westminster John Knox, 2007), 14.

48 Susan G. Eastman, *Recovering Paul's Mother Tongue: Language and Theology in Gala-tians* (Grand Rapids: Eerdmans, 2007), 6.

49 Kar Yong Lim, *Metaphors and Social Identity Formation in Paul's Letters to the Corin-thians* (Eugene, OR: Pickwick, 2017), 125.

50 J. Albert Harrill, *Slaves in the New Testament: Literary, Social, and Moral Dimensions* (Minneapolis: Fortress, 2006), 48.

51 On the text-critical issue in 1 Thess 2:7, see Jeffrey A. D. Weima, " 'But We Became Infants among You': The Case of ΝΗΠΙΟΙ in 1 Thess. 2.7," *New Testament Studies* 46 (2000): 547–64.

52 On Paul's self-characterization in 1 Thess 2, see Jennifer H. McNeel, *Paul as Infant and Nursing Mother: Metaphor, Rhetoric, and Identity in 1 Thessalonians 2:5–8*, ECL 12 (Atlanta: Society for Biblical Literature, 2014).

53 Reidar Aasgaard, "Paul as a Child: Children and Childhood in the Letters of the Apos-tle," *Journal of Biblical Literature* 126 (2007): 129–59, 113.

54 Martyn, *Galatians*, 421. I prefer to understand Paul as injured by persecution rather than sick, but Martyn's point still stands with this slight alteration.

55 Eastman, *Mother Tongue*, 120–1.

56 Bettina Shell-Duncan et al., "The Role of Older Women in Contesting Norms Associ-ated with Female Genital Mutilation/Cutting in Senegambia: A Factorial Focus Group Analysis," *PLoS One* 13 (2018), doi: 10.1371/journal.pone.0199217.

57 McCreary and Schutts, "Why Hazing?," 355–6. One survey question that was used to measure such a concern for solidarity amongst group members was how strongly they agreed with the statement "One of the main outcomes of our associate member process is to unify the group." For a complete listing, see Ibid., 351.

58 Keating et al., "Going to College," 116. The measure of social deviance involved in the initiation was not significantly predictive of this variable.

59 Cimino, "Evolution of Hazing," 252.

60 Ibid., 259.

61 Ibid., 261.

62 Ibid. See, for instance, Ernst Fehr and Simon Gächter, "Altruistic Punishment in Humans," *Nature* 415 (2002): 137–40.

63 "[Paul's] preaching included the conviction that, as he had himself suffered crucifixion with Christ, so in his present life he bears in his body physical scars . . . that are marks of his association with Jesus." Martyn, *Galatians*, 421. See also Basil S. Davis, "The Meaning of προεγράφη in the Context of Galatians 3.1," *New Testament Studies* 45 (1999): 194–212. I cite Gal 4:12 solely for the proposition that Paul presents himself as a model for the Galatians, but if we adopt Troy Martin's translation of the verse, Paul additionally describes himself as having been harmed by the Galatians yet continuing to serve them regardless. Martin translates 4:12 as follows: "Become as I am because I, in as much as you are brothers, need nothing from you. You wronged me." Troy W. Martin, "The Ambiguities of a 'Baffling Expression' (Gal 4:12)," *Filologia Neotestamentaria* 12 (1999): 123–38.

64 Eastman, *Mother Tongue*, 97.

65 Hans Betz understands this clause as part of Paul's counsel not to compare, commenting: "There is a temptation to develop self-righteousness and arrogance with regard to the wrongdoer." Hans D. Betz, *Galatians*, Hermeneia (Philadelphia: Fortress, 1979), 298.

Bibliography

Ancient Sources

Albeck, Chanoch and Henoch Yalon (eds), *Shishah Sidre Mishnah*, 6 vols. (Jerusalem: Mosad Byalik, 1952–1959).

Guggenheimer, Heinrich W. (ed), *The Jerusalem Talmud. Second order, Mo'ed. Tractates Šabbat and 'Eruvin* (Berlin: de Gruyter, 2012).

Josephus, "Opera", in B. Niese (ed), *Flavii Iosephi opera*, 6 vols. (Berlin: Weidmann, 1887–1895; repr. 1955).

Justinian, "*Corpus juris civilis. Digesta*", in Theodor Mommson and Paul Krueger (eds), *The Digest of Justinian*, 4 vols. (Philadelphia: University of Pennsylvania Press, 1938).

Lucian, "Opera", in M. D. Macleod (ed), *Luciani Opera*, 4 vols. (Oxford: Oxford University Press, 1975–1980).

Philo of Alexandria, "Opera", in Leopold Cohn and Paul Wendland (eds), *Philonis Alexandrini opera quae supersunt*, 6 vols. (Berlin: Reimer, 1896–1915).

Steinsaltz, Adin, Tzvi H. Weinreb, Shalom Z. Berger, and Joshua Schreier (eds), *Koren Talmud Babli*, 42 vols. (Jerusalem: Koren, 2012–2019).

Modern Sources

Aasgaard, Reidar. "Paul as a Child: Children and Childhood in the Letters of the Apostle." *Journal of Biblical Literature* 126.1 (2007): 129–59.

Abusch, Ra'anan. "Circumcision and Castration Under Roman Law in the Early Empire." Pages 75–86 in *The Covenant of Circumcision*. Edited by Mark, Elizabeth W. Lebanon, NH: Brandeis Press, 2003.

Allan, Elizabeth J., David Kerschner, and Jessica M. Payne. "College Student Hazing Experiences, Attitudes, and Perceptions: Implications for Prevention." *Journal of Student Affairs Research and Practice* 56 (2019): 32–48.

Barclay, John M. G. "Mirror-Reading a Polemical Letter: Galatians as a Test-Case." *Journal for the Study of the New Testament* 31 (1987): 73–93.

Belfiglio, Valentine. "Perioperative Anesthesia in Ancient Rome: 27 B.C.-A.D. 476." *Neurology and Neuroscience Reports* 1 (2018): 1–3.

Betz, Hans D. *Galatians*. Hermeneia. Philadelphia: Fortress, 1979.

Björklund, Fredrik. "Intuition and Ex-Post Facto Reasoning in Moral Judgment: Some Experimental Findings." *Lund Philosophy Reports* 2 (2004): 36–50.

Blackwell, Jennifer A. "*Spadones et Castrati*: Two Types of Eunuchs in Roman Literature and Law." MA thesis, University of Florida, Gainesville, FL, 2003.

Blaschke, Andreas. *Beschneidung: Zeugnisse der Bibel und verwandter Texte*. Texte und Arbeiten zum neutestamentlichen Zeitalter 28. Tübingen: Francke, 1998.

Bonner, Kate. "Male Circumcision as an HIV Control Strategy: Not a 'Natural Condom'." *Reproductive Health Matters* 9 (2001): 143–55.

Borgen, Peder. "Observations on the Theme 'Paul and Philo': Paul's Preaching of Circumcision in Galatia (Gal 5:11) and Debates on Circumcision in Philo." Pages 85–102 in *Die paulinische Literatur und Theologie*. Edited by Pedersen, Sigfred. Teologiske Studier 7. Aarhus: Aarhus University Press, 1980.

Boyarin, Daniel. *Unheroic Conduct: The Rise of Heterosexuality and the Invention of the Jewish Man*. Berkeley: University of California Press, 1997.

Cimino, Aldo. "The Evolution of Hazing: Motivational Mechanisms and the Abuse of Newcomers." *Journal of Cognition and Culture* 11 (2011): 241–67.

Davis, Basil S. "The Meaning of προεγράφη in the Context of Galatians 3.1." *New Testament Studies* 45 (1999): 194–212.

Durkheim, Émile. *The Elementary Forms of Religious Life*. Translated by Fields, Karen E. New York: Free Press, 1995.

Eastman, Susan G. *Recovering Paul's Mother Tongue: Language and Theology in Galatians*. Grand Rapids: Eerdmans, 2007.

Fehr, Ernst, and Simon Gächter. "Altruistic Punishment in Humans." *Nature* 415 (2002): 137–40.

Frajzyngier, Vera, George Odingo, Mark Barone, Paul Perchal, and Melinda Pavin. "Safety of Adult Medical Male Circumcision Performed by Non-Physician Clinicians in Kenya: A Prospective Cohort Study." *Global Health Science Practice* 9 (2014): 93–102.

Fredriksen, Paula. "Why Should a 'Law-Free' Mission Mean a 'Law-Free' Apostle?" *Journal of Biblical Literature* 134 (2015): 637–50.

Gaventa, Beverly R. *Our Mother Saint Paul*. Louisville: Westminster John Knox, 2007.

Goddard, A. J., and S. A. Cummins. "Ill or Ill-Treated? Conflict and Persecution as the Context of Paul's Original Ministry in Galatia (Galatians 4:12–20)." *Journal for the Study of the New Testament* 52 (1993): 93–126.

Haidt, Jonathan, Fredrik Björklund, and Scott Murphy. *Moral Dumbfounding: When Intuition Finds No Reason*, 2000. Available from http://theskepticalzone.com/wp/wp-content/uploads/2018/03/haidt.bjorklund.working-paper.when-intuition-finds-no-reason.pub603.pdf.

Harrill, J. Albert. *Slaves in the New Testament: Literary, Social, and Moral Dimensions*. Minneapolis: Fortress, 2006.

Hodges, Frederick Mansfield. "The Ideal Prepuce in Ancient Greece and Rome: Male Genital Aesthetics and Their Relation to Lipodermos, Circumcision, Foreskin Restoration, and the Kynodesme." *Bulletin of the History of Medicine* 75 (2001): 375–405.

Jacobs, Andrew. *Christ Circumcised: A Study in Early Christian History and Difference*. Divinations. Philadelphia: University of Pennsylvania Press, 2012.

Keating, Caroline F., Jason Pomerantz, Stacy D. Pommer, Samantha J. H. Ritt, Lauren M. Miller, and Julie McCormich. "Going to College and Unpacking Hazing: A Functional Approach to Decrypting Initiation Practices Among Undergraduates." *Group Dynamics: Theory, Research, and Practice* 9 (2005): 104–26.

Kerrigan, Deanna, Caitlin Kennedy, and Heena Brahmbhatt. *Strategic Assessment to Define a Comprehensive Response to HIV in Iringa, Tanzania: Voluntary Medical Male Circumcision*. John Hopkins Center for Global Health, 2014. Available from www.jhsph.edu/research/centers-and-institutes/research-to-prevention/publications/iringa/vmmc-brief-final.pdf.

Lim, Kar Yong. *Metaphors and Social Identity Formation in Paul's Letters to the Corinthians*. Eugene, OR: Pickwick, 2017.

Longenecker, Bruce W. *Remember the Poor: Paul, Poverty, and the Greco-Roman World*. Grand Rapids: Eerdmans, 2010.

Martin, Troy W. "The Ambiguities of a 'Baffling Expression' (Gal 4:12)." *Filologia Neotestamentaria* 12 (1999): 123–38.

Martyn, J. Louis. *Galatians*. Vol. 33a, AB. New York: Doubleday, 1997.

———. *Theological Issues in the Letters of Paul*. Edinburgh: T&T Clark, 1997.

McCreary, Gentry R., and Joshua W. Schutts. "Why Hazing? Measure the Motivational Mechanisms of Newcomer Induction in College Fraternities." *Journal of Cognition and Culture* 19 (2019): 343–65.

McNeel, Jennifer H. *Paul as Infant and Nursing Mother: Metaphor, Rhetoric, and Identity in 1 Thessalonians 2:5–8*. ECL 12. Atlanta: Society for Biblical Literature, 2014.

Mills, John. *Three Months' Residence at Nablus, and an Account of the Modern Samaritans*. London: John Murray, 1864.

Moss, Candida R. *Divine Bodies: Resurrecting Perfection in the New Testament and Early Christianity*. New Haven: Yale University Press, 2019.

Munck, Johannes. *Paulus und die Heilsgeschichte*. Aarhus: Aarhus University Press, 1954.

Nutton, Vivian. *Ancient Medicine*. 2nd ed. London: Routledge, 2013.

Rillera, Andrew. "Paul's Philonic Opponent: Unveiling the One Who Calls Himself a Jew in Romans 2:17." PhD diss., Duke University, Durham, 2021.

Rubin, Nissan. "*Brit Milah*: A Study of Change in Custom." Pages 87–97 in *The Covenant of Circumcision: New Perspectives on an Ancient Jewish Rite*. Edited by Mark, Elizabeth W. Hanover, NH: Brandeis University Press, 2003.

Shell-Duncan, Bettina, et al. "The Role of Older Women in Contesting Norms Associated with Female Genital Mutilation/Cutting in Senegambia: A Factorial Focus Group Analysis." *PLoS One* 13 (2018). doi: 10.1371/journal.pone.0199217.

Soon, Isaac T. "Satan and Circumcision: The Devil as the ἄγγελος πονηρός in Barn 9:4." *Vigiliae Christianae* 76 (2002): 60–72.

———. " 'In Strength' Not 'by Force': Re-Reading the Circumcision of the Uncircumcised ἐν ἰσχύι in 1 Macc 2:46." *Journal for the Study of the Pseudepigrapha* 29 (2020): 149–67.

Thiessen, Matthew. *Paul and the Gentile Problem*. Oxford: Oxford University Press, 2018.

Tong, M. Adrael. " 'Given as a Sign': Circumcision and Bodily Discourse in Late Antique Judaism and Christianity." PhD diss., Fordham University, New York, 2019.

Tougher, Shaun. *The Eunuch in Byzantine History and Society*. London: Routledge, 2008.

UNAIDS. *Making Decisions on Male Circumcision for HIV Risk Reduction: Modelling the Impact and Costs*, 2007. Available from www.unaids.org/sites/default/files/media_asset/jc1630_stellenbosch_report_en_2.

Weima, Jeffrey A. D. " 'But We Became Infants Among You': The Case of ΝΗΠΙΟΙ in 1 Thess. 2.7." *New Testament Studies* 46 (2000): 547–64.

West, Louis J. "A Psychiatric Overview of Cult-Related Phenomena." *Journal of the American Academy of Psychoanalysis* 21 (1993): 1–19.

4 Pain in Ancient Medicine and Literature, and Early Christianity

The Paradox of Inshareability and Agency

Helen Rhee

In this chapter, I will show that pain was understood and experienced in Greco-Roman medicine mainly as a physiological phenomenon but with affective and social implication with an attention to its relationship with language and (in-) expressibility. I will then examine construction of pain narrative and pain pedagogy,[1] in Greco-Roman literature that intersect with not only rational medicine but also early Christian narratives. It is in these literary texts, we detect the broadening construction and display of pain with specific ways to navigate and endure pain. I argue that drawing on this wider cultural milieu of pain construction and drawing up Jesus's passion as their fundamental pain narrative, early Christians framed pain as an operative meaning-making category, to be shared in their respective communities as co-sufferers in Christ.

Greco-Roman Medicine

We start with pain in Greco-Roman medicine with two medical writers. In the time of the early Roman Imperial period, there was a greater concern for rational medicine to integrate patients' reportage of their felt sensations of pain and narratives with more developed anatomical theories.[2] In that process, it developed a view of pain, which rather emphasized the combination of physiology, language, subjectivity, affective aspects, and interaction of the doctor–patient relationship.[3] In *On Medicine* by Aulus Cornelius Celsus, the Roman medical encyclopaedist in the first century (CE), the word pain (*dolor*) appears over 200 times at the core of every moment of medical practice from diagnosis, to therapeutics, to prognosis.[4] In diagnosis, as in the Hippocratic treatises, locating pain as a sign of an imminent illness is the first step towards potential recovery. Among the body parts, head is most prone to pain, especially because of headaches associated with fevers (45 times), followed by internal organs (28 times), eyes (22 times), and hips (14 times). Patient's pain is also a main factor in distinguishing one illness from another similar one: "But those called *myrmecia* are less prominent and harder than *thymion*; their roots are more deeply fixed and they are more painful" (5.28.14c). In the context of therapeutics, the word *dolor* appears in about half of the occurrences in the text, in two-thirds of which cases (about 70 times) the doctor or medical practitioner (*medicus*) chooses the best treatment or performs the proper surgical act based on

DOI: 10.4324/9781003080534-5

the presence of pain. In other cases, presence or absence of *dolor* is a contraindication to a treatment (1.5.2; 7.20.4); depending on an outbreak or persistence of *dolor*, treatment is to be stopped or modified (5.28.1b; 4.29.2); and if *dolor* ends, it is a criterion to stop the existing treatment or to begin a new remedial step (6.6.9c; 7.20.3). Hence patients' pain as experienced and expressed is carefully attended in every step of the therapeutic process. In prognosis, pain can help predict the result of a disease by its presence (4.13.1) or absence (5.26.27b). For example, "If there is a great swelling without pain, and dryness, there is no danger; if there is dryness, accompanied by pain, there is general ulceration, and at times the result is that the eyelid sticks to the eyeball" (6.6.1c).

In granting pain such importance in the medical art, however, Celsus recognizes two significant points: first, Celsus acknowledges that for all his efforts to classify various pains, pain is inherently the subjective experience depending on the sufferer. Each pain is specific to the person, and one's "moderate pain" (*dolor mediocris*) will be the other's "intolerable pain" (*dolor intelerabilis*) and vice versa. Furthermore, one can see that there is an unbridgeable gap between the pain perceived and the pain expressed, and the language of pain is inevitably ambiguous and always approximate between the patient and the doctor. Therefore, second, the context of a "pain dialogue" requires a mutual trust (*fides*) between them as a way to minimize this linguistic incommunicability and ambiguity of pain. Hence it is no surprise that Celsus promotes the medicine between friends (*amicis*) of equals rather than strangers in the Preface.[5] Even in that setting, the doctor's task is challenging—one must with compassion (*misericordia*) try to comprehend the subjective perception and feeling of the patient, which can never be translated and transmitted accurately.

The most famous and influential Imperial physician, Galen of Pergamum, further developed a complex understanding of pain embedded in a consistent natural physiology, perceived and expressed by the patient, and in close relationship with the patient. Largely following the Hippocratic Corpus (and Plato), Galen presents a much more elaborate theory of the generation of pain, arising when an overwhelming or a violent and contrary-to-nature experience takes place in our body and its natural state (*Symp. Caus.* 1.6; Kühn 7:115).[6] "In regard to the patient's symptoms, pain is either indicative of the composition of humours [*diathesis*] or it reveals the affected organ."[7] This localization of pain corresponds to his (general) structural and functional understanding of disease, which is "any condition [*diathesis*] contrary to nature by which function is harmed, primarily" (*Symp. Diff.* 1 Kühn 7:43). Galen's aetiology of pain presupposes first an organ to receive outside impressions, then a connecting passageway, and an organizational centre to transform the sensation into a conscious perception.[8] Using the terms, ἄλγημα, ὀδύνη, and πόνος interchangeably,[9] Galen places pain under the sense of touch, which is distinguished from other senses in the ways in which sensory organs interact with external and internal stimuli.[10] Although sight, sound, smell, and taste are all affected by external sensibilities, pain in the sense of touch arises from specific external stimuli such as things that warm, cool, cut, or bruise the sensory organ; *and* from internal ones such as humoural changes (*Symp. Caus.* 1.6 Kühn 7:116; *Symp. Diff.* 3 Kühn

7:57).[11] These two causes of pain then reveal pain's evident utility in his usual tele-ological understanding: "pain served to warn and to protect every living being, and these functions accounted for the arrangement of the nerves and membranes which enveloped the brain, the pia mater and dura mater in particular."[12]

Drawing on an Aristotelian system of classification, Galen then classified the different kinds of pain according to their character, location of the diseased organ, and a general humoural imbalance, which were used until modern times: sharp pain, tense pain, punctuating, dull or numb pain, pulsating (throbbing) pain from inflammations, pain of ulcerating character, and heavy or oppressive pain with a feeling of weightiness in organs like the kidneys, liver, lungs, and so on (*De locis affectibus* 2.2–4; Kühn 8:70–79).[13] Furthermore, he "differentiated a periosteal pain caused by inflammation of the membrane lining the bone, or pain resulting from external injury."[14] He even observed sympathetic pain (i.e. referred pain) spreading from the stomach to the heart often leading to the individual's collapse, reasoning that communication of painful irritation was through the nervous system.[15] As one can see, there is a rational system set up by Galen which almost establishes an "universal law" of human body's susceptibility to pain: there existed a direct link between each type of pain and each part afflicted, characterized by its own specific nature (φύσις).[16] With a correct analysis, "the symptom made it possible to identify the specific reality of the disorder."[17] While the Hippocratic treatises also drew indications from the regional localization of pain, the actual centre of the disorder had a much more precious anatomical significance in Galen.[18] Hence Roselyne Rey sums up the significance of Galen's contribution in this way: "The qualitative description of the different pains was closely linked to their presumed cause, and their meanings were part of a perfectly elaborated rational system of thought based on humours and qualities."[19]

Again, this rational system presupposes a trusting relationship between the patient and the doctor with the patient's voice and ability to perceive and com-municate pain in a diagnostic setting.[20] Recognizing the limit of scientific language describing only the common properties of pain, to obtain more precise and intimate sense of the pain symptoms and disease of the sufferer, the doctor has to rely on the metaphorical language used by his patients to explain what troubled them (*De locis affectibus* 2.9; Kühn 8:116). Galen asked his patients to describe clearly the different symptoms of pain and examine the changes in the affected parts. At the same time, in that setting, the doctor had a superior authority in interpreting and analysing patient's shared symptoms as in the Hippocratic Corpus. Discussing the importance of clear terminology in diagnosis and medical knowledge, Galen states:

[T]his is difficult to evaluate, since we have to reply on many other persons: either on those who suffer but do not understand clearly (σαφῶς) their experi-ences because their minds [souls] are weak, or on those who understand but are unfit to communicate clearly (σαφῶς), being totally unable to formulate their suffering in words [or rational discourse—λόγῳ], since it requires a considerable effort or it is inexpressible (τῷ μηδ'εἶναι ῥητὸν αὐτό). Con-sequently a person who wants to describe each type of pain (ἀλγημάτων)

should have experienced it personally, should also be a physician and able to speak clearly (ἑρμηνεῦσαι) to others, and should observe it with understanding while suffering, and with his mental powers [souls] intact.
       (*De locis affectibus* 2.7; Kühn 8:88–89; tr. Siegal with modification)

This passage is telling for several reasons. First of all, for all its emphasis on patient's voice and expression, Galen reveals a substantial suspicion on the patients' ability to express and articulate their pain perception in a rational discourse in contrast to the doctors' rational capacity in a hierarchical relationship. Pain resists easy explanation because its perception and communication requires a high level of ability, thought to be found rare among the patients, or because pain experience is inexpressible in words.[21] When the inexpressibility of pain is due to the patient's inability, the doctor can solve that problem by filling in the patient's various pain experiences since he rationally understands the patient's pain experienced and possesses a clear linguistic ability to express them. Thus, there still can develop a sense of "common experience" between patient and doctor as long as it is managed and controlled by the doctor (Galen himself) as the latter shapes the patient's narrative of pain.[22] In constructing a "common experience," Galen also paid a careful attention to patient's emotional responses to pain. As Daniel King notes, Galen commonly uses emotional experiences like distress (λύπη) and anxiety (ἀνία) in close association with pain and disease in general.[23] Distress and other emotions (πάθη) such as anger, fear, worry, and desire are "both antecedent causes of diseases and caused by them" so much so that "the boundary between the physiological aspects of pain (or disease in general) and its emotional or psychological elements was always fluid in Galen's work."[24] The notions of emotional or psychic repercussions of physical pain *and* the physicality of emotional states are pervasive in Galen's contemporary literary and philosophical works and even Galen's works to an extent. Nonetheless, Galen himself was rather reticent in engaging with the patient's pain as a sign of disease in any compassionate way.

Secondly, in the aforementioned quote, Galen moreover recognizes the inexpressibility of pain due to the nature or quality of pain itself. He often describes pain sensations as "unspeakable" (ἄρρητος) throughout his corpus[25] and, like Celsus, acknowledges that no adequate terms exist even to describe the various personal impressions. This leads him to note pain's irreducible subjectivity because no doctor has experienced all types of pain (*De locis affectibus* 2.7; Kühn 8:89)[26]: "It is evidently impossible to transmit the impression of pain by teaching, since it is only known to those who have experienced it. Moreover, we are ignorant of each type of pain before we have felt it" (2.9; Kühn, 8:117). Here Galen's aim is to discredit his rival Archigenes's approach to pain language as the latter wrote about the painful symptoms "as if he has experienced all forms of pain" (2.7, 9; Kühn 8:89–90, 117).[27] Still, beyond his polemic, Galen might have found agreeable Elaine Scarry's argument that pain is inherently unshareable because it essentially shatters language; (physical) pain has no referential content: "It is not *of* or *for* anything. It is precisely because it takes no object that it, more than any other phenomenon, resists objectification in language."[28] This inaccessibility to language with its fundamental subjectivity challenges the possibility of understanding and empathizing with pain of others, according to Scarry:

> [F]or the person in pain, so incontestably and unnegotiably present is it that "having pain" may come to be thought of as the most vibrant example of what it means to "have certainty," while for the other person it is so elusive that "hearing about pain" may exist as the primary model of what it is "to have doubt." Thus pain comes unsharably into our midst as at once that which cannot be denied and that which cannot be confirmed.[29]

This understanding of pain's inexpressibility, subjectivity, and inshareability, while challenging the possibility and expectation of the opposite (i.e. expressibility, objectivity, and shareability of pain), further compels others (ancients and moderns) to pursue ways of achieving that opposite and provides a context for the Imperial culture of representation of pain, including a Christian one.

Pain Narrative and Pedagogy in Greco-Roman Literature: *The Sacred Tales* (Aristides)

As we now move to pain narratives in literature and early Christianity, a few terminological notes are in view. As we have seen, pain in Greco-Roman medical texts was primarily a physiological sensation and perception but included emotional and even social dimensions in right contexts; and in diagnostic settings, the pained individual was also referred to as the suffering patient. It is in literary and theological texts that pain moves beyond its anatomical basis and structure and is treated as a (long-term) "hardship or trial to be endured and navigated" with one's perseverance and moral strength and also in connection with disaster (*symphora*) or some evil (*kakon*).[30] As Daniel King notes, this is a "moment when pain perception and symptoms move close to what some scholars have designated as 'suffering'" and are assimilated into suffering as such.[31] Pain indeed constitutes "suffering when it is overwhelming, uncontrolled, unexplained, or in some other way associated with a dire *meaning* that calls into question the continued, integrated existence of the personal self"[32] or community. Therefore, in these texts, the interchangeable use of "pain" and "suffering" has a more nuanced legitimacy unless the texts imply otherwise or distinguish them. In this context, it is also appropriate to speak of a "pedagogy of pain,"[33] a way to navigate, endure, overcome, structure, or deal with pain with a certain moral agency and even rituals "to school the human mind in extreme endurance, whether aided by human or divine example."[34] Hence, in what follows, I will use the terms pain and suffering interchangeably with this qualification in mind.

A Greco-Roman pedagogy of pain in a narrative form comes from the six orations of the *Sacred Tales*, a record and representation of Aelius Aristides' pained existence throughout his chronic illness and recovery by the divine power. Deeply concerned about the perception of pain, Aristides represents his pain, his experience, and his reactions to the doctors' treatment and regimen in ways akin to those contemporary medical texts—coughs, vomitings, swellings, blood-letting, fever, headache, shivering, intermittent inability to eat, breathe, or walk properly (*Or.* 48.37–45). He was very ill in 144 CE and "the doctors were wholly at a loss not only as to how to help, but even how to recognize what the whole thing was" (48.5; cf. 48.69). When his intestines swelled and his breathing was blocked, the doctors first purged him with elaterium and made an incision from chest to bladder and used cupping instruments, at which his breathing left him (48.62–3).

> [A]nd a pain, numbing and impossible to bear (ὀδύνη ναρκώδης καὶ ἄπορος φέρειν) passed through me, and everything was smeared with blood and I felt extreme pain (ὑπέρινος), and I perceived that my intestines were cold and hanging out, and the difficulty in my respiration was intensified.
>
> (48.63)

Here Aristides is hyper-aware of what is being done to his body deep inside, fully capable of understanding and expressing what he perceives and suffers with his mental acuity and diagnostic terminology—the very opposite of Galen's patient lacking "a high level of ability" in one's perception and communication of pain.[35]

Ironically, it is his linguistic ability and mental acuity in communicating his pain that enables him to construct his narrative highlighting the insurmountable enormity and incomprehensibility of his pain experience as both the sufferer and observer of his pain. This construction first involves doctors' failure to comprehend and treat his suffering in contrast to the treatment by Asclepius. In addition to the aforementioned episode, earlier at Smyrna, he says, doctors and gymnastic trainers were unable to help him, failing to recognize "the complexity of his disease" (48.69; cf. 48.5). On another occasion, when he developed a painful swelling in the groin, doctors urged surgery or cauterization by drug with a prognosis of death if not followed (47.62). In contrast, Asclepius commanded Aristides to "endure and foster the growth"; and for Aristides, there was no choice between obeying the doctors or the god (47.63). However, the growth worsened, and others alternately marvelled at his endurance or criticized his credulity in dream and his cowardice in the face of the knife. The god's explanation of the condition was that it was dropsy diverted downwards, so it was a safe and appropriate swelling. Asclepius then gave him a dramatic treatment: run a race barefoot in winter, ride horses, sail in stormy weather after eating honey and acorns, and then vomit (47.65). Lastly, Asclepius the "Savior" told his foster-father Zosimus in a dream to apply a certain drug containing salt to the growth, which led to its disappearance. While the doctors stopped their criticism, they still thought surgery was necessary to treat the loose skin left after the disappearance of the growth. The god then prescribed Aristides to smear on an egg, and it cured his disease to the extent that no one could even tell on which thigh the tumour had been (47.68). Asclepius's diagnosis of diverted dropsy is one that could have been given by doctors and Aristides continues to use doctors elsewhere in the *Tales*. However, as Helen King notes, Asclepius offers something that the doctors do not or cannot: "an explanation of suffering acceptable to the patient" and a "holistic" approach to the patient's condition as seen in this episode.[36] Going back to his illness in 144 CE when his breathing was blocked, Asclepius not only recognized that Aristides' main concern was his breathing, but he also understood his patient's anxieties about oratory. Thus, he not only gives Aristides medicine but also eases his inability to breathe convincing him that once he starts to speak, his problems will diminish (cf. 48.7–10; 71–3; 50.13).[37] Understanding that oratory is central to his patient's life, Asclepius in fact exhorts him back to the oratory he had abandoned in hopelessness and despondency (50.14). Just as the god told him, when Aristides starts to speak even with a shortness of breath, he finds that he is soon able to breathe well and eventually resumes his oratory (50.22). This last episode further confirms doctors' failure in contrast to Aslepius's holistic treatment of Aristides's suffering.

The second aspect of the incomprehensibility of his pain experience involves his rhetorical emphasis on his incapacity to narrate his pain experiences and thus his choice to keep silent. Modern studies of trauma reveal that testimonies of extreme trauma are often characterized by the vacillation between the sufferers' compulsion to speak and the inability to capture all of their experiences.[38] Aristides would have identified with that vacillation as his detailed narrative conveyed the overwhelming power of pain that undermined his capacity for narrative description.

> In the beginning it did not occur to me to write about any of these [events and experiences], because I did not believe that I would survive. Next my body was also in such a state that it did not give me leisure for these things. . . . . So I thought that it was better to *keep completely silent* than to spoil such great deeds. And for these reasons I made many excuses both to the god and to my friends, who from time to time asked me to speak and write about these things.
>
> (48.1; italics added)

In light of his central concern on oratory, it is important for us to recognize that the relationship between his overwhelming bodily pain and his choice to remain silent is closely linked with his incapacity to engage in oratory (*Or*. 48.6; 50.14). Thus, he describes his pain as "unspeakable" (ἄρρητος) in the same language used by Galen (48.23) and even inconceivable (49.17). Aristides's pain is language-shattering, silencing, and thus inexpressible in utter subjectivity similar to Scarry's argument; and doctors' inability to recognize "the complexity of his disease" further heightens this incommunicability and incomprehensibility of pain.[39] Paradoxically, however, "in Aristides' hands, the ineffability that undermined medical accounts of pain becomes a way of communicating the nature of his experiences."[40]

Indeed, compelled by Asclepius, Aristides chooses to excavate his past and narrate his experiences (48.2). Suffering the ineffable pain and facing loss of his public career, he comes to believe that it is the god who offered him an explanatory framework for his suffering in contrast to doctors, understood his anxieties about oratory, and helped him speak, breathe, and eventually recover his oratory. As he submitted himself to the god's orders to endure painful experiences contrary to the demands of doctors and even a common sense at times, the result was not pain but well-being and union with the divine (*Or.* 48.19–23).[41] Therefore, Aristides comes to understand that his suffering, "seemingly incoherent mass of symptoms"[42] and "tempests of my body" (47.1; cf. *Or.* 42.7) has meaning.

> If someone should take these things into account and consider with how many and what sort of sufferings and with what necessary result for these he bore me to the sea and rivers and wells, and commanded me to contend with the winter, he will say that all is truly beyond miracles, and he will see more clearly the power and providence of the god, and will rejoice with me for the honor which I had, and would not be more grieved because of my sickness.
>
> (*Or.* 48.59)

Aristides narrates the full extent of his suffering because for him it is teleological and redemptive in that his readers and audience will not grieve his suffering but "see more clearly the power and providence of the god" which he experienced for himself and also "the honor which [he] had" (48.59). Thus, his pain becomes not only expressible but also sharable through his narrative; and his pain narrative becomes his pedagogy of pain through which he endures and makes sense of his pain in his intimate relationship with Asclepius. In the words of Helen King:

> The body, susceptible to pain, disease, old age, and death, seems to be a sign of distance from the divine world, but [Aristides'] creation of a story from the minute details of its physicality paradoxically seeks to transcend its materiality and make it into a sign of divine favor.[43]

Therefore, Aristides's pain narrative makes his pain sharable and offers a unique pain pedagogy, different from that of Galen's.

A Christian Ascetic Text (Syncletica): Shareability of Pain and Community of Co-sufferers

As we come to the early Christian texts of pain, we see a similar transformation of pain as something sharable through their respective pedagogies of pain. The first text, *The Life and Regimen of Blessed and Holy Teacher Syncletica*, is a fifth-century work in the era of post-Constantinian Christianity of the fourth-century desert mother from Alexandria; it showcases Syncletica's holiness not only through her rigorous ascetic regimen (ἄσκησις) and teaching but also through her bearing of decaying illness and bodily pain described in graphic detail.[44] This *Life* portrays the saint's illness and pain "as a shared way of living rather than as solitary suffering" for her ascetic co-sufferers and as a means of constructing communal subjectivities.[45] As such, this text illustrates pain "as a social relationship" as pain is part of what creates the particular conditions of action and experience according to Talel Asad.[46] Firstly, in her teaching, she sees a pedagogical value of pain in ascetic austerities (e.g. fasting) "because every sprig of virtue grows straight as a result of pain (πόνον) " (41)[47]; but the pain of *askēsis* can also be harmful and even evil as it can lead the ascetic to be self-deceived and prideful (52–4). The painful *askēsis* is a remedy (φάρμακον) and virtue, but it must be accompanied by humility, which is the critical virtue and remedy of the soul (54–8). Furthermore, "the evil originating from God" such as famines, droughts, plagues, poverty, and other misfortunes are "for the salvation of the soul and the training of the body" (84). The determinists falsely regard these as evils of the soul, but these are in fact saving remedies offered to those who believe in free will for conversion by the Almighty (84). Thus, it is the self-mastery of will through lifelong painful *askēsis* in humility that benefits from the seemingly evil afflictions coming from God. However, the Devil also uses the suffering such as illness and disease to weaken the ascetic's resolve (98). Still, in that case, illness functions as a medication and remedy, helpful to the ascetic because it is allowed for the destruction of pleasures. Just like martyr texts, the suffering, pained body becomes a site of spiritual battle and healing; and beyond body–soul dualism, attainment of spiritual health "demands the complete engagement with the human body," particularly in pain and suffering[48]; the great *askēsis* and marker of holiness is then "to persevere in illness and to keep sending up hymns of thanksgiving to the Almighty" (99). Asceticism here goes beyond renunciation but is about "self-formation"[49] worthy of transformation not only of the sufferer but also of the community.

Secondly, Syncletica indeed exemplifies this transformative "self-formation" in bearing of her terrible disease not alone but in community. The Devil first strikes her lung making her cough up pieces of her lungs bit by bit and suffer unremitting fevers for seven years (105) and strikes again her inner organs with unceasing torment for another three and half years to the extent that her suffering is said to surpass that of the martyrs (106). While nobly enduring her disease, she fights against the Enemy through her teaching, that is, by her teaching she keeps healing those in her community wounded by the Enemy. Here, her teaching, as it has always been, is a means of saving remedy for her ascetic community, so the Enemy then afflicts her speaking organ that she cannot teach. Nevertheless, "as the women *contemplated* her suffering *with their own eyes*, they were strengthened in their will; the wounds in her body healed their afflicted souls" (110; italics added). Here her pained body becomes a "spectacle" and as such, itself an instrument of healing of her community, and while it is she herself who is still suffering, her disciples are joined to her suffering through their contemplation and observation.

The Enemy then hits a final blow into her mouth, inflicting pain in one tooth and causing infection in her gum.

The bone deteriorated and the sore spread through the whole jaw and became the source of infection for the adjacent body parts. Within forty days the bone decayed, and after a period of two months a hole appeared. . . . Putrefaction (σῆψις) and a very foul-smelling stench overpowered her body throughout so that those women who tended her *suffered more than she did* (πλέον αὐτῆς πάσχειν). They used to withdraw for quite long periods of time, unable to endure the inhuman stench (δυσωδίας ἀπάνθρωπον).

(111; italics added; *PG* 28.1556)

Notice the progression of the depth of community's co-suffering as her pain and suffering grows ever intolerable and unbearable. And a particular cause of their co-suffering is the "inhuman stench"; this is significant. Earlier in the text, the same women smelled "the sweet fragrance (εὐωδία) of her most glorious sufferings (εὐκλεστάτων αὐτῆς πόνων)," that is, her stringent *askēsis* (fasting, praying, etc.) (21). Now they suffer with her and even more than her not only seeing her transformed (i.e. decayed and decomposing) body but also smelling Syncletica's "inhuman stench" in her ultimate *askēsis* (i.e. persevering in her illness). We see here Syncletica's female body with ascetic virility becoming (further) porous and permeable with her illness and emission of her scent and stench; and her disciples also experience permeability of their bodies by being receptacles of Syncletica's emission. As Peter Mena notes, "[t]he permeability of bodies" to bodily traumas and suffering—"Syncletica's and those who attend to her—is the central feature" of how they suffer together and thus "how holiness is transmitted in the *Life*."[50] Here suffering and sanctity are united in the co-suffering of Syncletica and her disciples. Thus, her apparent solitary illness and experience of pain indeed mark "a construction of communal ascetic identity" as her caring disciples become a part of her and she a part of them through the shared suffering.[51]

Augustine: Pain in This Age and Solidarity in (Affective) Pain

As just about every topic in Augustine's theology, Augustine sees pain within his grand vision of the creation, fall, redemption, and the eschaton. While absent in the original creation, pain (*dolor*) emerges from (original) sin as its manifestation and punishment (e.g. *Mor.* 1.35; *Civ. dei* 1.10; *Ep.* 130.12 *En. Ps.* 136.14).[52] Even in the fallen state of this world, however, pain, "whether it is in the mind or the body, cannot exist except in good natures" as evil can exist only in something good (*The Nature of the Good*, 20). Pain is a sign of life in this age (*Civ. dei.* 21.3). Only a healthy enough body can feel pain when it hurts (21.3). There is no pain in an unconscious body and no pain in an immortal (glorified) body; but the health of a person in pain, is closer to immortality than is the insensitivity of one who cannot feel pain. Why is that? For Christ the Lord and God himself felt (*in his soul and body*) a deep and anguishing sorrow to the point of death (Mt 26.38; Mk 15.34)—in carrying our own weakness, Christ bore our wounds and sorrows (*En. Ps.* 55.6; 63.18; 87.3; cf. Isa 53.4). Born from Mary, "scourged was He who expelled from the bodies of man the scourges of all distresses; crucified was He who put an end to our crucial pains (*omnium dolorum*); dead did He become who raised the dead" (*Cat. rud.* 40). Buried, risen, ascended into heaven, and now sitting at the Father's right hand, he is the head and we are the body. As such, Augustine speaks of the *totus Christus*, "the whole Christ," with Christ as Head and the Church as Body sharing in one life and one identity on account of the incarnation, the Word of God uniting himself to humanity even to the point of embracing pain and suffering in order to transform humanity into himself (e.g. *En. Ps*. 30.3).[53] Therefore, Augustine says the following in a mystical manner:

> [W]hatever he suffered, we too suffered in him, and whatever we suffer, he too suffers in us. Think of an analogy: if your head suffers some injury, can your hand be unaffected? Or if your hand is hurt, can your head be free from pain? . . . When any one of our members suffers, all the other members hasten to help the one that is in pain. This solidarity meant that when Christ suffered, we suffered in him; and it follows that now that he has ascended into heaven, and is seated at the Father's right hand, he still undergoes in the person of his Church whatever it may suffer amid the troubles of this world, whether temptations or hardship, or oppression (for all these are the necessary means of our instruction, and through them the Church is purified, as gold is by fire).
>
> (*En. Ps*. 62.2)

Christ's pain, that is, his assumption of our weakness by identifying us with himself, is the basis of our pain in mimetic identification with Christ. The suffering Christ is the model of our suffering and at the same time the healer of our pain. We are united with Christ in our mutual and co-suffering with Christ, which requires our ability to feel pain in this life; for Christ, our head, the victorious one, continues to experience pains and sufferings of the world through his body, the church, until the coming of the new age. Then our (vertical) solidarity with Christ in suffering necessarily binds the members of Christ's body in co-suffering with one another. Again, pain's shareability lies in a particular relationship that enables and mediates sociality.[54] Since our union with Christ through our mutual and co-suffering with Christ is contingent upon our capacity to feel pain, our capacity to feel one another's pain is the vital sign of the collective health and sanctification of the body—and even the health of the head because Christ binds himself to his body. This is what Paul was speaking about, says Augustine: "Is anyone weak, and I am not weak too? Is anyone tripped up, without my being afire with indignation?" (2 Cor 11.29). If Paul "had been unmoved and immune to pain" by some scandal, or the ruin of some weak person, that would have been callousness, not tranquillity (i.e. *apatheia*) (*En. Ps*. 55.6).

Augustine then pursues this horizontal shareability and pedagogy of pain through compassion (*misericordia*) in the *City of God* (9.5). The Stoics consistently regarded compassion (*eleos*; *misericordia*) a morally bad species of emotion (e.g. Cicero, *Tusc*. 3.9.20).

> Within our [Christian] discipline, then, we do not so much ask whether a pious soul is angry, as why he is angry; not whether he is sad, but whence comes his sadness; not whether he is afraid, but what he fears. For I do not think that any right-minded person would condemn anger (*irasci*) directed at a sinner in order to correct him; or sadness (*contristari*) on behalf of one

who is afflicted in order to liberate him, or fear (*timere*) for one in peril, lest he perish. The Stoics, indeed, are wont to reproach even compassion (*misericordia*); . . . What is compassion but a kind of fellow-feeling in our hearts for the misery of another which compels us to help him if we can? This impulse is the servant of right reason (*rationi*) when compassion (*misericordia*) is displayed in such a way as to preserve justice (*iustitia*), as when alms are distributed to the needy or forgiveness extended to the penitent. (*sive cum indigent tribulitur, sive cum ignoscitur paenitenti*) (9.5).

Augustine here endorses compassion as the distinctive feature of his (Christian) ethics, in the context of endorsing other emotions such as anger and fear, all of which the Stoics regarded as reactionary and arising from false judgements. Defined as "a kind of fellow-feeling in our hearts for the misery of another," compassion's goal is to "liberate" from vice and fear lest someone "perish" (cf. *Civ. dei* 14.9). Thus, it is good to commiserate (*contristari, conpati*) with one who is afflicted, judged by reason in preserving justice. This combination of reason and justice is significant for Augustine. Stoics (Seneca in particular) reproach compassion as something that acts from feelings of pity clouding the judgement without regard for justice; this leads to sentimental people wanting to throw open the prion doors and let out the most harmful criminals if once they see them cry without any proper judgement or regard for justice (Seneca, *Clem.* 2.4.1).[55] Against that Seneca praises mercy or clemency (*clementia*), a tendency or act to pardon from punishment in such a way as to preserve the principles of justice without any affective involvement (*Clem.* 1.18–1–2; 2.6.1). Augustine, while agreeing with Seneca's justice-oriented *clementia* to an extent, redefines it as compassion, that is, a good emotion (*eupatheia*) spurring or accompanying good works such as almsgiving and forgiveness; and this compassion is a proper, just response to bodily and moral afflictions—this is Christian pedagogy of pain. Augustine is basically saying that "a concern for virtue as such will entail that the sage has emotional reactions to others' virtue or lack thereof"; that is, "the sage *ought to* have concern for virtue as such—but that the Stoic sage does *not* actually have this."[56] As we have seen in Augustine, pain is indeed an affect and is predicated in social relationship. Whereas the Stoics are trying to avoid affective pain caused by involvement with the other in the name of self-sufficiency and self-mastery, Christians not only acknowledge but also embrace that affective pain is a regular, necessary part of life (even for the sage)—thus Christians "feel fear and desire, pain and gladness, but in a manner consistent with the Holy Scripture and wholesome doctrine; and because their love is righteous, all these emotions are righteous in them" (*Civ. dei* 14.9).

That is why Christians feel sad "on behalf of one who is afflicted" and "fear for one in peril, lest he perish" (*Civ. dei* 9.5; 14.9); they feel pain for their own sins and gladness in their own good works and also on account of those whose liberation they desire (14.9); Christians are troubled and anxious by (their friends') famine, war, disease, or captivity, fearing that in slavery they may suffer evils beyond (the Christians') powers of imagination (19.8). A Christian love command demands us our solidarity in pain: not only to grieve *for* the ills and impairments in our neighbour's well-being, but also to grieve *with* our neighbour in his/her grief (cf. 19.8; 19.4)[57]: "if we felt no [negative] emotions at all while subject to the infirmity of this life, we should then certainly not be living rightly" (*Civ. dei* 14.9). A Christian pain and suffering is a condition of one's relationship because by virtue of Christ's pain and suffering, she always lives in tangible, inseparable vertical and horizontal relationships; it is something that includes her ability to respond compassionately to the pain of other sufferers, both vertical and horizontal.[58] For Augustine, sadness, anger, fear, grief, pain, and the like are not goods in one's life as such, for there will be no *pathē* in the life to come. However, in this present life with its "great mass of evils" (*Civ. dei* 19.8), sharing one another's pain and suffering through compassion unites Christians as co-sufferers as Christ himself feels pain, anger, fear, and grief when they suffer from the effects of the fall (14.9; cf. *En. Ps.* 62.2).

Conclusion

In conclusion, we have seen in Greco-Roman medical texts, pain's centrality in both diagnosis and therapeutics in a complex patient–doctor relationship with its affective and social implication through language (expressibility) and also its challenge due to its inaccessibility to language. Celsus and Galen both emphasize inshareability of pain due to its essentially subjective and inexpressible nature that cannot be mediated through patient's expression. However, in Greco-Roman literature, we have seen transformation of pain as something sharable and teleological. In Christian pain narratives, their particular openness to pain constituted itself "a form of agency"[59] and transformed the uniquely subjective unshareable pain narrative of Jesus into something repeatedly shareable by his followers. In this process, they expanded the application of the Christological pain and suffering beyond pain under torture and violence to illness and other afflictions that would require moral agency. Based on these narratives and pedagogy of pain, early Christians forged their unique communal identity as the community of co-sufferers in mimetic identification with Christ, in which pain and suffering became a constitutive part of sustaining that relationship and identity.

Notes

1 Pain pedagogy here means a way to navigate, overcome, and endure pain with moral agency and rituals. See p. 5 under "Pain Narrative and Pedagogy in Greco Roman Culture: *The Sacred Tales* (Aristides)."
2 Daniel King, *Experiencing Pain in Imperial Greek Culture*, Oxford Classical Monographs (Oxford: Oxford University Press, 2018), 36.
3 King, *Experiencing Pain in Imperial Greek Culture*, 37.
4 This section draws on Aurélien Gautherie, "Physical Pain in Celsus' *On Medicine*," in Brigitte Maire (ed.) *'Greek' and 'Roman' in Latin Medical Texts: Studies in Cultural Change and Exchange in Ancient Medicine* (Leiden and Boston: Brill, 2014), 137–54.
5 " [P]resuming their state to be equal, it is more useful to have in the practitioner a friend (*medicum esse amimum*) rather than a stranger (*extraneum*)" (Prooem. 73; Marx 29).
6 Cf. King, *Experiencing Pain in Imperial Greek Culture*, 71.

7 Quoted in Rudolph E. Siegel, *Galen on Sense Perception: His Doctrines, Observations and Experiments on Vision, Hearing, Smell, Taste, Touch and Pain, and Their Historical Sources* (Basel, Switzerland and New York: S. Karger, 1970), 185. See *De locis affectibus* 2.1 (8.70K): "Pain is symptomatic of a certain condition or location, cough of others, and in this manner [we diagnose the source of] vomiting, bleeding, loose stools, cramps, chills, shivering and delirium." See also *Ars medicinae*, 356–7. K: "Pain (*algēma*) strongly established in a particular place indicates dissolution of continuity or a sudden complete change."

8 R. Rey, *The History of Pain* (Cambridge: Harvard University Press, 1995), 32.

9 Helen King Peregrine Horden, "Religion in the Ancient World Pain in Hippocratic Medicine," in *Religion Health & Suffering* (London: Routledge, 2013), 308.

10 Cf. Siegel, *Galen on Sense Perception*, 184–93.

11 Cf. King, *Experiencing Pain in Imperial Greek Culture*, 74. See *Symp. Diff.* 3 (Kühn 7:57): "In the case of touch, pain comes not only from what is external, but also far more from conditions in the body itself, and often in fact so strongly that some who are overcome by suffering may kill themselves. . . . The most severe pains happen to the sense of touch."

12 Rey, *The History of Pain*, 33. See On the Utility of the Parts, 5.9.

13 Siegel, *Galen on Sense Perception*, 190.

14 Siegel, *Galen on Sense Perception*, 190.

15 Siegel, *Galen on Sense Perception*, 187–8.

16 Rey, *The History of Pain*, 35.

17 Rey, *The History of Pain*, 35.

18 Rey, *The History of Pain*, 35.

19 Rey, *The History of Pain*, 35.

20 On this aspect of patient–physician relationship in Galen and his "patient-centeredness," which Galen himself challenges it at times (see the paragraphs following), see Susan P. Mattern, *Galen and the Rhetoric of Healing* (Baltimore, MD: Johns Hopkins University Press, 2008), 124–5, 138–58.

21 See also *De locis affectibus* 2.6–9 (Kühn 8.86–87).

22 Cf. King, *Experiencing Pain in Imperial Greek Culture*, 80; Mattern, *Galen and the Rhetoric of Healing*, 124–5.

23 King, *Experiencing Pain in Imperial Greek Culture*, 89. On emotion in Galen's case histories, see Mattern, *Galen and the Rhetoric of Healing*, 132–6; Susan P. Mattern, *The Prince of Medicine: Galen in the Roman Empire* (Oxford: Oxford University Press, 2013), 249–56. On distress (*lupē*) and anxiety (*ania*) in Galen in particular, see Clare K. Rothschild and Trevor W. Thompson (eds.), *Galen's De indolentia: Essays on a Newly Discovered Letter*, STAC 88 (Tübingen: Mohr Siebeck, 2014).

24 King, *Experiencing Pain in Imperial Greek Culture*, 89; *De symptomatum causis* 1.6. Also, Mattern, *The Prince of Medicine*, 255.

25 For example, *De locis affectibus* 2.9 (Kühn 8.117); *De method medendi* 9.2, 10.11, 12.1 (Kühn 10:604, 731, 810).

26 Horden, "Pain in Hippocratic Medicine," 308.

27 See the discussion in King, *Experiencing Pain in Imperial Greek Culture*, 80–8, versus Courtny Roby, "Galen on the Patient's Role in Diagnosis: Sensation, Consensus, and Metaphor," in G. Petridou and C. Thumiger (eds.) *Homo Patiens: Approaches to the Patient in the Ancient World* (Leiden: Brill), 304–24.

28 Elaine Scarry, *The Body in Pain: The Making and Unmaking of the World* (Oxford: Oxford University Press, 1985), 5.

29 Scarry, *The Body in Pain*, 4.

30 King, *Experiencing Pain in Imperial Greek Culture*, 109.

31 King, *Experiencing Pain in Imperial Greek Culture*, 110. Cf. Howard Brody in his *Stories of Sickness*, 2nd edition (Oxford: Oxford University Press, 2003), 49, explains the relationship between pain and suffering as follows: "[P]ain per se does not equal

suffering . . ., but pain may constitute suffering when it is overwhelming, uncontrolled, unexplained, or in some other way associated with a dire *meaning* that calls into question the continued, integrated existence of the personal self " (italics original).

32 Brody, *Stories of Sickness*, 49, italics original.

33 This phrase itself comes from Antigone Samellas, "Public Aspects of Pain in Late Antiquity: The Testimony of Chrysostom and the Cappadocians in Their Graeco-Roman Context," *Zeitschrift für antikes Christentum* 19.2 (2015): 279. Cf. Talal Asad suggests pain not merely as a passive state but also as action itself and intentionally collapses (or at least reduces) the distinction between physical pain and psychological or social suffering in *Formations of the Secular: Christianity, Islam, Modernity* (Stanford, CA: Stanford University Press, 2003), 79–80, 81–5.

34 Susanna Elm, "Roman Pain and the Rise of Christianity," in *Quo Vadis Medical Healing: Past Concepts and New Approaches* (New York: Springer, 2009), 51.

35 See also Aristides, *Or.* 48.39: "[D]octors gave up and finally despaired entirely, and it was announced that I would die immediately. However, even here, you could use the Homeric phrase, 'his mind was firm.' Thus I was conscious of myself as if I were another person, and I perceived my body ever slipping away, until I was near death."

36 Helen King, "Chronic Pain and the Creation of Narrative," in James I. Porter (ed.) *Constructions of the Classical Body* (Ann Arbor: University of Michigan Press, 1999), 279–80.

37 Cf. King, "Chronic Pain and the Creation of Narrative," 280.

38 Dominick LaCapra, *History and Its Limits: Human, Animal, Violence* (Ithaca, NY: Cornell University Press, 2009), 60–2, in King, *Experiencing Pain in Imperial Greek Culture*, 143.

39 See David Morris, *The Culture of Pain* (Berkeley and Los Angeles: University of California Press, 1991), 72–3: "The normal failure of language under the assault of acute pain, . . . is a common but not devastating experience. . . . [But a chronic pain] constitutes a radical assault on language and on human communication. There is simply nothing that can be said."

40 King, *Experiencing Pain in Imperial Greek Culture*, 144.

41 See *Or.* 48.21–3: "When we reached the river, there was no need for anyone to encourage us. But being still full of warmth from the vision of the god, I cast off my clothes, and not wanting a massage, flung myself where the river was deepest. . . . When I came out, all my skin had a rosy hue and there was a lightness throughout my body. There was also much shouting from those present and those coming up, shouting that celebrated phrase, 'Great is Asclepius!' . . . [T]here was a certain inexplicable contentment, which regarded everything as less than the present moment, so that even when I saw other things, I seemed not to see them. Thus I was wholly with the god."

42 C. A. Behr, *Aelius Aristides and the Sacred Tales* (Amsterdam: A. M. Hakkert, 1968), 162.

43 King, "Chronic Pain and the Creation of Narrative," 282.

44 On Synletica's illness as the great asceticism, see Andrew Crislip, *Thorns in the Flesh: Illness and Sanctity in Late Ancient Christianity* (Philadelphia: University of Pennsylvania Press, 2013), 100–6.

45 Peter A. Mena, "Scenting Saintliness: The Ailing Body, Chicana Feminism, and Communal Identity in Ancient Christianity," *Journal of Feminist Studies in Religion* 33:2 (2017): 7–8, 5–20. Mena in this study reads the *Life* using the Chicana Feminist theorists' construction of communal subjectivity in their theories of health, pain, illness, and the body.

46 See Asad, *Formations of the Secular*, 85.

47 Unless it is noted otherwise, translation of this text comes from Elizabeth Bryson Bongie, *The Life & Regimen of the Blessed & Holy Syncletica by Pseudo-Athanasius*, trans. with notes (Toronto, ON: Peregrina Publishing Co., 1999).

48 Cf. Elizabeth A. Castelli, "Mortifying the Body, Curing the Soul: Beyond Ascetic Dualism in the Life of Syncletica," *Differences: A Journal of Feminist Cultural Studies* 4.2 (1992): 137.

62   *Helen Rhee*

49 Castelli, "Mortifying the Body, Curing the Soul," 140.
50 Mena, "Scenting Saintliness," 13.
51 Mena, "Scenting Saintliness," 15.
52 *Contra* Julian of Aeclanum, who regarded (moderate) pain as "part of the human nature as created by God in the beginning" in Josef Lössl, "Julian of Aeclanum on Pain," *Journal of Early Christian Studies* 10.2 (2000): 221, 223, 233.
53 On Augustine's doctrine of *totus Christus*, see Kimberly Baker, "Augustine's Doctrine of the Totus Christus: Reflecting on the Church as Sacrament of Unity," *Horizons* 37.1 (2010): 7–24; Tarsicius van Babel, "The 'Christus Totus' Idea: A Forgotten Aspect of Augustine's Spirituality," in Thomas Finan and Vincent Twomey (eds.) *Studies in Patristic Christology: Proceedings of the Third Maynooth Patristic Conference* (Portland, OR: Four Courts Press, 1998), 84–94; Bernard Bruning, "Die Einheit des Totus Christus bei Augustinus," in Cornelius Petrus Mayer and Willigis Eckermann (eds.) *Scientia Augustiniana: Studien über Augustinus, den Augustinismus und den Augustinorden* (Wurzburg: Augustinus-Verlag, 1975), 43–75; David Vincent Meconi, *The One Christ: St. Augustine's Theology of Deification* (Washington, DC: The Catholic University of America Press, 2013), 194–216.
54 Cf. Asad, *Formations of the Secular*, 89.
55 Comparing Augustine and Seneca in this paragraph, I am indebted to Sarah Byers, "The Psychology of Compassion: Stoicism in *City of God* 9.5," in James Wetzel (ed.) *Augustine's City of God: A Critical Guide* (Cambridge: Cambridge University Press, 2012), 135–7.
56 Byers, "The Psychology of Compassion," 138, italics original; cf. *Civ. dei* 14.9.
57 Cf. Nicholas Wolterstorff, "Augustine's Rejection of Eudaimonism," in James Wetzel (ed.) *Augustine's City of God: A Critical Guide* (Cambridge: Cambridge University Press, 2012), 161.
58 I am using a phrase from Asad and applying it to Augustine, *Formations of the Secular*, 82.
59 Asad, *Formations of the Secular*, 87.

Bibliography

Ancient Sources

Aelius Aristides. (1976) "Sacred Tales," in C. A. Behr (ed.) *P. Aelii Aristidis Opera Quae Extant Omnia*, Leiden: Brill. English translation in Behr, C. A. (1981–1986) *P. Aelius Aristides: The Complete Works*, vol. 2, Leiden: Brill.
Augustine. (1955) "De Civitate Dei," in B. Dombart and A. Kalb (eds.) *Sancti Aurelii Augustini De Civitate Dei*, Corpus Christianorum Scriptorum Latinorum 47 and 48, Turnout: Brepols.
———. (1956) "Enarrationes in Psalmos," in D. Dekkers and J. Fraipont (eds.) *Enarrationes in Psalmos*, LI-C, Corpus Christianorum Scriptorum Latinorum 39, Turnout: Brepols.
Celsus. (1915) "De medicina," in Frederick Marx (ed.) *A. Cornelii Celsi quae supersunt*, Corpus Medicorum Latinorum 1, Leipzing: Teubner.
Galen. (1821–33) "De Locis Affectibus," in Carl Gottlob Kühn (ed.) *Claudii Galeni Opera Omnia*, vol. 20, Leipzig: Libraria Karl Knobloch, 8:1–452; English translation in Siegel, Rudolph E. (1976) *Galen on the Affected Parts: Translation from the Greek Text with Explanatory Notes*, Basel: Karger.
Galen. (1821–33) "De Symptomatum Causis," in Carl Gottlob Kühn (ed.) *Claudii Galeni Opera Omnia*, vol. 20, Leipzig: Libraria Karl Knobloch, 7:85–272.
Galen. (1821–33) "De Symptomatum Differentiis," in Carl Gottlob Kühn (ed.) *Claudii Galeni Opera Omnia*, vol. 20, Leipzig: Libraria Karl Knobloch, 7:42–84.

Galen of Pergamon. (2016) "Ars medicina," in Ian Johnston (ed. and trans.) *Galen. On the Constitution of Medicine, on the Art of Medicine, a Method of Medicine to Glaucon*, Loeb Classical Library 523, Cambridge, MA: Harvard University Press, 156–318.
Pseudo-Athnasius. *Vita S. Syncletiae*, PG 28:1488–1558; English translation in Bongie, Elizabeth Bryson. (1999) *The Life & Regimen of the Blessed & Holy Syncletica by Pseudo-Athanasius*, trans. with notes, Toronto, ON: Peregrina Publishing Co.

Modern Sources

Asad, Talal. (2003) *Formations of the Secular: Christianity, Islam, Modernity*, Stanford, CA: Stanford University Press.
Baker, Kimberly. (2010) "Augustine's Doctrine of the Totus Christus: Reflecting on the Church as Sacrament of Unity," *Horizons* 37: 7–24.
Behr, C. A. (1968) *Aelius Aristides and the Sacred Tales*, Amsterdam: Adolf M. Hakkert Publisher.
Brody, Howard. (2003) *Stories of Sickness*, second edition, Oxford: Oxford University Press.
Bruning, Bernard. (1975) "Die Einheit des Totus Christus bei Augustinus," in Cornelius Petrus Mayer and Willigis Eckermann (eds.) *Scientia Augustiniana: Studien über Augustinus, den Augustinismus und den Augustinorden*, Wurzburg: Augustinus-Verlag, 43–75.
Byers, Sarah. (2012) "The Psychology of Compassion: Stoicism in *City of God* 9.5," in James Wetzel (ed.) *Augustine's City of God: A Critical Guide*, Cambridge: Cambridge University Press, 130–48.
Castelli, Elizabeth A. (1992) "Mortifying the Body, Curing the Soul: Beyond Ascetic Dualism in *The Life of Syncletica*," *Differences: A Journal of Feminist Cultural Studies* 4: 134–53.
Crislip, Andrew. (2013) *Thorns in the Flesh: Illness and Sanctity in Late Ancient Christianity*. Philadelphia: University of Pennsylvania Press.
Gautherie, Aurélien. (2014) "Physical Pain in Celsus' *On Medicine*," in Brigitte Maire (ed.) *'Greek' and 'Roman' in Latin Medical Texts: Studies in Cultural Change and Exchange in Ancient Medicine*, Leiden and Boston: Brill, 137–54.
King, Daniel. (2018) *Experiencing Pain in Imperial Greek Culture*, Oxford Classical Monographs, Oxford: Oxford University Press.
LaCapra, Dominick. (2009) *History and Its Limits: Human, Animal, Violence*, Ithaca, NY: Cornell University Press.
Lössl, Josef. (2000) "Julian of Aeclanum on Pain," *Journal of Early Christian Studies* 10: 203–43.
Mattern, Susan P. (2013) *The Prince of Medicine: Galen in the Roman Empire*, Oxford: Oxford University Press.
Meconi, David Vincent. (2013) *The One Christ: St. Augustine's Theology of Deification*, Washington, DC: The Catholic University of America Press.
Mena, Peter A. (2017) "Scenting Saintliness: The Ailing Body, Chicana Feminism, and Communal Identity in Ancient Christianity," *Journal of Feminist Studies in Religion* 33: 5–20.
Roby, Courtny. (2016) "Galen on the Patient's Role in Diagnosis: Sensation, Consensus, and Metaphor," in G. Petridou and C. Thumiger (eds.) *Homo Patiens: Approaches to the Patient in the Ancient World*, Leiden: Brill, 304–24.
Rothschild, Clare K. and Thompson, Trevor W. (eds.) (2014) *Galen's De indolentia: Essays on a Newly Discovered Letter*, STAC 88, Tübingen: Mohr Siebeck.

Samellas, Antigone. (2015) "Public Aspects of Pain in Late Antiquity: The Testimony of Chrysostom and the Cappadocians in Their Graeco-Roman Context," *Zeitschrift für Antikes Christentum* 19: 260–96.

Siegel, Rudolph E. (1970) *Galen on Sense Perception: His Doctrines, Observations and Experiments on Vision, Hearing, Smell, Taste, Touch and Pain, and Their Historical Sources*, Basel, Switzerland and New York: S. Karger.

van Babel, Tarsicius. (1998) "The 'Christus Totus' Idea: A Forgotten Aspect of Augustine's Spirituality," in Thomas Finan and Vincent Twomey (eds.) *Studies in Patristic Christology: Proceedings of the Third Maynooth Patristic Conference*, Portland, OR: Four Courts Press, 84–94.

Wolterstorff, Nicholas. (2012) "Augustine's Rejection of Eudaimonism," in James Wetzel (ed.) *Augustine's City of God: A Critical Guide*, Cambridge: Cambridge University Press, 149–66.

Part Two

Defining Patients, Delimiting Communities

5   To Be, or Not to Be Sterile

That Is a Question of Well-being in
Byzantine Medical Discourse of the
Sixth Century AD

Elisa Groff

Introduction

This contribution is framed by three issues of ancient sexual health and gender identity: (1) whether sterility and infertility were framed as diseases in medical discourses of late antiquity; (2) who, from a medical perspective, was to bear the societal burden of childlessness; and (3) which kind of treatments were envisaged if the man and/or the woman were unable to conceive, or when childbirth was too hazardous a risk for a mother-to-be. The discussion will focus on two chapters in Aëtius of Amida's Book 16 on gynaecology and obstetrics.[1] In particular, we shall concentrate on the medical differentiation of *atokía* (contraceptives) and *phthoría* (abortifacients) in chapter 16.16 and in chapter 16.26 dealing with the causes on account of which men and women may not conceive.

These late antique narratives of sterility (*impotentia concipiendi*) and infertility (*impotentia gestandi*) will show that early Byzantine culture had a medicalized knowledge of sex and reproduction. Moreover, they will well exemplify Aëtius' *modus operandi*, which is characterized by (a) critical use and reuse of earlier medical material,[2] (b) a philosophical understanding of the human body and its functions, (c) an overarching attention to body–mind balance, and (d) an emphasis on women's self-well-being in relation to sexuality and reproduction.[3]

From the analysis of the medical texts, it will emerge that Aëtius qualifies sterility not as a single disease entity but as a range of factors related to body and mind which hinder the ability of man and/or woman to conceive. In addition to this first diagnosis, sterility can also be recommended as a preventive treatment in women whom labour would put in more jeopardy due to their constitutionally unfit body shape. That will be the case of a temporary sterility induced through the medically supervised intake of contraceptives (*atokía*) with the aim of preventing a pregnancy. Furthermore, Aëtius qualifies a condition of permanent irreversible sterility, which in clinal practice is defined more properly as infertility in terms of *impotentia gestandi*. While Aëtius describes sterility also as an irreparable change of the woman's reproductive system induced by an overdose of contraceptives, he never addresses a genetically based infertility as a moral problem—although he acknowledges the social burden it brings with it.[4] We shall show that Aëtius' treatment in sexual and reproductive health (1) includes therapy for the soul as

DOI: 10.4324/9781003080534-7

well as body, and (2) may be culturally determined, but (3) also subverts gender expectations in that it cuts against the biblical line that usually describes women as infertile, but men as merely "old."[5]

Ultimately, this chapter aims for three further goals: (1) to demystify the language around disorders of the reproductive system by being appropriate to an ancient context while avoiding ideological loads and ableist biases[6]; (2) to bring a new voice to the discussion of infertility in medical history and sexual ethics; (3) to locate the study of late antique narratives of sterility and infertility within the study of Global Health over the long term, likewise within the remit of promoting women's health and well-being in order to bridge the current divides between historical studies and contemporary healthcare concerns.

Aëtius Amidenus: Life, Work, Medical Discourse

The main source for Byzantine medicine and women's sexual and reproductive health in the sixth century AD is the medical author and physician Aëtius of Amida.[7] Unfortunately, Aëtius' medical encyclopaedia and biography are a conundrum. What can be said which have not been disputed amongst modern scholars are the following: (i) Aëtius was a native of Amida[8]; (ii) he lived after Oribasius (born in AD 325) and before Alexander of Tralles (ca. AD 525–605)[9]; (iii) he was a medical student in Alexandria[10]; (iv) he served as a physician[11]; and (v) during his career as a doctor, he wrote a medical encyclopaedia in 16 books known as βιβλία ἰατρικὰ ἑκκαίδεκα, or *Tetrabiblos* since it is divided in four parts, or *Libri Medicinales*. This work was very well received in the Middle Ages to the Renaissance but is, alas, very poorly served by modern editions.[12] With regard to the contents, the *Tetrabiblos* meshes rational medicine with isolated examples of Christian mysticism and elements of superstition.[13] This may well lie with the fact that mystical ideas and superstition "were deeply rooted in Byzantine popular thinking."[14] Nevertheless, these few textual references to Christian customs are too thin a piece of evidence to describe Aëtius as a declared Christian.[15] I would say that Aëtius was a man of his time, "Christian enough to use Christian forms of incantation,"[16] and open-minded enough to believe that effective medicine blended together rational and popular understanding. Furthermore, early Byzantine medicine portrayed the debating culture of late antiquity as endangering a process of continuation of, and distance from, a revered medical prehistory. Aëtius' *oeuvre* perfectly exemplifies the Byzantine pattern of continuation and disjuncture from a previous medical tradition.[17] For instance, book 16 on gynaecology and obstetrics, on which this chapter focuses, emerges as the product of cross-fertilization of ideas transferred from philosophy, Aristotelian in great part, to Aëtius understanding of medicine.[18] Despite relying on earlier authors, Aëtius amalgamated together the contents of different authors and re-elaborated them. What is more, he appears to call upon in his writings what he learnt as of physician in actual medical practice, and expanded on that, as we shall see as follows: in chapter 16.16 about women who cannot deliver safely and in chapter 16.26 about both physiological and psychosomatic causes of sterility.

Aëtius' Medical Terminology: Sterility versus Fecundity, Infertility versus Fertility

"Sterility may be either due to the man or to the woman, or to both," [Ἀσυλληψί α γίνεται ἢ περὶ τὸν ἄνδρα ἢ περὶ τὴν γυναῖκα ἢ καὶ περὶ ἀμφοτέρους]. So reads the first line in Aëtius' Book 16, chapter 26 (Zervos 1901: 16.26, 24) on the causes through which men and women may not conceive.

From the very beginning, Aëtius makes it clear what is the subject he is addressing: he uses the term *a-sullepsia*, "no-conception," which in modern terms means "absence (failure) of fertilization."[19] This etymological precision is of relevance since by using the term *asullepsia*, Aëtius clarifies that he is not tackling here matters of infertility, that is, the inability to carry a pregnancy to term after fertilization. In modern clinical terms, infertility refers to a spectrum of pathological (usually genetic) malformations of the reproductive system which may hinder the process of development of the embryo after fertilization and prevent it from developing all the way through the stages of gestation (embryogenesis, organogenesis) up to delivery and the moment of birth.

Instead, with *a-sullepsia*, Aëtius means here "sterility," that is, the permanent "incapability of conceiving/fertilising" and the opposite of fecundity. This is a noticeable point since the terms "sterility" and "infertility" are often wrongly interchanged even in modern terms, both in medical and popular usage.[20] On the contrary, Aëtius is most precise and he has an accurate word choice defining sterility as the opposite of fecundity, that is "the potential for fertilization, the capability of conceiving," and infertility as the opposite of fertility.[21] In terms of modern demographic analysis, Aëtius understands fertility as the "marker for the attainment of adulthood" versus sterility (*impotentia concipiendi*), which can be a permanent condition[22]; and he links fertility versus infertility (*impotentia gestandi*) to the life and menstrual cycle of every woman.[23] Aëtius' differentiation conforms to the modern procedure of in vitro fertilization that aims at reproducing the biological process of conception outside of the body, in couples where fertilization does not occur naturally. If the fertilized embryo can then be implanted into the woman's uterus, this means that the woman is not only fecund but also fertile, namely she is able to carry the pregnancy to term potentially. If the woman were infecund (or genetically barren), in fact, no treatment could ever be successful, so even in vitro fertilization would be done in vain.

Since in vitro fertilization is usually presented as a method to "treat fertility problems," it is here to be observed that in modern clinical terms "fertility" is often used as a synonym for "fecundity." However, understanding the difference between the two terms is highly important, especially in relation to the different consequences they imply. With regard to those, Aëtius will keep the distinction between sterility and infertility clear and consistent in his text, as well as in other chapters of the treatise, confirming that this is a cornerstone in his theory of sexuality and reproduction and that he is fully aware of the implications of the two different diagnoses. For example, in chapter 16.67, Aëtius profiles those who present symptoms of uterine suffocation[24] as "young women inclined to lasciviousness" and women who have become "infecund" (and so "infertile"), στείραις, after taking φαρμακείαι ἄτοκοι, that is, "drugs" that hinder conception and so "cause (immediate) sterility." Once more, the use of Aëtius' medical language is not accidental: ἀτόκιον comes from τίκτω meaning "to generate, to produce offspring," from which also οἱ τεκόντες, "the parents," derive and which links to the definition of "fertility" we have given earlier as "the actual product of offspring."[25]

Physiological Causes of Sterility in Men and Women

Aëtius' chapter on the failure to conceive (16.26 Zervos), which meshes an understanding of fecundity with medical cases and elements that are not strictly clinical, is an excellent example to gain insights into the late antique medicalized knowledge of reproduction and women's sexual well-being.[26]

According to the title, the chapter deals with "the causes through which men and women may not conceive" as well as "the signs and treatment of conception"; it provides the reader with a detailed and fascinating list of factors pro fecundity and contra sterility that moves from sheer biology, through romantic issues and lifestyle, to sexual rights and beauty tips.

While the causes that can endanger woman's safety during labour are of a genetic nature, and concerned with women only, the causes that hinder conception can be due to the man, the woman, or both. Aëtius explains that when it comes to the failure to conceive, it cannot be said without further investigation who is responsible.[27] At first glance, the man and the woman are potentially responsible all the same, so the physician must be familiar with the whole spectrum of symptoms and signs of sterility in each gender. If it is due to the man, the problem is an abnormal sperm production linked to the fact that the semen is either too warm, too cold, too thick, or too weak, for the man is too fat, too old, has a genital birth defect, or his penis is too short and "it is not capable of ejaculating the semen in the innermost part of the womb" [οὐκ ἰσχύειν εἰς τὸ ἐντὸς τῆς μήτρας τὸ σπέρμα ἐξακοντίζειν].[28]

Of salience is that amongst the conditions that may affect the male reproductive system impeding fertilization, some causes can be cured, such as gonorrhoea, some require a surgical intervention, such as for some cases of hypospadias, but for others there is no cure: for example, for those men who have undergone an operation to remove gallstones, for those who cannot emit semen due to an irreversible (inoperable) condition of hypospadias, or for those who have too narrow genital ducts. For these men, there is no cure.[29]

On the other hand, if the failure to conceive is due to the woman, the problem lies with the quality of her womb, which may be too warm, too cold, too moist, or obstructed, so the woman is not menstruating properly, or the cervix is not in place.[30] Furthermore, the problem can lie with the woman being too fat or too thin, with her working too much or with the fact that she is idle or she eats food that is difficult to digest.[31]

In Aëtius' symptomatology, a pathological dysfunction is of particular interest, namely the twisting of the cervix, as it refers to the theory of conception in the *Historia Animalium* (*HA*). The author of *HA* X 634b28–30 identifies the places of seminal emission and sexual pleasure in the woman's body, and he explains that in order to conceive, man and woman have to emit their seminal seeds in the same place before the uterus, that is the cervix. It is thus logical that if the cervix is twisted, the uterus cannot draw the concocted seed inside and fertilization cannot take place. Basically, if the penis is too short to ejaculate the semen inside the womb, or the cervix is not in a straight line to let the semen come through, the result is the same, namely fertilization cannot occur in the womb and fecund semen gets wasted.

Further in the text, Aëtius writes that sterility may also be caused by age: so the man and the woman should not have sexual intercourse when they are too young or too old; the most suitable age is 30 for the man and 18 for the woman, and this is because the body of a younger woman—namely younger than 18—is not suitable for conception because it is not yet fully developed (Aëtius 16.26, lines 2–5, Zervos).[32]

It is worth drawing a parallel here with Aristotle's *History of Animals* IX 581b11–21.[33] In this passage, Aristotle suggests marriage should not take place at too early an age because the memories of pleasant sexual experiences may arouse sexual desire. The bottom line is that the later the people start having sexual intercourse, the longer they will be able to control their sexual desires. Now, although in Aëtius (16.26, 2–5, Zervos) the age at marriage is linked to conception, whereas in Aristotle it is linked to sexual pleasure, the arguments of the two authors seem to fit conceptually like pieces of a jigsaw puzzle. Hence when compared to the Hippocratic culture, in Aëtius' context of sexual and reproductive health, what is "closely joined in societal and medical thinking" are not only "the two moments of marriage and menarche" but also the experience of sexual arousal.[34]

After explaining the physical conditions that in women can hinder conception, Aëtius lays down for his reader the profile of the fecund (and fertile) woman, ἐπίτεκνον γυναῖκα (16.26, l. 5–8): ideally, she should be

proportionate in size, hips and abdomen must be rather broad, the nates must be pronounced, the upper-abdomen of good size, narrow chest and well-developed mammary glands; women of this sort get pregnant rapidly, κυΐσκειν, while the opposite are less fecund, ἀτεκνότεραι.[35]

In the last section of the chapter, Aëtius provides those who wish to have children with a final prescription, which sounds like common-sense advice from our modern perspective. In line with his general approach of balanced preventive medicine, Aëtius prescribes a healthy and moderate lifestyle, and recommends that parents-to-be should take good care of their body and keep themselves fit: "neither a fat woman nor a fat man are suitable for conception . . . for that they cannot accommodate their genitals to each other . . . in addition, fat men produce little semen"; the man and the woman should know what to eat and drink, that is, food "stimulating intercourse and generating semen," for example,

amongst the herbs sage, rocket, mallow but . . . not rue and mint since mint stimulates an over-production of semen and rue destroys it; they should drink wine instead of water, and be aware that the most suitable moment for conception is close to the beginning of the monthly period.

(Zervos 1901: 16.26, 39–40)

Psychosomatic Causes of Sterility in Men and Women

After looking at age and the anatomy as well as physiology of the reproductive system in men and women, Aëtius adds that "if the woman and the man are healthy in all respects," the physician should look for other causes that are not of a physical nature.[36] In other words, diagnosed incurable dysfunctions apart, if the man and the woman are still not able to conceive, it might lie in other factors that are germane to what modern society understands as the remit of self-regulation, sexual rights, and well-being.

With regard to sexual rights, Aëtius writes that "the woman (who is) having intercourse with a man through force and unwillingly" "may also be a hindrance to conception," since when she is in love, she brings the seed into harmony, and for this reason intercourse with desire is readily productive of children [τὸ ἀγάγκη καὶ μὴ ἐθέλουσαν μίσγεσθαι τῷ ἀνδρὶ τὴν γυναῖκα, γάρ ἀγαπῶσα συναρμόζει τὴν γονὴν, καὶ διὰ τοῦτο αἱ μετ' ἔρωτος μίξεις ταχυτεκνόταταί εἰσι].[37]

These lines are of particular interest because on the one side, they can be read in parallel with *HA* X 5.636a22 stating that a reproductive woman needs to be at ease and in the right frame of mind; but on the other side, they echo indirectly Soranus *Gyn.* 1.37 asserting that if a woman has conceived after being raped, she must have enjoyed it. This is one of those passages in the *Libri Medicinales* where Aëtius does not (feel forced to) take a clear stand in support or in opposition to a previous author; he decides to acknowledge both positions instead.

In terms of hindrance to conception due to lack of an overall state of well-being in the man, Aëtius says: "So then, men who spoil their semen through their depraved life habits or customs, will have fecund semen [γόνιμον] if they make use of a healthier change of habits and ordered lifestyle." It is worth underlining that Aëtius is giving here prominence to an overall state of well-being in the man by recommending patterns of self-regulation. Furthermore, he adds that "those who are not in tune [i.e., sexually] with their wives, will produce children, once they have substituted their wife with another woman [οἱ ἀσυμφώνως πρὸς τὰς ἑαυτῶν γυναῖκας διακείμενοι, παιδοποιήσονται, μεταλαβόντες ἄλλας]."[38]

Aëtius' account of these additional causes because of which a healthy man and a healthy woman may be childless is of relevance for several reasons, starting with the consideration that early Byzantine medicine believed that conception could be affected by factors of mental and emotional well-being. It is compelling to note that the WHO classifies such non-physical causes under the spectrum of "involuntary infertility," while modern medical ethics qualifies "relational infertility" due to sexual reproductive incompatibility between man and woman as a status that can be cured with a change in partner.[39]

Further considerations emerge from the textual analysis and investigation of *loci paralleli.* Cross-references are to be found in ancient treatises of medicine, philosophy, and socio-economics, which is not too surprising. For instance, I argue that the expression "συναρμόζει τὴν γονὴν" refers to man and woman reaching orgasm at the same time, as stated in *HA* X 636b10–11.[40] A brief excursus on the conceptualization of mutual orgasm in ancient medical and philosophical authors will give us the measure of its value for the theory of sexuality and reproduction in antiquity.

Indeed, mutual orgasm is not only acknowledged by Aëtius and the Aristotelian author(s), or by their common source. For Plato, it was not even an option but the only possible way. He considered, in fact, sexual satisfaction in man and woman as biologically determined since by nature men and women were made to seek completeness; and the latter could be only achieved through sexual union. As long as the "two sexes" were not united in mutual completeness—"their desire and love satisfied"—they were thought of as incapable of finding peace.[41] High commendation of mutual orgasm came also from Hippocrates' and Galen's model of conception. *On Generation* 4.2, the Hippocratic author describes the ideal heterosexual intercourse aiming at reproduction as culminating in both partners' sexual arousal. Nonetheless, the Hippocratic model understood female sexual drive as in need of male heat/penetration to be initiated since women were cooler than men by nature (φύσει).[42] Simultaneous achievement of the sexual peak in man and woman was so designed to open the womb and give way to successful reproduction. Hence, provided that it could occur soon after the male sperm entered the womb, orgasm in woman exploded "like a flame that flares when wine is sprinkled upon it."[43] Furthermore, the author of *HA* X 636b17–21 explains that

> the partners must keep pace with one another. Thus if the man ejaculates too quickly and the woman with difficulty . . . that prevents conception; and that is why partners who do not produce children with one another *do* produce children when they meet with partners who keep pace with them during intercourse.[44]

If it is difficult to clinically prove the latter assumption right, the rhythmic muscular contractions that characterize orgasm in a woman corroborate the former. In the medical context of *Tetrabiblos*' 16.26, this is what Aëtius may mean when he suggests that man should change her wife and substitute her with another woman if they are unable to have children together.[45]

In sum, far from being the reward for sexual moderation, reproduction and the failure to conceive are approached first and foremost as a physical matter by Aëtius: society needs offspring to thrive and not die out; if reproduction does not come about, a physician must be summoned who will investigate the entire spectrum of causes that hinder conception, and find a solution for the sake of society, of man and of woman—in this order.[46] The factors that determine the failure to conceive can be of physical, mental, or emotional nature. The physician is thus in charge of giving instructions as to what can be cured, what can be operable, and all that is necessary to do in order to facilitate conception. Changing wives, μεταλαβόντες, is one path that can lead to the goal.[47]

Temporary Induced Sterility versus Irreversible Permanent Sterility

In antiquity, established sterility was a condition that society had to fight against with every available tool.[48] If incurable, every contract which was stipulated on the basis of fecundity (i.e. the capability of having children) and with the promise of fertility (i.e. the actual number of children) could be legally nullified as Nero's ground for divorce from Octavia and the diatribe between the ancient Roman jurists Labeo and Trebatius teach us.[49] The latter is reported, for example, in Aulus Gellius' *Noctes Atticae* and it deals in general, with the difference between a "permanent defect" (*vitium perpetuum*) and a "disease" (*morbus*) which arises and can be cured [4.2, 13][50]; and in particular, with an aediles' edict that established whether infecund slave women could be returned [4.2, 9–10]:

> [N]o action could be taken . . . if the woman had been born barren. But if her health had failed, and in consequence such a defect had resulted that she could not conceive, in that case she appeared to be unsound and there was ground for returning her.

But what if the woman was not born barren (infecund), only unfit to go into labour and deliver safely? Chapter 16 in Aëtius' Book 16, "Treatments/drugs to cause Sterility and Methods to destroy [a Foetus]" ["ΠΕΡΙ ΑΤΟΚΙΩΝ ΚΑΙ ΦΘΟΡΙΩΝ"] provides us with a piece of an answer.

This chapter is of relevance for our discussion of ancient women's well-being in relation to sexuality and reproduction because it addresses the issue of what ought to be done when the woman is unfit to conceive and cannot delivery safely. Surely, this is a topic ancient authors did not like to dwell upon as it depicts a threatening scenario that questions the very existence of society. Presumably, this is one reason why ancient sources are not teeming with mentions of acceptance of childless women, and especially for those who wanted to remain that way. Aëtius' account is then all the more remarkable, also because he diagnoses female childlessness, that is, infertility, not as a moral problem but as a genetic issue, that is, a fact determined by a woman's constitution to which she should adapt the best she could.

On this account, Aëtius is as much concerned about the well-being of woman as about that of society, and he suggests that the physician should help the infertile (but fecund) woman to find out a behavioural adaptation to survive if pregnant or to be able to have a sexual life without the risk of becoming pregnant. According to Aëtius, case one is accomplished through the use of abortifacients (φθορίου), and case two through the intake of contraceptives (ἀτόκιον). In both cases, the doctor's prescription and supervision are essential in order not to harm the woman, for example, making her involuntarily infertile like one of the patients afflicted with uterine suffocation (16.67 Zervos).

The introductory section of passage 16.16 in the words of Aëtius follows: "Some women who conceive, they are endangered during labour" [Τινες τῶν γυναικῶν ἐν γαστρὶ λαμβάνουσαι, κινδυνεύουσινἐν ταῖς ἀποτέξεσιν][51]; "for those (women) it would be much better if they do not conceive" [αἷς πολλῷ μὲν ἄμεινον ἐστὶ τὸ μὴ συλλαβεῖν]. It is worth highlighting here, once again, the legacy of Aristotle behind the diagnosis of abnormal formations in the cervix (cf. *HA* X 634b28–30) and at the mouth of the womb (*GA* 728a31–34).

Despite everything, if these women "should conceive, it would be better to destroy the embryo rather than to cut the foetus out of the womb (later)" [βέλτιον ἐστὶ τοῦ ἐμβρυοτομηθῆναι τὸ φθεῖραι]; "on this account we must deal with the methods to destroy the embryo and to cause sterility."

In fact, "contraceptive methods (i.e. methods that cause temporary sterility) [Ἀτόκιον δὲ φθορίου διαφέρει] differ from abortifacients (i.e. methods to destroy a foetus)" as follows: "while contraceptive(s) do not allow conception (i.e. fertilisation) to occur," "abortifacient(s) destroy and expel the product of conception" [τὸ μὲν γὰρ ἀτόκιον οὐκ ἐᾷ γίγνεσθαι σύλληψιν, τὸ δὲ φθόριον φθείρει τὸ συλληφθὲν καὶ ἐκβάλλει].[52]

Therefore, in the cases of those women who are not able to deliver safely due to congenital malformations affecting their reproductive system, the physician should first prescribe ἀτοκία, "contraceptive methods to prevent conception from taking place," because it is better to prevent than cure. Abortifacients are in fact presented as a second-choice solution.

If the goal is to hinder delivery, since childbirth can constitute a health hazard for those women, the process of reproduction must be stopped at its onset. Therefore, τίκτω describes the whole process of reproduction from fertilization, through embryogenesis, to organogenesis, until birth. Since τίκτω includes in itself the primary generative stage (fertilization) which is defined with συλλάμβανω, the word ἀτοκία comes to hold the same conceptual significance as ἀσυλληψία here.[53] In modern terms, if a woman is taking a contraceptive pill, she is currently sterile or not fecund, namely she is not able to conceive because the pill is impeding fertilization. Nevertheless, she is not permanently infecund for the pill does not nullify her capability of conceiving (fecundity). Hence, when induced through contraceptive methods, sterility is not an illness, but a temporary condition of barrenness (infecundity).

Along with the conceptualization of the spectrum of female fertility in late antiquity, this passage is of salient interest because it condenses information about the use of birth-control methods in antiquity, which is by now historically established on the basis of ancient medical writings, legislative texts, and therapeutic amulets.[54]

Aëtius' differentiation of *atokía* and *phthoría* follows Soranus' argument partly (*Gyn.* 1.20), but he expands the focus on the congenital causes of infertility in woman (by integrating Aristotelian observations), and he makes no mention of concern for beauty or adultery on the woman's side as reasons for moral blame. Having said that, I am by no means arguing that Aëtius' omission of blame stands by itself as evidence that he believes women should be allowed to procure an abortion whenever they wanted one. Moreover, Aëtius does not use his discussion of contraceptives and abortifacients as a blanket acceptance for women to choose to remain childless if they wish so on a whim. As much as not every abortion is a crime, not every abortion is condoned. Every case is different and needs to be taken into account according to the nature of the woman's body and the social circumstances. Whatever the case, Aëtius gives women with gynaecological health issues an ethically legitimised option.[55]

Therefore, although we ought to bear in mind that Aëtius' prescriptions were not within the reach of everyday women, his writings reveal that as a doctor he was very wary of childbirth and conscious that "there [were] particular things that [happened] to women" in the ancient cultural context of sexual health and reproduction simply by virtue of their being women.[56]

On a philological note, Aëtius acknowledges the prehistory of the *materia medica* he is dealing with but the contents of 16.16 are the outcome of his own reasoning. Indeed, although his discussion of the right of a woman to prevent pregnancy or to procure an abortion is upheld by Soranus, Aëtius headlines the circumstances in which the woman's own life is in danger directly at the beginning of his chapter, and from there he develops his argument. On the contrary, in Soranus, the reference to endangered conditions for a pregnant woman is mentioned *en passant* in the middle of the account. The fact that Aëtius decided not to repeat Soranus' structure but to reorganize his own argument instead reveals his own priorities.[57] In other words, the structure of his argument is functional to the message he wants to get through. We may dare to say that Aëtius draws attention to the woman as human being, and he deals with aspects related to a woman's reproductive autonomy and her sexual self-well-being. Thus, in 16.16, his discussion of contraceptives and abortifacients concentrates not so much on the mechanism and efficacy of these methods as on the therapies available to medicine to safeguard the woman's health. Ultimately, Aëtius provides the infertile woman and the woman whose health was endangered at childbirth with medically legitimized options that have at their core the well-being of women first and foremost, and then that of society. In the context of late antique syncretism, Aëtius acts first and foremost as a physician. Aëtius' medicine does not serve theological purposes; his medical treatment is not based on religious prescriptions for he is primarily concerned with the well-being of his female patients according to their constitution.

As it is within the scope of this contribution, I would like to conclude this paragraph by drawing a parallel to the WHO definition of sexual and reproductive health which makes the effort to minimize the health hazards for a pregnant woman a right. The analogies are for the readers to reflect upon:

> Reproductive health implies . . . the rights of men and women to be informed and to have access to safe, effective, affordable and acceptable methods of family planning . . . which are not against the law, and the right of access to appropriate healthcare services that will enable women to go safely through pregnancy and childbirth and provide couples with the best chance of having a healthy infant.[58]

Conclusions

This chapter has shown which kinds of sterility ancient medicine in the sixth century AD qualified as permanent and which as temporary medical conditions of infertility, which warranted treatment for the sake of society and which for the sake of the woman.

We have seen that the early Byzantine medical author Aëtius of Amida describes sterility as a spectrum disorder encompassing a wide variation in the type and severity of symptoms, some of which possess features clinical practice too associate today with infertility and sterility. Thus, in early Byzantine medical discourse, some cases of sterility qualify disorders due to failures of biological functions in the woman and/or in the man or due to psychosomatic factors. These cases can be potentially cured. Other cases involve sterility induction (i.e. infertility) through a medically supervised intake of contraceptives (*atokía*), and irreversible sterility caused by an unsupervised overdose of contraceptives.

What are we to make out of this late antique medical evidence? This bulk of information is significant because it gives a direct answer to the questions we have asked in the introduction of this chapter, namely whether infertility and sterility were a disease in late antiquity and to whom it did matter. Indeed, Aëtius does not categorize any form of sterility as a disease but as a range of factors affecting body and mind whose therapy aims at restoring an overall state of physical, mental, and emotional well-being. In so doing, Aëtius' treatment pins down the remit of early Byzantine medicine not as simply concerned with curing but rather as concentrating on the whole process of healing, which resonates with the WHO's definitions of sexual and reproductive health. What is more, Aëtius' holistic view on fertility measures, which he grants as culturally determined, subverts gender expectations in that it cuts against the biblical line that usually describes infertility as a failing on the woman's part—while if anything, men are just "old."

Finally, even though it would be anachronistic to say that Aëtius makes reproductive autonomy a constitutionally protected right in the sixth century AD, he certainly takes a proactive approach to patient care. His medical discourse envisages in fact an alternative to childbirth for women with reproductive issues, for instance, those who could not deliver without harm. We can therefore safely conclude that Aëtius understands the question of childbearing as concerning with equal importance safety issues for the woman and reproductive duty towards the husband and society.

Ultimately, early Byzantine medical conceptualizations of sterility and infertility enable us to address specific issues which fall within the remit of preventive medicine, ethical dilemmas, and the promotion of women's physical, mental, and emotional well-being in relation to sexuality and reproduction. On this basis, I argue that ancient medical discourses of disease, disability, and healing affecting the reproductive system of men and women can be successfully complemented by modern discussion of fertility in clinal practice and research, and vice versa. In fact, ancient medical evidence of infertility proves illuminating for our current public debates today which affect different parts of the world and different gender categories, as it makes no claims regarding "normal" reproductive bodies or one-size-fits-all approach to fertility treatments. Equally, ancient medical narratives can be comforting in the long run when it comes to demystifying a language around disorders of the reproductive system and choosing how to frame past and present stories of people's fertility in medical academic publications and higher education.

Notes

1 Aëtius' Book 16 on gynaecology, obstetrics, and surgical procedures of the female reproductive system is available in four modern translations: Skévos Zervos, *Aetii Sermo
   Sextidecimus et Ultimus. Erstens aus Handschriften veröffentlicht*. Leipzig: Anton Man-
   gkos, 1901; J. Ricci, 1950, *Aetius of Amida: The Gynaecology and Obstetrics of the VIth
   Century AD*. Blakiston Co. Philadelphia, based on the Latin translation by Cornarius,
   1533, numbering 123 chapters; text available online at http://babel.hathitrust.org/cgi/
   pt?id=mdp.39015071062593;view=1up;seq=93. A German translation by the physician
   Max Wegscheider, complete only through chapter 113, was published in 1901, *Geburtshilfe und Gynäkologie bei Aëtios von Amida*, Berlin. The most recent translation is by
   Roberto Romano 2006, 251–553.
2 See, for example, King 2011: 124.
3 While drawing on earlier medical and philosophical authors, Aëtius does expand on previous material and calls upon in his writings his own autoptic experience as a physician.
   On this point, see also Betancourt 2020: 69.
4 Strikingly, those distinctions mirror the modern medical understanding of infertility versus sterility and so the practice of in vitro fertilization.
5 See, for example, the Biblical example of Sarah and Abraham.
6 Chouinard 1997.
7 Nutton 1996: 209–210; Van der Eijk 2010.
8 Today Diyarbakir (Turkey). See about *Tetrabiblos'* Books I, II, III, V, VI, IX, and XI: for
   details about his life and career, see Calà 2012a; 2012b. See also Photius' *Bibliothèque*
   Tome III (cod. 221, ed. R. Henry, Paris 2003): Ἀνεγνώσθη **Ἀετίου Ἀμιδηνοῦ ἰατρικὸν
   ἐν λόγοις ιϛ´**; Nutton 1996; Scarborough 2013.
9 Alexander of Tralles quotes Aëtius in his treatise *De Febribus* 7 [= Puschmann I, 437],
   Ἐκ τοῦ Ἀετίου περὶ τῶν ἐν τοῖς σπλάγχνοις ἐρυσιπελατωδῶν διαθέσεων: about see
   Calà 2012a: 11, n. 10. For the chronology of Alexander of Tralles, see also Guardasole
   2006, 557–8 and Jonathan Zecher, in this volume.
10 See *Tetrabiblos'* Book 9.15. See also Scarborough 2010.
11 See Groff 2019. About the title of *comes obsequii* attributed to Aëius as "personal/royal
   physician" with the rank of *comes*, see Nutton 1996, *NP*; Hunger 1978; Ricci 1950;
   Shaw 1998, 71 versus Martindale 1980; Treadgold 1988, 112, 119, 129; Wegscheider
   1901, ix. See also Scarborough 2013 for his alleged affiliation to the court of the emper-
   ors Justinian and Theodora.
12 The *editio princeps* of the first eight books was printed by the Aldine press in Venice
   in 1534, which remained the only available edition until Alessandro Olivieri's critical
   edition for the *Corpus Medicorum Graecorum* in 1935. Of the entire treatise, only two
   Latin translations are available: by the Italian doctor Giovan Battista Montanus (1534
   Venice): www.biusante.parisdescartes.fr; and by the German doctor Janus Cornarius
   (1533; 1542, Basel), www.biusante.parisdescartes.fr. Currently, Irene Calà and Matthias
   Witt at the Ludwig-Maximilian University in Munich are preparing the first critical editions of Aëtius' book 10 and 14, as well as of book 9 with translation. A research team
   at the Humboldt University in Berlin led by Prof. Philip Van der Eijk is working on the
   translations of books 1 and 2.
13 Aëtius 8.54; 13.13; 15.15. See Calà 2012a: 14–16.
14 Duffy 1984: 22, n. 9 about the place occupied by superstition in the "upper class" of
   Byzantine society.
15 Aëtius 8.54; 13.13; 15.15. See Calà 2012a: 14–16.
16 Nutton 1996.
17 See, for example, Calà 2012: 20–47 for a comparative study of Aëtius' sources in *Tetrabiblos'* book 1.
18 According to the *pinax*, chapter 16 is based on the work of Soranus (first–second century AD), Hippocrates (fifth century BC), Galen (second century AD), Aspasia (? BC),

Philumenus (before fourth century BC), Asclepiades Pharmacon (first century AD), Archigenes (first–second century AD), Leonidas (second–third century AD), Theodorus Priscianus (fourth century AD), Rufus of Ephesus (first century AD), and Oribasius of Pergamon (fourth century AD). The names of the referred authors are mentioned by Aëtius either implicitly, which means the author is not acknowledged in the text but the contents are clearly borrowed, or explicitly, meaning fragments of the contents are reported and the name of the author whom Aëtius is referring to is explicitly mentioned in the main body or as often in the chapters' title or, for example, ch. 25 (Zervos), ΠΕΡΙ ΕΠΙΜΕΛΕΙΑΣ ΜΕΤΑ ΤΗΝ ΕΜΒΡΥΟΤΟΜΙΑΝ, ΑΣΠΑΣΙΑΣ, "Management of the patient after embryotomy, Aspasia."

19 See, for example, the *Invitra* magazine specialized in assisted reproduction and pregnancy, available at www.invitra.com. Cf. Rochon et al. 1986.

20 In demography, it is said that fertility is the actual production of offspring, meaning the actual number of foetuses that a woman is able to bring to term during her life, whereas fecundity is the physiological capability of conceiving. See Chamberlain 2006: in part. 2,17, 27, 35, 54.

21 For discussions of causes of and remedies against Ἀσυλληψία before Aëtius, see, for example, the Corpus Hippocraticum: *Mul.* 3.8, 408 fll; 1, 75.8, 162, fll.; 1, 85.210; *Aer.* 21.2, 74 fll.; *Genit.* 2.7, 472 fll.; Dioscorides Pedanius: *De Materia Medica* 1.104, 1,4; 3.34, 2 l. 3; 4.185, 1 l. 8; 5.80, 1 l. 2; 5.106, 6, l. 5: 5.146, 1 l. 5; *De simplicibus medicinis* 2.100, 1 l.1; Soranus: *Gyn.* 1.61, 2 fll; 3.50, 3, 18; Oribasius: *Libri ad Eunapium* 4.114. A detailed study of *loci paralleli* in ancient medical writings dealing with "sterility" and "infertility" is beyond the purpose of the present work. However, an in-depth analysis is worth considering for further development in a future study.

22 Chamberlain 2006: 17.

23 Steinberg 1955: 169.

24 Zervos 1901: 16,67, 95–103. The suffocation (pnix) of the womb (hysterike) is diagnosed as a retention of chilled seed in the womb affecting the woman's overall state of well-being.

25 Cf. Chesi 2014: 20, 44, 100, 104, 120, 160, 165 for τίκτω with the meaning of "giving life" referred to Clytemnestra's motherhood in Aeschilus' Oresteia. The "reproductive power" of Clytemnestra is bound together with both her mind (44) and her "reproductive agency" (166, 175, 185).

26 Zervos 1901: 36–40 (Ch. 29 in the *Thesaurus Linguae Graecae*). Ch. 23 ms. *Laur. Plut.* 75.07; ch. 23 ms. *Par Suppl. Gr.* 632; ch. 26. Cornarius' edition in Latin; ch. 26 Montanus' edition in Latin as well as Horozco 1540; ch. 26 Wegscheider's German translations 1901: 39–42; ch. 26 Ricci's English translation 1950: 36–8.

27 Cf. Taymor 1990: 12. "[T]he significance of the couple as a unit plays an important role as to whether or not each individual will or will not be considered as having a 'fertility problem'."

28 A dysfunction which recalls Aristotle's theory in *GA* 2.716a5–7.

29 Hypospadias is a birth defect, "a congenital abnormality in which the opening of the urethra is on the underside of the penis" (instead of at the tip). Surgery can usually restore the normal appearance of the penis. With successful treatment, most male patients can have normal urination and reproduction. Hypospadias impairs reproduction and modern medicine lists it amongst the causes of male infertility: *Concise Medical Dictionary* 2015, s.v. "hypospadias." It is here to be noted that the Greek text in Zervos 1901: 37, l. 4–5, and 38, l. 15–16 reads ὑποσπαδιαίους, like Wegscheider 1901: 39, "die an Hypospadie leiden." Contra Montano 1533–35: 129 and Cornarius 1549: 875 transmit *viri semispadones*, which Ricci 1950: 36 translates as "of the eunuchoid type."

30 Cf. Steinberg 1955 about the role of the cervix in sterility and infertility in modern clinical practice.

31 This conceptualization of the womb as *malorum causa* is not unusual in the ancient medical landscape and here in the background we can hear distinctly the voices of Hippocrates, Galen, Soranus, and Pseudo-Aristotle.

80   *Elisa Groff*

32 Zervos 1901: 38.
33 Balme 1991: 418–21.
34 Hanson 1990: 322–3 n. 65. See also Dean-Jones 1992: 77 explaining that in the Aristotelian model "the quantity of pleasure a woman was allowed to take in intercourse proceeded . . . from political expediency."
35 Zervos 1901: 38. Cf. Cornarius 1549: 875, he also translates ἐπίτεκνον with *foecunda*. The idea of a fecundity's diagnosis is not an invention of late antiquity. For instance, a number of rather interesting fertility tests are described in the Kahun/Petrie Gynaecological Papyrus (1850–1700 BC) about the health of mother and baby; whereas Soranus uses fumigations to test if the fianceé examined by the midwife was fecund and thus worth being married (*Gyn.* 1, 34,36,46).
36 Zervos 1901: 38, 16.26, l. 20–2.
37 Zervos 1901: 37, 19–21. Cf. Ricci 1950: translating ἀγαπῶσα with "Love presides over generation."
38 Zervos 1901: 38, 14–15. The English translation is mine. It is here worth noting that Ricci's translation (1950: 36–8) from the Latin text by Cornarius (1549: 971) is misleading. Indeed, Cornarius does not report Zervos' line μεταλαβόντες ἄλλας, but "at qui alienis foeminis delectati propriis uxoribus non conveniu servata temperantia genrabunt": *these men who do not cohabit with their own wives, but find pleasure with strange women, will beget when they observe moderation* (Ricci 1950: 37). In this way, the text takes on a moral character which we do not find in Zervos' Greek text.
39 Wilcox 2010: 69. See also Maung 2019: 48–9.
40 In *GA* 2.4.739a 29–30; 1.19.727b 6–11, Aristotle explains that a woman may become pregnant without reaching orgasm and that both partners may experience a mutual orgasm but not conceive. In *HA* X 636b10–11, then the point is made that the key to conception is that men and women dance at the same coital rhythm which is essential to achieve a simultaneous orgasm leading to reproduction.
41 Plato, *Timaeus* 91a-c.
42 Dean-Jones 1992: 83.
43 *On Generation*, 319.
44 Cf. *HA* X 1.634b 28. We have seen that attention is also drawn to the importance of pre-lubrification in women before coitus.
45 In the ancient world, the production of offspring with more than one woman for men was also envisaged within the framework of strategies for socio-economic development. For example, amongst the reforms introduced by Lycurgus in Sparta to regulate marriages and the birth of children, one norm states (Plutarch, *Lycurgus* 15.6) that men were freed "from the empty and womanish passion of jealous possession" and it was "honourable for them, while keeping the marriage relation free from all wanton irregularities, to share with other worthy men in the begetting of children." Indeed, children were regarded not as "the particular property of their fathers, but rather as the common property of the state" (*Lyc.* 15.8). The concern of fertility was paramount for Jewish people as well, so much so that the patriarch Abraham is entitled in the Bible to turn to his wife's handmaid Hagar for Sarah was barren (she will bear a child in older age after all). As with Sparta, the first Israelite communities needed desperately to thrive and survive "for they began as a small tribe in a harsh, infertile upland frontier country": Clark 2008: 36. And like Sparta with its children, the last surviving fertile women in the dystopian world of "The Handmaid's Tale" are also treated as property of the state. In this fictive totalitarian society with zero population growth, all fertile women are sexually enslaved to repopulate the world: Atwood 1985.
46 See Wakefield 2014: 664 about the definition of "dysfunction" as a condition that directly harms the individual in the first place, not the society or other people.
47 Wilcox 2019: 69.
48 Cf. the pursuit of a pronatalist policy to raise the number of births in socialist governments. See also national family planning promoting systematic compulsory sterilization. As for modern history, see, for example, Bock 1986 about the violent national

population policy and compulsory sterilization adopted by the NSDAP in Germany during 1933–1945. See also Vasquez del Aguila 2020 about the forced sterilization policy imposed in Peru on indigenous women during the former president Alberto Fujimori's dictatorship between 1996 and 2000.

49 Nero divorced Octavia, the daughter of Claudius and Messalina, in AD 62 for sterility. Our sources report that he had tried with adultery in the first place, but he failed in his attempt. Fundamental for the purpose of the present discussion is that the Roman law allowed Nero to "use sterility" as a legitimate ground for divorce.

50 Cf. Wakefield 2014 about the difference between dysfunction and disorder.

51 Aëtius 16.16 in Zervos 1901: 17, lines 18–20: "because either the cervix is narrow or the uterus is small and it is neither in a good shape (lit. in a state of ruin) nor is able to make the foetus thrive until completion (i.e. end of gestation), or a lump or something similar has developed at the *os uteri,* and it causes an hindrance for delivery."

52 Zervos 1901: 17–18. In Zervos. the chapter is divided into two parts, with the second starting under the subtitle "ΠΕΡΙ ΑΤΟΚΙΩΝ ΚΑΙ ΦΘΟΡΙΩΝ" contra mss *Laur. Plut.* 75.07 and *Par. Suppl. Gr.* 632 where the chapter ends with part one in the Zervos's edition and it presents a different title: *Quomodo opem ferre oportet his quae non tuto concipiunt,* translated by Ricci as "What aid is necessary for those who are not able to conceive safely." The second part subtitled in Zervos "Contraceptives and abortifacients" belongs in the codices to the next chapter: Ch. 13–14 ms. *Laur. Plut.* 75.07; ch. 13–14 ms. *Par. Suppl. Gr.* 632; ch. 16. Cornarius' edition in Latin; ch. 16 Montanus' edition in Latin as well as Horozco 1540; ch. 16 Wegscheider's German translations 1901: 17–18. Wegscheider presents the same layout as Zervos. Ch. 26 Ricci's English translation 1950: 24. Ricci, translating from Cornarius, presents the text as one single unit with no subtitled section. Cf. Soranus, *Gyn.,* 1.20, ed. Gourevitch 2003: 59.

53 See the meaning of *syllepsin* as "conception" and *kuophorian* as "pregnancy" referring to the Virgin Mary in Photius, *Homily* 5: discussion in Betancourt 2020: 32–3.

54 Hopkins 1965a, 1965b; Riddle 1994, 2010. See also Caldwell 2004; Scarborough 2010, 2013, especially 761 "Appendix Drugs and the Law"; Totelin 2007, 2016. In particular, on therapeutic amulets related to aspects of sexual and reproductive health in Aëtius' treatise, see Calà 2012: 48–51.

55 Cf. Maung 2019: 46–7 discussing the bias of social values in a particular society which affect both the personal and social perception of infertility as a disorder or as a disease with implications for modern clinical practice.

56 Adichie 2014: 44–5. The same is true for men.

57 See Betancourt 2020: 69.

58 UN Programme of Action adopted at the International Conference on Population and Development, Cairo, 5–13 September 1994, Para 7.2a.

Bibliography

Aetius of Amida's Latin Translations

Cornarius, J. 1542, Basel.
Montanus, G.B. 1533–1535, Venice.

Aëtius of Amida's Modern Translations

Ricci, J.V. 1950. *Aëtius of Amida: The Gynaecology and Obstetrics of the Sixth Century AD.* Philadelphia and Toronto.
Romano, R. 2006. "Aezio Amideno libro XVI". In A. Garzya (ed.), *Medici Bizantini.* Torino, pp. 251–553.

Wegscheider, M. 1901. *Geburtshilfe und Gynäkologie bei Aëtios von Amida.* Berlin.
Zervos, S. 1901. *Sermo Sextidecimus et Ultimus.* Leipzig.

Modern Sources

Adichie, N.C. 2014. *We Should All Be Feminists.* London.
Atwood, M. 1985. *The Handmaid's Tale.* Toronto.
Balme, D.M. 1991. *Aristotle: History of Animals Book VII-X,* ed. and trans. Loeb Classical
    Library. Cambridge, Mass.
Betancourt, R. 2020. Byzantine Intersectionality: Sexuality, Gender and Race in the Middle
    Ages. Princeton and Oxford.
Bock, G. 1986. *Zwangssterilisation in Nationalsozialismus.* Opladen.
Calà, I. 2012a. "Per l'edizione del primo dei Libri medicinales di Aezio Amideno". PhD
    thesis University of Bologna.
——— 2012b. "La fortuna dei 'Libri medicinales' di Aezio Amideno nell'Europa rinasci-
    mentale: le 'Annotationes' di Cristobal de Horozco". *Les Études Classiques* 80, 187–205.
Caldwell, J.C. 2004. "Fertility Control in the Classical World: Was There an Ancient Fertil-
    ity Transition?" *Journal of Population Research* 21(1), 1–17.
Chamberlain, A. 2006. *Demography in Archaeology.* Cambridge.
Chesi, G.M. 2014. *The Play of Words. Blood Ties and Power Relations in Aeschylus' "Orest-
    eia".* Berlin.
Chouinard, V. 1997. "Making Space for Disabling Difference: Challenging Ableist Geogra-
    phies". *Environment and Planning D: Society and Space* 15, 379–87.
Clark, A. 2008. *Desire: A History of European Sexuality.* London.
Dean-Jones, L. 1992. "*The Politics of Pleasure:* Female Sexual Appetite in the Hippocratic
    Corpus". *Helios* 19, 72–91.
Duffy, J. 1984. "Byzantine Medicine in the Sixth and Seventh Centuries: Aspects of Teach-
    ing and Practice". *Dumbarton Oaks Papers* vol. 38, Symposium on Byzantine Medicine,
    pp. 21–27.
Groff, E. 2019. "S.v. Excision". In L. Bodiou and V. Mehl (eds.), *Dictionnaire Anthro-
    pologique du Corps Antique.* Rennes.
Hanson, A.E. 1990. "The Medical Writers Woman". In D.M. Halperin, J.J. Winkler and F.I.
    Zeitlin (eds.), *Before Sexuality: The Construction of Erotic Experience in the Ancient
    Greek World.* Princeton, pp. 309–38.
Hopkins, K. 1965a. "Contraception in the Roman Empire". *Comparative Studies in Society
    and History* 8(1), 124–51.
——— 1965b. "Textual Emendation in a Fragment of Musonius Rufus: A Note on Contra-
    ception". *The Classical Quarterly* 15, 72–4.
Hunger, H. 1978. *Die Hochsprachliche profane Literatur der Byzantiner,* vol. 2. München,
    p. 294.
King, H. 2011. "Sex, Medicine and Disease". In M. Golden and P. Toohey (eds.), *A Cultural
    History of Sexuality, vol. 1: Cultural History of Sexuality in the Classical World.* Oxford
    and New York, pp. 107–24.
Martindale, J.R. 1980. *The Prosopography of the Later Roman Empire,* vol. 2. Cambridge.
Maung, H.H. 2019. "Is Infertility a Disease and Does It Matter?" *Bioethics* 33(1), 43–53.
    Available online at: https://doi.org/10.1111/bioe.12495.
Nutton, V. 1996. *Der neue Pauly: Enzyclopädie der Antike,* band I. Stuttgart and Weimar, *ad
    vocem* "Aetios", coll. 209–10.

Riddle, J.M. 1994. *Contraception and Abortion from the Ancient World to the Renaissance*. Cambridge.

———. 2010. *Goddesses, Elixirs, and Witches: Plants and Sexuality Throughout Human History*. New York.

Rochon, M., et al. 1986. "Sterility and Infertility: Two Concepts". *Cahiers de Sociologie et de Démographie Médicales* 15(1), 27–56.

Scarborough, J. 2010. "Teaching Surgery in Late Byzantine Alexandria". In H.F.J. Horstmanshoff (ed.), *Hippocrates and Medical Education: Selected Papers Read at the XIIth International Hippocrates Colloquium*. Leiden, 24–26 August.

———. 2013. "Theodora, Aëtius of Amida, and Procopius: Some Possible Connections". *Greek, Roman, and Byzantine Studies* 53(4), 742–62.

Shaw, T. 1998. *The Burden of the Flesh: Fasting and Sexuality in Early Christianity*. Minneapolis.

Steinberg, W. 1955. "Cervical Aspects in Sterility and Infertility". *Fertility and Sterility* 6(2), 169–79.

Taymor, M.L. 1990. *Infertility: A Clinician's Guide to Diagnosis and Treatment*. New York.

Totelin, L.M.V. 2007. "Sex and Vegetable in the Hippocratic Gynaecological Treatise". *Studies in History and Philosophy of Biological and Biomedical Sciences* 38, 531–40.

———. 2016. "Technologies of Knowledge: Pharmacology, Botany and Medical Recipes". *Oxford Handbooks Online*. Available online at: www.oxfordhandbooks.com/view/10.1093/oxfordhb/9780199935390.001.0001/oxfordhb-9780199935390-e-94 (accessed 4 November 2022).

Treadgold, W. 1988. *The Byzantine Revival 780–842*. Standford, CA.

Van der Eijk, P. 2010. „Principles and Practices of Compilation and Abbreviation in the Medical "Encyclopedia" of Late Antiquity. In M. Horster and C. Reitz (eds.), *Condensing Texts-Condenses Text*. Stuttgart, pp. 519–544.

Vasquez Del Aguila, E. 2020. "*Precarious Lives:* Forced Sterilisation and the Struggle for Reproductive Justice in Peru". Available online at: https://doi.org/10.1080/17441692.2020.1850831 (accessed 4 November 2022).

Wakefield, J.C. 2014. "The Biostatistical Theory Versus the Harmful Dysfunction Analysis, Part 1: Is Part-Dysfunction a Sufficient Condition for Medical Disorder?" *Journal of Medicine and Philosophy* 39, 648–82.

Wilcox, A.J. 2010. *Fertility and Pregnancy: An Epidemic Perspective*. Oxford.

6 The Negotiation of Meaning in Late Antique Clinical Practice

Alexander of Tralles and "Natural Remedies"

Jonathan L. Zecher

Treatment is a matter of negotiation of viewpoints and attitudes.
This discards immediately old authoritarian views of treatment.
W. S. Muncie, "The Psychobiological Approach"[1]

Alexander of Tralles is probably the most famous physician most of us haven't heard of. Right down to the early modern period, his *Therapeutics* were standard reading for European doctors in Latin,[2] for Alexandrian medical students in Arabic,[3] and Byzantine practitioners in Greek. Even in the eighteenth century, though he fell afoul of Enlightenment narratives of scientific progress, he so captured the imagination of Dr Edward Milnard, a Fellow of the Royal Society, that the latter wrote public letters to the Royal College of Physicians arguing that Alexander demonstrated the vivacity of medicine after Galen.[4] Dr Milnard's pleas were unsuccessful, however, and Alexander has been largely ignored, even as recent years have seen resurgence of interest in Galenic and late antique medicine. In this chapter, I make two intertwined arguments: first, that Alexander is not a "Christian" in any meaningful sense, and second, that his clinical practice exemplifies openness to negotiating meaning and means of healing with his patients. The first argument is a small historical contribution to our understanding of medicine in Christian late antiquity; the second puts Alexander's work in conversation with emerging trends in the health humanities that focus on the co-construction of meaning in clinical encounters.

Alexander is an encyclopaedist as well as a practising physician. His *Therapeutics* liberally extracts from Galen and other physicians in *capite ad calcem* order, and so participates in the same discourses and impulses as do other late antique physicians like Aëtius of Amida, Oribasius, and Paul of Aegina. More unusually, Alexander regularly interjects his own discoveries among the authorities he cites, or else alters their recipes and therapies according to his experience. The few scholars who have spent time with Alexander—John Duffy,[5] John Scarborough,[6] and, recently, Alessia Guardasole,[7] Petros Bouras-Vallianatos,[8] and Barbara Zipser— have all pointed to Alexander's relentless emphasis on "experience" as key to his composition, self-presentation, and medical thought. Additionally, they have noted what is perhaps most unusual in his work: a frequent reliance on healing techniques

DOI: 10.4324/9781003080534-8

that Hippocratic, professional physicians, would have labelled "non-medical," and which Alexander calls either φυσικὰ ἰάματα or even περίαπτα/περιάμματα. No other physician from Galen on refers to frequently or positively to amulets, incantations, inscriptions, and other "folk" remedies.

In studying Alexander, I am seeking what sort of cultural commitment(s) underlie his approach to medicine, his patients' approach to him, and what sort of meaning is being constructed between them. In this regard, it matters very much whether Alexander is a Christian as well as *why* he accepts "folk" remedies. For example, a 2016 article in *Clinical Trials* hailed Alexander's use of amulets as the first example of a "placebo" in medical history.[9] This article presumes that Alexander administered a therapy he knew was ineffective on the rationale that his patients' mistaken belief in its efficacy could prove clinically effective. Leaving aside the problematic application of the very modern concept of a "placebo" to ancient medicine, this article raises the question of *meaning* in Alexander's clinical practice.[10] What, in fact, did Alexander think an amulet *meant*? What did his patients think it meant? What did later readers, such as Theophanes Nonnus Chrysobalantes, who copied Alexander's "natural remedies" for epilepsy but nothing else, make of them?[11] What does his language of "natural" remedies say about the epistemology of medical science and its relation to medical clinical practice and therapy?

In order to answer these questions, I will examine first the content of Alexander's natural remedies—what is included, what is not, and what can be made of both. I will then explore the implications of his characterization of remedies as "amulets" (περίαπτα/περιάμματα), which he justifies by his experience of their success and by the authority of other physicians; and as "natural" (φυσικά), by which he draws supposedly non-medical healing into the sphere of "scientific medicine." I will demonstrate, first, that Alexander likely lived earlier than is often assumed and that, contrary to expectation, Christianity seems not to have influenced his practice at all. I will then argue that his characterization and defence of "non-medical" healing constitutes an attempt to translate between professional and lay explanatory models of illness, which is open to multiple interpretations by readers, and that Alexander's humane and practical approach to medical care led him to a more capacious notion of medical science.

Life and Times

Alexander is conventionally dated to the sixth century and is presumed to have been a Christian. He came from a wealthy and well-connected provincial family. His father, Stephen, was a physician, as was his brother Dioscorus. His other brother Metrodorus was a grammarian, and Olympius a jurist who assisted in the compilation of Justinian's *Digests*. The most famous family member was Anthemius, the other brother, who built Hagia Sophia. Alexander himself was likely educated in medicine through apprenticeship, first with his father and then abroad. He travelled extensively—his *materia medica* come from across the Mediterranean and beyond, and he shows himself familiar with many locales. He came to "dwell in Old Rome, having been called thither because of his surpassing reputation."[12] He lived during Justinian's reign, and his brothers were active in the imperial building and legal projects of the 530s. All were known as contemporaries of the historian Agathias, who wrote of them in the early 560s. That is the sum of our certainties and Alexander provides few hints to add to them, despite Félix Brunet's gleeful assertions that Alexander was a personal physician to Justinian, that he accompanied Belisarius on campaign, and so on—none of these claims is true.[13] Nevertheless, as Bouras-Vallianatos concludes, "Alexander should not be seen as a marginal provincial figure, but as a well-connected member of the sixth-century establishment."[14] What this means is a point to which we will return.

He wrote several works, of which *Therapeutics* in 12 books, *On Fevers*, and a letter on intestinal worms survive. The treatises *On Eyes* and *On Pulses and Urine* are likely spurious, although Alexander did write more than what survives.[15] Both *On Fevers* and the *Therapeutics* were written in Alexander's later years. In the dedicatory letter transmitted with *On Fevers*, he refers to himself as an "old man no longer able to practise," who has, therefore, written "this book, having set in order my experiences collected with much careful practice in human diseases."[16] *Therapeutics* is a reference guide, organized *capite ad calcem*, and filled with descriptions of diseases, their diagnostic signs, prognostic indications, and known therapies. Alexander is fondest of pharmacological therapies. In these respects, his works are perfectly ordinary examples of the medical "encyclopaedias" being produced in late antiquity, by physicians like Oribasios, Aëtios of Amida, and Paul of Aegina.[17]

Alexander is not a mere "compiler" (though I doubt that such a creature ever existed).[18] More than many late antique encyclopaedists, he inserts his own recipes, some of which rely on spice trade extending well beyond the Byzantine borders.[19] He incorporates his own scholia, too, perhaps a quick note on a therapy, or a description of its effects. For these, he uses the first-person singular. He engages actively with his sources, and criticizes even Galen, who is otherwise his most cited medical authority and almost sacrosanct in other encyclopaedias.[20] Petros Bouras-Vallianatos concludes that "He is an active physician, who having already travelled a great deal and with an awareness of the ancient literature on the subject, tries to evaluate, adjust and adopt earlier therapeutic agents from a broad variety of sources."[21] For Alexander, experience is not merely an aspect of self-presentation, but a principle of medical practice through *testing*. Although he operates basically within Galenic humouralism, he is less committed to a theoretical model than to the care of patients, whatever the means. Thus, while Alexander insists that "it is absolutely necessary that the expert who uses natural remedies confirm scientific principle and the method of the Art"—but continues, "the same must mobilize everything that conduces to delivering the sufferer from prolonged and painful disease. For my part, I like to use everything."[22] In fact, he elsewhere claims it would be *impious* (ἀσεβές) not to use any and all means of healing at one's command.[23] This principle of openness and inclusion, founded on a relentlessly empirical mindset, not only sets Alexander's literary output apart from his contemporaries, but, as we shall see, it also sets his practice apart, since he is led to include means of healing that stood at the margins of medical arts, if not outside their self-definition.

Natural Remedies

By Alexander's time, mainstream medicine was largely dominated by Galen's version of humoural theory, his anatomical teleology, his interpretation of Hippocratic writings, and his approaches to diagnosis, prognosis, and therapy. Two caveats. First, this does not mean that the "medical marketplace" was less populous than it had been in the high Roman Empire. One could still employ root-cutters, midwives, dream-diviners, and other, seemingly marginal healers.[24] Asclepian priests could still be found, though by Alexander's day one more often encountered Christian priests mediating the power not of Asclepius, but of healing saints. The term "non-medical" refers, therefore, only to a distinction maintained by Galenic or Hippocratic physicians in seeking to police the often blurred boundaries of their art.[25] Second, Galenic hegemony does not mean stagnation, as has been claimed in the past,[26] but that physicians' creative additions to medicine were largely fitted to a Galenic framework.[27] This framework delimited disease causation within the bounds of nature—either humoural imbalance or an environmental impact of some kind. Galen believed in gods but did not believe they or any spiritual being caused disease.[28] Such methodological materialism is programmatic for Galenic medicine. Likewise, therapy fell into the three-tiered hierarchy that Galen inherited, visible already in Celsus and others: regimen, including diet; pharmacology; finally, surgery.[29] One moves from least invasive to most and, if possible, avoids surgery altogether.[30] Each of these is intended to answer the *cause* of disease which, as we have seen, is natural. Alexander and other late antique physicians follow suit.[31] To draw these points together, the Galenic self-presentation and definition of "medical art" circumscribed the "scientific" and "methodical" approach to healing by recourse to naturalistic psycho-physiology and corollary techniques of diagnosis and therapy. The range of techniques was legitimized by the authority of "the ancients"—Hippocrates and texts thought to be by Hippocrates, but filtered now through Galen's commentaries and interpretation. What counts as "medical," at least in the eyes of physicians, is constrained by humoural theory, therapeutic hierarchy, and traditional authority. Despite Alexander's enlisting his support, Galen is generally quite dismissive of amulets, charms, and other ritual techniques. While discussing Pamphilos' study of plants, Galen admits with chagrin that the old philosopher was "given to old wives' tales and some superstitious Egyptian sorcerers, together with some songs that they recited as they picked the plants."[32] Concerning these, Galen says:

> And so he used for amulets and other trickery not only curiosities that lie outside the medical art, but all sorts of lies. We, however, will say nothing of them or of their ridiculous transformations. For we do not consider such tales to be useful even to little children, let alone to those striving to pursue to practice of medicine!
>
> [Κ]αὶ δὴ κέχρηται πρὸς περίαπτα καὶ ἄλλας μαγγανείας οὐ περιέργους μόνον, οὐδ' ἔξω τῆς ἰατρικῆς τέχνης, ἀλλὰ καὶ ψευδεῖς ἁπάσας. ἡμεῖς δὲ οὔτε τούτων οὐδὲν οὔτε τὰς τούτων ἔτι ληρώδεις μεταμορφώσεις ἐροῦμεν.

οὐδὲ γὰρ τοῖς μικροῖς παισὶ κομιδῇ χρησίμους ὑπολαμβάνομεν εἶναι τοὺς τοιούτους μύθους, μήτι γε δὴ τοῖς μετιέναι σπεύδουσι τὰ τῆς ἰατρικῆς ἔργα.³³

Galen here draws a bright line between "curiosities" (περιέργους) and "lies" on the one hand, and the "medical art" (τῆς ἰατρικῆς τέχνης) on the other. Charms and songs sung over plants, not to mention the amulets made in the same way, belong in the first category, and the only value Galen can see for such things is as a diverting tale for children—and even then he is not sure they are really beneficial. These practices and the remedies made with them do not belong to medicine.

It is unsurprising, then, that Alexander's colleagues in Rome ridiculed therapies that fell outside the range delimited by Galenic naturalism: in therapy, the medicine must match the malady.³⁴ What is perhaps more surprising is that he calls them "uneducated" for doing so, and avers his own willingness to use "natural remedies," despite his scientific preference for dietetic and pharmacological approaches. He says:

> Because many of my contemporaries are uneducated and condemn those using natural [remedies], I have continually had recourse to using things that are able by their nature to operate and I have striven to overcome diseases by the medical method. I have known not only epilepsies but many other diseases as well to be cured through diet and drugs.
>
> Διὰ δὲ τοὺς πολλοὺς τοὺς ἐν τῷ νῦν χρόνῳ ἀμαθεῖς ὄντας καταμέμφεσθαι τοῖς χρωμένοις τοῖς φυσικοῖς, ἔφυγον συνεχῶς χρῆσθαι τοῖς φύσει δρᾶν δυναμένοις καὶ ἔσπευσα τεχνικῇ μεθόδῳ περιγενέσθαι τῶν νοσημάτων. καὶ οἶδα οὐ μόνον ἐπιληπτικὰς νόσους, ἀλλὰ καὶ ἄλλα νοσήματα πολλὰ διὰ διαίτης καὶ φαρμακείας ἰαθέντα.³⁵

This passage suggests that the dismissal of "natural remedies"—the sort of dismissal we have just read from Galen!—demonstrates a failure of the medical art, rather than its preservation. If only other physicians were better educated, they would know to use the "medical method" *and* whatever works by its nature. The latter category might include not only diet and drugs, but other, more "curious" objects and practices.

So, what are the "natural remedies" that Alexander accepts? They are usually amulets (Alexander frequently calls them by the technical terms περίαπτα and περιάμματα)—inscribed objects applied to patients' bodies. They may also be other objects, but always applied topically. Such remedies fall, as Alessia Guardasole has shown, into four categories: stones and metals, animals, plants, and humoural fluids.³⁶ Metals especially might be inscribed with formulae consonant with magical texts:

> Taking a sheet of gold at the waning of the moon, write on it the words below . . . 'mei, threu, mor, phor, teux, za, zôn, the, lou, chri, ge, ze, ôn. As the sun is restored in these names and is renewed each day, so restore this creation to his former state: now, now, quickly, quickly, for behold! I speak the great

name, in which things that have died are restored: iaz, azuph, zuôn, threngx, bain, chôôk. Restore this creation, just was he was before, now, now, quickly, quickly.[37]

Plants also might be inscribed and applied to sufferers of quotidian fevers.[38] From humans, the blood of a strangled gladiator,[39] or a virgin's first menses[40] could assist with epilepsy or gout, respectively. Some cures require specific astrological conditions, others benefit even from incantations. Of particular importance is the following:

Sacred plant, that is, henbane: when the moon is in Aquarius or Pisces dig up the plant before sunset, without touching the root, digging with two fingers of your right hand, and the doctor's finger [the pinky[41]] of your left,[42] say: "I tell you, I tell you, sacred plant, soon I will call you to my friend's house, that you may staunch the discharge in his feet and his hands, whether this or the other. But I adjure you in the great name Iaôth, Sabaôth, the God who fixed firm the earth and established the sea from abundant flowing rivers, who desiccated Lot's wife and turned her to salt. Receive the spirit of your mother, the earth, and her power, and dry up the discharge in his hands and feet, this or that."

Ἱερὰν βοτάνην, ἥτις ἐστὶν ὑοσκύαμος, σελήνης οὔσης ἐν ὑδροχόῳ ἢ ἰχθύσι περιορύξας τὴν βοτάνην, πρὶν ἢ δῦναι τὸν ἥλιον, μὴ ἁψάμενος τῆς ῥίζης, ὀρύξας αὐτοῖς τοῖς δύο δακτύλοις τῆς ἀριστερᾶς χειρός, τῷ ἀντιχειρὶ καὶ τῷ ἰατρικῷ δακτύλῳ, λέγε· "λέγω σοι, λέγω σοι, ἱερὰ βοτάνη, αὔριον καλῶ σε εἰς τὸν οἶκον τοῦ φιλεᾶ, ἵνα στήσῃς τὸ ῥεῦμα τῶν ποδῶν καὶ τῶν χειρῶν τοῦδε ἢ τῆσδε. ἀλλ' ὁρκίζω σε τὸ ὄνομα τὸ μέγα Ἰαώθ, Σαβαώθ, ὁ θεὸς ὁ στηρίξας τὴν γῆν καὶ στήσας τὴν θάλατταν ῥεόντων ποταμῶν πλεοναζόντων, ὁ ξηράνας τὴν τοῦ Λὼτ γυναῖκα καὶ ποιήσας αὐτὴν ἁλατίνην. λάβε τὸ πνεῦμα τῆς μητρός σου γῆς καὶ τὴν δύναμιν αὐτῆς καὶ ξήρανον τὸ ῥεῦμα τῶν ποδῶν ἢ τῶν χειρῶν τοῦδε ἢ τῆσδε."[43]

In this instance, zodiacal as well as sidereal time is important, and the adjuration of the plant combines biblical theology and stories with nature worship. The result is an incantation worthy of any magical text. And this Alexander recommends for gout.

We should not be seduced by the biblical language here. This is the only time Alexander uses it, and it is common to find Hebrew names for God in magical texts, whatever their provenance. Another cure for gout requires writing a line from Homer on a sheet of gold,[44] and a cure for epilepsy records lines from the Pythian Oracle.[45] In short, there is nothing in Alexander's oeuvre to suggest an interest in Christian theology or practice, or even in Christianized healings—no relics, no rose water, no holy water, no holy oil, no saints, no Christ. Even the construction of amulets betrays no sign of Christian influence—octagonal rather than cruciform, lines from Homer rather than Psalms. This absence is not decisive, but suggestive, since, as Jeffrey Spier has argued, the sixth century saw a general shift towards

Christianized forms of carving, inscription, and incantation.[46] By way of example, at least one late Byzantine manuscript gives a natural remedy to aid the expulsion of afterbirth. Pennyroyal root is boiled and drunk, during which the physician says over the woman's head "holy, holy, holy [ἅγιος, ἅγιος, ἅγιος]."[47] In this addition, the incantation is recognizable as a prayer, the *Trisagion* hymn sung in churches and homes. Later Christian copyists and physicians clearly felt willing to approach natural remedies in keeping with Alexander's, but the language is Christianized. What can we make of all this?

I think we need to adjust the dating of Alexander's life, and drop his characterization as a "Christian" physician. We have only Agathias' brief notice, which suggests that he knew Alexander's *family* but not necessarily Alexander himself; the use of aorist verbs may mean that Alexander was deceased. That was written around 560 if not a bit before. In Alexander's own work, there is no reference to the Plague of Justinian, which hit Rome by 543.[48] This is surely a curious omission in a physician who so emphasizes his first-hand experience of diseases. Adding this consideration to the lack of any discernible Christian influence, it seems likely that he practised the first half of the sixth century, and not right through Justinian's reign. He probably died before 540. Secondly, it is not meaningful to call Alexander a "Christian" physician. That is, neither Christian theology nor Christianized practices, geography, or cult has left a mark on Alexander's medical practice, despite Johannes Fabricius' conclusion that "nevertheless, I do not believe Alexander Trallianus was a stranger to the rites of Christ."[49] He is a faithful Galenist, a collector of recipes and therapies, educated, and likely more Hellene than Christian.

The first point is of interest only to the chronographer. The second is directly relevant to this chapter. His cultural commitments and presuppositions in medical practice can be understood without reference to Christianity. Moreover, Alexander's acquaintances and informants share his largely a-Christian cultural outlook. He did not invent the incantations he suggests. He learned them from others. Alexander tells us at one point that his clients, especially the "wealthy ones," refuse the more unsavoury drugs, they "compel" Alexander "to assuage their pain with natural amulets."[50] Of course, this passage suggests that Alexander is embarrassed by his use of amulets but, weighed against his warm regard for them in passages already quoted, this can only mean that he is frustrated to have to give them to appease pickiness, rather than because of their superior efficacy. The import of this passage, though, is that interest in "non-medical" healing is not only found among Roman elites, but it is actually fomented by wealthy lifestyles averse to certain medical approaches. Alexander's resort to amulets is certainly not a placebo. Rather, it is usually governed by pragmatism—if something works, use it. In other cases, it is governed by a willingness not to domineer the patient—if they cannot or will not use Alexander's preferred treatment, he finds something that they will accept. And that something is, very often, an object we might term "magical." Thus, we may conclude that, firstly, Alexander negotiates a tension between Galenic science and a cultural acceptance of "non-medical healing," secondly, his clientele shares that cultural acceptance, and thirdly, neither they nor he is particularly interested in its implications for Christian belief or practice, or even in Christianizing its form.

Amulets versus Natural Remedies

To return, however, to Alexander's language for "non-medical" healing, it is worth asking what status he accords them. We have seen already that he is, above all, a pragmatist, for whom efficacy governs use. We can, however, go further and conclude that in fact Alexander is shifting the boundaries of "medicine" so as to incorporate amulets as *medical* rather than "non-medical" means, and to translate between professional and lay explanatory models.

When Alexander describes some remedies as "amulets," he uses a term common outside of medical texts, but almost never used by other late antique physicians. The word has no status among medical writers, except as a pejorative—as Alexander's comments on his compatriots show. But Alexander regularly introduces them as discovered or tested "through experience" (διὰ πείρας).[51] Of one he says that, if executed properly, "you will marvel at it! [καὶ θαυμάσεις]."[52] Such claims will likely please like-minded physicians, but at other points, Alexander appeals also to the authority of Galen and other physicians. After all, medical knowledge was guaranteed by its agreement (or supposed agreement) with the Hippocratic tradition and, by Alexander's time, the Galenic interpretation and expansion of that tradition. Thus, Alexander claims that "the most divine Galen and those before him" used every means at their disposal—and so exemplified the principle of pragmatism that he himself follows.[53] Elsewhere he goes further and, quoting an otherwise lost work, claims that Galen may have derided "incantations" (ἐπῳδαί) as "old wives' tales" (οἱ τῶν γραῶν μῦθοι) but he "learned by long experience that there is potency in them [τῆς μακρᾶς πείρας εὗρε μεγάλως δύνασθαι αὐτάς]." He quotes "the supremely divine Galen":

> Certainly, some deem chants to be like old wives' tales, and so did I for a long time. However, with time, I was persuaded by things vividly seen that there is power in them. For I discovered benefit through chants in those stung by scorpions and, no less, for spitting out bones lodged in the throats of others. For there are many excellent things in each case and chants that hit the mark.
>
> ἔτι δὲ καὶ ὁ θειότατος Γαληνὸς μηδὲν νομίσας εἶναι τὰς ἐπῳδὰς ἐκ τοῦ πολλοῦ χρόνου καὶ τῆς μακρᾶς πείρας εὗρε μεγάλως δύνασθαι αὐτάς. ἄκουσον οὖν αὐτοῦ λέγοντος, ἐν ᾗ περὶ τῆς καθ' Ἔνιοι γοῦν οἴονται τοῖς τῶν γραῶν μύθοις ἐοικέναι τὰς ἐπῳδάς, ὥσπερ κἀγὼ μέχρι πολλοῦ· τῷ χρόνῳ δὲ ὑπὸ τῶν ἐναργῶς φαινομένων ἐπείσθην εἶναι δύναμιν ἐν αὐταῖς· ἐπί τε γὰρ τῶν ὑπὸ σκορπίου πληγέντων ἐπειράθην ὠφελείας, οὐδὲν δ' ἧττον κἀπὶ τῶν ἐμπαγέντων ὀστῶν ἐν τῇ φάρυγγι δι' ἐπῳδῆς εὐθὺς ἀναπτυομένων. καὶ πολλὰ γενναῖα καθ' ἕκαστόν εἰσι καὶ ἐπῳδαὶ τυγχάνουσαι τοῦ σκοποῦ.[54]

Given what we have read from Galen, this admission would mark a dramatic change of mind, indeed! Perhaps Galen really did come to value chants and other "natural remedies" in later life, although Heinrich von Staden rightly questions the authenticity of the passage.[55] Nevertheless, Alexander believes that this is really Galen's final position on the matter, and adds to Galen's testimony the authority of "wisest Didymos,"[56] the physician Archigenes,[57] Democritus,[58] Marsinus of Thrace,[59] Strato,[60] and "the ancients."[61] Alexander's language of amulets fits his self-presentation, summed up by Guardasole: "Alexandre interprète son rôle de 'médiateur' entre le savoir médical des prédécesseurs, notamment de Galien, et sa propre expérience, qui est la vraie clef de voûte de son enseignement."[62] On this double basis, then, Alexander asks, "What hinders us from writing out for you things which we have learned from our own experience and that of our close friends?"[63] Both efficacy and authority guarantee the status of amulets as medical practice, while the language of περίαπτα and περιάμματα remains comprehensible to clientele who might seek them. Alexander legitimates, translates, and incorporates "non-medical" healing into medicine.

His other, certainly preferred, description of "non-medical" healing is as "natural." Sometimes Alexander speaks of "natural remedies" (ἰάματα φυσικά) but most frequently of "natural things" as such (φυσικά).[64] These are objects or practices that "are able by their nature to operate [τοῖς φύσει δρᾶν δυναμένοις]."[65] This language is, I think, of the utmost significance for Alexander's understanding of medicine as science, but has not been noticed even by scholars like Guardasole and Bouras-Vallianatos. The question is—why should Alexander refer to amulets and other seemingly magical means as "natural"?

Hippocrates, and later Galen, would insist that "nature is the creator, the physician her assistant."[66] Drawing on Aristotelian natural science, Galen emphasized the purposiveness of natural construction, according to which form follows function—bodies, soul, and their parts are constructed teleologically. According to Galen, medicine, too, is ordered teleologically, to the restoration and preservation of health, which means the proper function of bodies, souls, and their respective parts.[67] The organizing principle behind all of this is nature: medicine merely imitates and assists what nature does. When Alexander calls seemingly "non-medical" techniques "natural," his readers would have seen in this a strong claim that even those practices which seem to fall outside the medical art are, in fact, part of the nature that medicine imitates and assists. He explains their working in Aristotelian fashion as "things that are naturally able to work."[68] Some remedies are φυσικά because their capacity for action is φύσει. This description matches what Alexander claims from Galen—that he found by experience that some things, like incantation, have a δύναμις, a capacity, in themselves. Galen, and the other ancient witnesses Alexander calls, could not explain the origin of that capacity, and Alexander never attempts to explain the operation of amulets. But by calling them natural Alexander claims their efficacy—whatever its hidden explanation— as part of the "method of the art"—by which he means its Galenic pretension to scientific standing. Alexander's understanding of the art as driven especially by experience blurs its definitional boundaries. At those points where Galen might decry the charms and spells of "magicians" or "soothsayers," Alexander is not only silent but open to their practices. For a physician like Alexander, the difference between "medicine" and "magic" is neither clear nor consistent, but the principles of experience and efficacy are.

Conclusion

What, then, can we conclude from Alexander's language of amulets and natural remedies? He is trying to translate between the language of his clientele, who know amulets and incantations, and authoritative physicians, who study nature and its creations. Alexander is not merely sympathetic to his patients, nor is he merely a pragmatist—though he is certainly both. Rather, he uses the principles of Galenic medicine to extend its boundaries to include and incorporate means of healing that neither Galen nor any other late antique writer thought of as part of the art. In doing so, Alexander hints at a wider aetiological range for disease—therapies still answer cause, but if the therapy's mechanism is unknown, so too perhaps is the disease's cause. In the end, Alexander negotiates between different cultural commitments—not between Christianity and Hellenistic religions, but between a professionalized medical community and its lay clientele. In doing so, Alexander's overwhelming care for his patients' healing as well as his openness to their experience led him to craft a more expansive medical science than is otherwise known in antiquity. Since medical culture is in practice predicated on its self-definition, and largely worked out through opposition and competition with other healing arts, Alexander's expansion of the art's domain has significant consequences for its cultural production and practice. Alexander works with his patients, co-constructing the art by translating and embracing "what works," to redefine how the physician interacts with patients and with other healers.

What, if anything, does Alexander's broadening of medical experience have to do with narrative health? Alexander does not seem to have been uniquely interested in patients' lives as stories, let alone constructing with them a narrative framework within which to locate and understand their illness. *Sensu strictu*, Alexander's interest in amulets is not narrative medicine.

However, I believe it does speak to the epistemic underpinnings of narrative health. Narrative medicine presumes that the co-construction of meaning, shared between healer and patient, is an integral component not only of clinical encounters but of the healing process. Much of that construction is done around understanding why and how the illness has come about. Patient and healer both import and together craft "explanatory models," which underpin treatment and also make sense of suffering. Alexander's admission that not only his patients want amulets and other "natural remedies" but also these work in ways unknown to the physician point us towards competing explanatory models of illness. The remedy implies the cause of disease and physicians would exclude amulets because they would exclude divine, daimonic, sympathetic, or other non-humoural causation. His use of amulets admits a wider range of causation, which does not necessarily include, but certainly does not *preclude*, those causes that might be termed "magical" or "divine." Alexander shows an openness to ranges of causation that his patients accept, and in prescribing amulets or other natural remedies, he is stretching medical practice to accommodate their meaning. There is, therefore, a subtle "co-construction" of meaning at work in Alexander's curious prescription.

I think Alexander raises a more profound issue for those of us interested in generating conversation between ancient texts and modern healthcare. Here the issue is not so much the categories within which Alexander's patients understood his prescriptions, but the categories within which later readers fit them. I pointed in the introduction to a recent article claiming that they were placebos. Those authors treat Alexander like a contemporary physician and use the categories and practices of modern clinical medicine to explain his practices. Other assessments have been less kind. Johannes Fabricius expressed surprise that "among tried and true medicines [Alexander] gives place to other, even superstitious, ones."[69] For Fabricius, a consummate Enlightenment scholar and former medical student, natural remedies could not but be "superstitious," even if applied for the noblest of motives. They represent a failure of medical nerve. Certainly, Alexander's medical practice sat uneasily within the scientific categories emerging in the Enlightenment, and to which medicine was increasingly laying claim. The "placebo" explanation could then be understood as a rehabilitation of Alexander within a similar conceptual frame: he is not superstitious, his patients are, and he like a good doctor today knows the powerful effects of belief.

Both "placebo" and "superstition" describe Alexander's practice in categories utterly foreign to him, but quite natural to their respective users. This raises an issue of *translation* in the interpretation of medical practice. As Byron Good put it, "Interpretations of the nature of an illness always bear the history of the discourse that shapes its interpretation, and are always contested in settings of local power relations."[70] Good's point is that the very categories within which illness (or, in this case, treatment) is understood have histories: is it purely "biological"? or "psychosomatic"? These terms not only privilege one kind of meaning by foreclosing others but do so by invoking larger discourses of bio-medicine, clinical practice, and their apparatus, which have been forged through dramatic changes in every respect over the last two centuries. Reading ancient authors in conversation with contemporary practices and concerns inevitably requires translating them into contemporary language, but this may distort or erase the ancient meaning. In Alexander's case, we have seen that between his patients, himself, and his readers, "natural remedies" mean very different things and carry equally different connotations for the nature and limits of medical practice. We cannot simply import Alexander's practice into narrative medicine, nor can we dismiss it outright. His lack of interest in patients' lives is problematic. His capacious understanding of medicine, and his emphasis on experience and openness, is valuable. Between these, we read Alexander (and other ancient healers) in tension. Unable to dismiss them, unable to idolize them, we read them in tension with our own commitments and concerns. It is a creative tension, though, which disrupts narratives of progress, breaks accepted categories, raises new possibilities, and poses uncomfortable questions for our own experience, both as historians and as health humanists.

Notes

1   In S. Arieti (ed.), *American Handbook of Psychiatry*, vol. 1 (New York: Basic Books, 1974).
2   D.R. Langslow, *The Latin Alexander Trallianus: The Text and Transmission of a Late Latin Medical Book* (London: Society for the Promotion of Roman Studies, 2006).

3 Theodor Puschmann, *Handbuch der Geschichte der Medizin* (Jena: Fischer, 1903), 537–8.

4 Edward Milnard, *Trallianus Reviviscens: Or, an Account of Alexander Trallian: One of the Greek Writers that Flourished after Galen: Shewing that These Authors Are Far from Deserving the Imputation of Meer Compilers . . .* (London: F. Gyles, 1734); Edward Milnard, *A Letter to the Honourable Sir Hans Sloane, Bart. President of the College of Physicians, and President of the Royal Society. In Vindication of the Character of Those Greek Writers in Physick that Flourished after Galen, but Particularly that of Alexander Trallian . . .* (London: Blackwell, 1733).

5 John Duffy, "Byzantine Medicine in the Sixth and Seventh Centuries: Aspects of Teaching and Practice", *Dumbarton Oaks Papers* 38 (1984), 21–7, at 25–6.

6 John Scarborough, "The Life and Times of Alexander of Tralles", *Expedition Magazine* 39 (1997), 51–60, at 53–4.

7 Alessia Guardasole, "Alexandre de Tralles et les remèdes naturels", in Franck Collard and Évelyne Samama (eds.), *Mires physiciens, barbiers et charlatans: Les marges de la médecine de l'Antiquité au XVIᵉ siècle* (Paris: Dominique Guéniot, 2005), 81–99.

8 Petros Bouras-Vallianatos, "Clinical Experience in Late Antiquity: Alexander of Tralles and the Therapy of Epilepsy", *Medical History* 58 (2014), 337–53.

9 Francesco M. Galassi, Frank Rühli, and Gutan Ashrafian, "Alexander of Tralles and the First Portrayal of a Placebo by Illusion in the 6th Century AD", *Clinical Trials* 13 (2016), 450.

10 I approach Alexander through what Byron Good calls the " 'meaning-centered' tradition" of illness representations. This approach emphasizes the role of culture—as symbolic network, as *habitus*, and as individual performance—in organizing and constructing the experience of illness and healing. That is, I am less interested in the biomechanical efficacy of natural remedies than in what Alexander thought he was offering, and what his patients thought they were requesting. See Byron I. Good, *Medicine, Rationality, and Experience: An Anthropological Perspective*, The Lewis Henry Morgan Lectures 1990 (Cambridge: Cambridge University Press, 1994), 52–6.

11 Theophanes Nonnus Chrysobalantes, "Epitome de curatione morborum", in I.O. Steph. Barnard (ed.), *Theophanis Nonni Epitome de curatione morborum graece ac latine*, vol. 2 (Gotha: C.W. Ettinger, 1795), 1:156–64; on which Guardasole, "Alexandre de Tralles et les remèdes naturels", 98.

12 Agathias, *Historiae* 5.6.5: Καὶ μακαρίσαιμι ἂν ἔγωγε αὐτῶν τὴν μητέρα, οὕτω ποικίλης παιδείας ἀνάπλεων γονὴν ἀποκυήσασαν. τούτω τε γὰρ τὼ ἄνδρε τέτοκε καὶ Ὀλύμπιον, νόμων τε ἀσκήσει καὶ ἀγώνων δικαστικῶν ἐμπειρίᾳ προεσχηκότα, καὶ πρός γε Διόσκορον καὶ Ἀλέξανδρον, ἄμφω ἰατρικῆς δαημονεστάτω. τούτων δὲ Διόσκορος μὲν ἐν τῇ πατρίδι κατεβίω, τὰ ἐκ τῆς τέχνης μάλα εὐστόχως ἐπιδεικνύμενος ἔργα· **ἅτερος δὲ ἐν τῇ πρεσβύτιδι Ῥώμῃ κατῴκησεν ἐντιμότατα μετακεκλημένος.** Ἀνθεμίου δὲ καὶ Μητροδώρου τὸ κλέος ἁπανταχοῦ περιιόμενον καὶ ἐς αὐτὸν ἀφῖκται τὸν βασιλέα.

13 Brunet's claims are summarized in Brunet Félix, "Le médecin byzantin du VIe siècle Alexandre de Tralles, sa personne, son œuvre: Influence historique de ses écrits", *Comptes rendus des séances de l'Académie des Inscriptions et Belles-Lettres* 78(1934), 87–8. See, however, Theodor Puschmann, *Alexander von Tralles: Original-Text und Übersetzung nebst einer einleitenden Abhandlung: ein Beitrag zur Geschichte der Medicin*, vol. 2 (Vienna: Wilhelm Braumüller, 1878–79), 1:75–87. John Duffy offers a creative but well-grounded reading of Alexander's likely educational and practical life: Duffy, "Byzantine Medicine in the Sixth and Seventh Centuries", 25–6.

14 Bouras-Vallianatos, "Clinical Experience", 339.

15 Alexander's works are all edited by Theodor Puschmann in *Alexander von Tralles*. Puschmann did not, however, provide a critical apparatus or discussion of the manuscripts used; Brunet's French translation offers no information whatsoever. Barbara Zipser has identified the most important, but a proper critical edition is not forthcoming. See Barbara Zipser, "Die *Therapeutica* des Alexander Trallianus: Ein medizinisches Handbuch und seine Überlieferung", in Rosa Maria Piccione and Matthias Perkams

(eds.), *Selecta Colligere. II. Beiträge zur Methodik des Sammelns von Texten in der Spätantike und in Byzana (Collana Hellenika)* (Alessandria: Edizioni dell'Orso, 2005), 211–34. As Langslow (*The Latin Alexander Trallianus*) has shown, the Latin tradition may preserve earlier readings, and so must also be taken into account.

16 *Dedicatio ad Cosmam*: "διὸ καὶ γέρων λοιπὸν πειθαρχῶ καὶ κάμνειν οὐκέτι δυνάμενος τοῦτο τὸ βιβλίον ἔγραψα συντάξας τὰς μετὰ πολλῆς τριβῆς ἐν ταῖς τῶν ἀνθρώπων νόσοις καταληφθείσας πείρας."

17 Although it is true that he includes a wider range of sources than others, while his Hippocratic material is all found in quotes from Galen. Even as a compilation, Alexander's choices can tell us much about his preferences as a physician, and his understanding of medical science.

18 *Pace* Vivian Nutton's famous description of Alexander and others as the "refrigerators of late antiquity": "From Galen to Alexander: Aspects of Medicine and Medical Practice in Late Antiquity", *Dumbarton Oaks Papers* 38 (1984), 1–14, at 2. I would note, however, that Nutton does not for this reason dismiss late antique encyclopaedists. See also Philip J. van der Eijk, "Principles and Practices of Compilation and Abbreviation in the Medical 'Encyclopaedias' of Late Antiquity", in Marietta Horster and Christiane Reitz (eds.), *Condensing Texts—Condensed Texts*, Palingensia 98 (Stuttgart: Franz Steiner Verlag, 2010), 519–54, especially 519–25. Van der Eijk does not discuss Alexander.

19 Scarborough, "Life and Times", 58–9. On this basis, perhaps, and a remark by Johannes Fabricius (*Bibliotheca Graeca*, 12:595), Puschmann tentatively identified the dedicatee as Cosmas Indicopleustes (*Alexander von Tralles*, 1:83). Fridolf Kudlien finds that implausible, though it is suggestive: "Alexander of Tralles", in Charles Gillespie and Noretta Koertge (eds.), *Complete Dictionary of Scientific Biography*, vol. 27, rev. ed. (Detroit: Charles Scribner's Sons, 2008), 1:121.

20 *Ther.* 8.2 (Puschmann, *Alexander von Tralles*, 2:343); see Alessia Guardasole, "L'heritage de Galien dans l'oeuvre d'Alexandre de Tralles", in *La médecine grecque antique. Actes du 14ème colloque de la Villa Kérylos à Beaulieu-sur-Mer les 10 & 11 octobre 2003* (Paris: Académie des Inscriptions et Belles Lettres, 2004), 219–34; see also Duffy, "Byzantine Medicine," 25–6.

21 Bouras-Vallianatos, "Clinical Experience," 352–3.

22 *Ther.* 1.15 (Puschmann, *Alexander von Tralles*, 1:571–3): "καὶ δεῖ πανταχόθεν βοηθεῖν τὸν ἐπιστήμονα καὶ φυσικοῖς χρώμενον ἐπιστημονικῷ λόγῳ καὶ μεθόδῳ τεχνικῇ καὶ τὸ λεγόμενον πάντα κινεῖν τὰ καλῶς σπεύδοντα μακρᾶς νόσου καὶ μοχθηρᾶς ἀπαλλάξαι τὸν κάμνοντα. ἐγὼ δὲ φιλῶ πᾶσι κεχρῆσθαι." So too *Ther.* 11 (Puschmann, *Alexander von Tralles*, 2:473): "τοσαῦτα καθόλου καὶ κατὰ μέρος εἰρήσθω σοι κατὰ μέθοδον ἐπιστημονικὴν ἐκτεθέντα." See also passages in *Ther.* 8.2, 10, 12 (2:375, 441, 461, 535, 585).

23 *Ther.* 7.9 (Puschmann, *Alexander von Tralles*, 2:319): "εἰ δὲ πολλῶν καὶ ποικίλων γενομένων ἀπαραμύθητος ὁ κάμνων εἴη, μηδενὸς τῶν ἀπὸ τῆς τέχνης ἰσχύοντος βοηθῆσαι τῇ δυστροπίᾳ τοῦ νοσήματος, καὶ τοῖς φυσικοῖς περιάπτοις οὐδὲν ἄτοπον κεχρῆσθαι χάριν τοῦ σῶσαι τὸν κάμνοντα· καὶ γὰρ **ἀσεβές** ἐστι τοιοῦτον παραλιπεῖν καὶ γενέσθαι κώλυσιν τῶν εἰς σωτηρίαν συντελούντων τῷ κάμνοντι."

24 On this see Vivian Nutton, "Healers in the Medical Marketplace: Towards a Social History of Graeco-Roman Medicine", in Andrew Wear (ed.), *Medicine in Society: Historical Essays* (Cambridge: Cambridge University Press, 1992), 15–58; Rebecca Fleming, *Medicine and the Making of Roman Women: Gender, Nature, and Authority from Celsus to Galen* (Oxford: Oxford University Press, 2000), 33–79; Heidi Marx (Marx-Wolf), "Religion, Medicine, and Health", in Josef Lössl and Nicolas J. Baker-Brian (eds.), *Blackwell Companion to Religion in Late Antiquity* (Oxford: Blackwell, 2018), 511–28.

25 Peter van Nuffelen, "Galen, Divination, and the Status of Medicine", *Classical Quarterly* 64 (2014), 337–52.

26 See, for example, Owsei Temkin's influential *Galenism: Rise and Decline of a Medical Philosophy* (Ithaca, NY: Cornell University Press, 1973).

27 It is worth repeating that Alexander is unusually independent in this regard, showing, as Guardasole puts it, "une autonomie sans pareille dans la médecine byzantine" (Guardasole, "Alexandre de Tralles at les remèdes naturels", 85).

28 See Philip van der Eijk, "Galen and the Early Christians on the Role of the Divine in the Causation and Treatment of Health and Disease", *Early Christianity* 5 (2014), 337–70. It is true that some Neoplatonists (Porphyry) and some Gnostics (*The Gospel of Mary*) believed that *daimones* were responsible for human health and even different parts of the body, but it is far from clear that these beliefs influenced Galenic medicine in any meaningful way. The cult of Asclepius is, perhaps, a rather different matter. Gods can intervene in human health but do not *cause* disease as such. See Marx (Marx-Wolf), "Religion, Medicine, and Health", 511–28.

29 Celsus, "De medicina, Proem.9", in Frederick Marx (ed.), *A. Cornelii Celsi quae supersunt*, CML 1 (Berlin: Teubner, 1915), 18.

30 Galen certainly saw it as the sign of a good physician that he could accomplish with diet and drugs what others needed surgery for: *opt. med. cog.* 10.1, in Albert Z. Iskandar (ed.), *Galeni de optimo medico cognoscendo libelli versionem Arabicam*, CMG Supplementum Orientale 4 (Berlin: Akademie-Verlag, 1988), 116.

31 *De febribus* 3 (Puschmann, *Alexander von Tralles*, 1:329): "Ἄνευ γὰρ διαγνώσεως οὐχ οἷόν τε ἁρμόσασθαι καλῶς πρὸς ἑκάστην αἰτίαν". So Celsus, *De medicina* Prol.30 (Marx, CML 1:22); Paul of Aegina (7th c.), *Epit. Med.* Prol. (CMG 9.1:4.12–15); etc.

32 Galen, *SMT* 6.Prol (Kühn 11:792,11–14): [Ἀ]λλ' ἐκεῖνος μὲν εἴς τε μύθους γραῶν τινας ἐξετράπετο καί τινας γοητείας Αἰγυπτίας ληρώδεις ἅμα τισὶν ἐπῳδαῖς, ἃς ἀναιρούμενοι τὰς βοτάνας ἐπιλέγουσι.

33 Galen, *SMT* 6.Prol (Kühn 11:792, 14–793, 2).

34 A principle of utmost importance from Hippocratic medicine through to Alexander. See Guardasole, "Alexandre de Tralles et les remèdes naturels", 89–90.

35 *Ther.* 1.15 (Puschmann, *Alexander von Tralles*, 1:573): "Διὰ δὲ τοὺς πολλοὺς τοὺς ἐν τῷ νῦν χρόνῳ ἀμαθεῖς ὄντας καταμέμφεσθαι τοῖς χρωμένοις τοῖς φυσικοῖς, ἔφυγον συνεχῶς χρῆσθαι τοῖς φύσει δρᾶν δυναμένοις καὶ ἔσπευσα τεχνικῇ μεθόδῳ περιγενέσθαι τῶν νοσημάτων. καὶ οἶδα οὐ μόνον ἐπιληπτικὰς νόσους, ἀλλὰ καὶ ἄλλα νοσήματα πολλὰ διὰ διαίτης καὶ φαρμακείας ἰαθέντα."

36 Guardasole, "Alexandre de Tralles et les remèdes naturels", 94–7.

37 I have left out some of the preparatory instructions. The full passage reads: "Λαβὼν πέταλον χρυσοῦν σελήνης ληγούσης γράφε ἐν αὐτῷ τὰ ὑποκείμενα καὶ ἐνδήσας εἰς νεῦρα γεράνου, εἶτα ὅμοιον τῷ πετάλῳ σωληνάριον ποιήσας κατάκλεισον καὶ φόρει περὶ τοὺς ἀστραγάλους 'μεί, θρεύ, μόρ, φόρ, τεύξ, ζά, ζών, θέ, λού, χρί, γέ, ζέ, ών. ὡς στερεοῦται ὁ ἥλιος ἐν τοῖς ὀνόμασι τούτοις καὶ ἀνακαινίζεται καθ' ἑκάστην ἡμέραν, οὕτω στερεώσατε τοῦτο τὸ πλάσμα, καθὼς ἦν τὸ πρίν, ἤδη, ἤδη, ταχύ, ταχύ· ἰδοὺ γὰρ λέγω τὸ μέγα ὄνομα, ἐν ᾧ ἀναπαυόμενα στερεοῦνται, ἰάζ, ἀζύφ, ζύων, θρέγξ, βαίν, χωώκ. στερεώσατε τὸ πλάσμα τοῦτο, καθὼς ἦν τὸ πρῶτον, ἤδη, ἤδη, ταχὺ, ταχύ" (*Ther.* 12 [Puschmann, *Alexander von Tralles*, 2:583]).

38 *Feb.* 6 (Puschmann, *Alexander von Tralles*, 1:407); cf. astrologically determined applications of plants: *Ther.* 1.15 (I:565,11–15), etc.

39 *Ther.* 1.15 (Puschmann, *Alexander von Tralles*, 1:565, 8–10).

40 *Ther.* 12 (Puschmann, *Alexander von Tralles*, 2:581, 12–13).

41 A curious term! Alexander glosses it at *Ther.* 12 (Puschmann, *Alexander von Tralles*, 2:475, 23–4): "τῷ μικρῷ ἢ ἰατρικῷ δακτύλῳ."

42 An operation recalling a cure for worms recorded by Julius Africanus: *Cesti*, 3.19.

43 *Ther.* 12 (Puschmann, *Alexander von Tralles*, 2:585, 6–15). One then repeats part of the adjuration, with two additional Hebrew names of God, after sunrise: 'ὁρκίζω σε κατὰ τῶν ἁγίων ὀνομάτων Ἰαώθ, Σαβαώθ, Ἀδωναί, Ἐλωί' (*Ther.* 12 [Puschmann, *Alexander von Tralles*, 2:585, 7–18]).

44 *Ther.* 12 (Puschmann, *Alexander von Tralles*, 2:581, 20–9); the line is *Il.* 2,95: "Τετρήχει δ᾽ ἀγορή, ὑπὸ δὲ στεναχίζετο γαῖα."

45 *Ther.* 1.15 (Puschmann, *Alexander von Tralles*, 1:569, 1–23); the cure is ascribed to Democritus.

46 Jeffrey Spier, *Late Antique and Early Christian Gems* (Wiesbaden: Reichert, 2007), 183; so too Nils Hallvard Korsvoll, "Official Teaching and Popular Practice: Are Church Opinions on Magic Reflected in the Surviving Amulets from the Early Middle Ages?" in Sarah Kiyanrad, Christoffer Theis, and Laura Willer (eds.), *Bild und Schrift auf "magische" Artefakten* (Berlin: De Gruyter, 2018), 149–63.

47 Florence, Biblioteca Medicea Laurenziana cod. Plut. 74.10, f. 333v, quoted from Michael Zellmann-Rohrer, "Tantalaus and Hemorrhage: An Inscribed Hematite Gem and Its Tradition", in Emily Mackil and Nikolaos Papazarkadas (eds.), *Greek Epigraphy and Religion: Papers in Memory of Sara B. Aleshire from the Second North American Congress of Greek and Latin Epigraphy*, Brill Studies in Greek and Roman Epigraphy 16 (Leiden: Brill, 2021), 310–34, at 323.

48 According to Marcellinus Comes' *Chronicon, an.* 543 (6th ind., 3rd cons. Basil), s.2: *Mortalitas magna Italiae solum devastat, Orientem iam et filyricum peraeque attritos.* In Brian Croke, *The Chronicle of Marcellinus: A Translation and Commentary*, Byzantina Australiensia 7 (Leiden: Brill, 1995), 50.

49 Fabricius, *Bibliotheca Graeca* (Hamburg: Theodorus Christophorus Felgerinus, 1724), 12:597: *A CHRISTI sacris tamen alienum suisse Alexandram Trallianum non crediderim.*

50 *Ther.* 8.2 (Puschmann, *Alexander von Tralles*, 2:375, 10–16): "Ἀλλ᾽ ἐπειδὴ τῶν περιοδευομένων πολλοὶ **καὶ μάλιστα τῶν πλουσίων** οὔτε πίνειν ὅλως θέλουσι φάρμακον οὔτε κλύσμασι θεραπεύειν τὴν γαστέρα, **διὰ δὲ περιάπτων φυσικῶν ἀναγκάζουσιν ἡμᾶς ἀποπαύειν αὐτῶν τὴν ὀδύνην,** ἐσπούδασα καὶ περὶ τούτων ἐκθέσθαι ὑμῖν, ὧν τε αὐτὸς ἔσχον πεῖραν καὶ ὅσα παρὰ φίλων ἀληθινῶν ἔγνων ὠφελεῖν δύνασθαι."

51 As, for example, at *Ther.* 1.15 (Puschmann, *Alexander von Tralles*, 1:557, 13–17); 7.9 (2:319,4–8), 8.2 (2:375,15; 375,21; 375,26), and 12 (2:581,11).

52 *Ther.* 12 (Puschmann, *Alexander von Tralles*, 2:579,25).

53 *Ther.* 7. (Puschmann, *Alexander von Tralles*, 2:319,8–10): "Καὶ γὰρ ἀσεβές ἐστι τοιοῦτον παραλιπεῖν καὶ γενέσθαι κώλυσιν τῶν εἰς σωτηρίαν συντελούντων τῷ κάμνοντι, ὁπότε καὶ ὁ θειότατος Γαληνὸς καὶ οἱ πρὸ αὐτοῦ τούτοις ἐχρήσαντο."

54 *Ther.* 11.1 (Puschmann, *Alexander von Tralles*, 2:475,7–13).

55 Heinrich von Staden, "Galen's Daimon: Reflections on 'Irrational' and 'Rational'", in Nicoletta Palmieri (ed.), *Rationnel et irrationnel dans la médecine ancienne et médiévale: aspects historiques, scientifiques et culturels* (Saint-Étienne: Publications de l'Université de Saint-Étienne, 2003), 15–43, at 19–20.

56 *Ther.* 7.9 (Puschmann, *Alexander von Tralles*, 2:319,10–11).

57 Twice in *Ther.* 1.15 (Puschmann, *Alexander von Tralles*, 2:557, 567).

58 *Ther.* 1.15 (Puschmann, *Alexander von Tralles*, 1:569,1–571, 2).

59 *Ther.* 1.15 (Puschmann, *Alexander von Tralles*, 1:565).

60 Twice in *Ther.* 1.15 (Puschmann, *Alexander von Tralles*, 1:565, and 571, 2–575, 9).

61 *Ther.* 8.2 (Puschmann, *Alexander von Tralles*, 2:375,16–19); cf. also 12 (2:579, 13).

62 Guardasole, "L'heritage de Galien", 226.

63 *Ther.* 11.1 (Puschmann, *Alexander von Tralles*, 2:475, 14–15).

64 In references above, but also at, for example, *Feb.* 7 (Puschmann, *Alexander von Tralles*, 1:407), 7 (1:437); *Ther.* 8.2 (2:375), 11.1 (2:475); 12 (2:579,15, 20), etc.

65 *Ther.* 1.15 (Puschmann, *Alexander von Tralles*, 1:573).

66 *Ars med.* 26, in Ian Johnston (ed.), *Galen. On the Constitution of the Art of Medicine. The Art of Medicine. A Method of Medicine to Glaucon*, Loeb Classical Library 523 (Cambridge, MA: Harvard University Press, 2016), 262 (= Kühn 1:378).

67 Galen, "De sectis", 1, in Georg Helmreich, *Claudii Galeni Pergameni scripta minora*, vol. 3 (Leipzig: Teubner, 1893), 1,1–2 = I,64K); *Exhortatio* 9.1 (CMG 5.1.1:130, 23–26); *Thras. 5* (Helmreich, *Scripta Minora* 3:36 = Kühn 5:811.13–14); *Ars Med.*, Praef. (Kühn 1:306.3–5); so too *MM* 1.7 (Kühn 10:58–9); *CAM*, Praef.8–9 (CMG 5.1.3:56.11–18). He is followed, for example, by Oribasios, *coll. med.* 1.proim.2 (CMG 6.1, 1:4, 6–12).

68 *Ther.* 1.15 (Puschmann, *Alexander von Tralles*, 1:573, 3–4): "ἔφυγον συνεχῶς χρῆσθαι τοῖς φύσει δρᾶν δυναμένοις καὶ ἔσπευσα τεχνικῇ μεθόδῳ περιγενέσθαι τῶν νοσημάτων."

69 *Bibliotheca Graeca*, 12:595: *Inter praeclara ac probata medicamenta aliquibus etiam superstitiosis dat locum.*

70 Good, *Medicine, Rationality, and Experience*, 53.

Bibliography

Ancient Sources

Agathias, "Historiae", in R. Keydell (ed), *Agathiae Myrinaei historiarum libri quinque*, Corpus Fontium Historiae Byzantinae. Series Berolinensis 2 (Berlin: De Gruyter, 1967).

Alexander of Tralles, "De febribus (Febr.)", in Theodor Puschmann (ed), *Alexander von Tralles: Original-Text und Übersetzung nebst einer einleitenden Abhandlung: Ein Beitrag zur Geschichte der Medicin*, vol. 2 (Vienna: Wilhelm Braumüller, 1878–79), 1:290–439.

———, "Therapeutica (Ther.)", in Theodor Puschmann (ed), *Alexander von Tralles* (Vienna: Wilhelm Braumüller, 1878–79), 1:440–617, 2:2–499.

Celsus, "De medicina", in Frederick Marx (ed), *A. Cornelii Celsi quae supersunt*, CML 1 (Berlin: Teubner, 1915).

Galen, "De sectis", in Georg Helmreich (ed), *Claudii Galeni Pergameni scripta minora*, vol. 3 (Leipzig: Teubner, 1893), 1–32.

———, "De optimo medico cognoscendo", in Albert Z. Iskandar (ed), *Galeni de optimo medico cognoscendo libelli versionem Arabicam*, CMG Supplementum Orientale 4 (Berlin: Akademie-Verlag, 1988).

———, "Exhortatio", in Adelmo Barigazzi (ed), *Galeni de optimo docendi genere, Exhortatio ad medicinam (Protrepticus)*, CMG 5.1.1 (Belin: Akademie-Verlag, 1991), 111–51.

———, "De Constitione Artis Medicinae (CAM)", in Stefania Fortuna (ed), *Galeni de constitutione artis medicae ad Patrophilum*, CMG 5.1.3 (Berlin: Akademie-Verlag, 1997).

———, "Ars medicinae (Ars med.)", in Ian Johnston (ed), *Galen. On the Constitution of the Art of Medicine. The Art of Medicine. A Method of Medicine to Glaucon*, Loeb Classical Library 523 (Cambridge, MA: Harvard University Press, 2016).

———, "De methodo medendi (MM)", in Carl Gottlob Kühn (ed), *Claudii Galeni Opera Omnia*, vol. 10 (Leipzig: Libraria Karl Knobloch, 1821–33).

———, *Thrasybulus* (*Thras.*), in Georg Helmreich (ed), *Claudii Galeni Pergameni scripta minora*, vol. 3 (Leipzig: Teubner, 1893), 33–100.

Marcellinus Comes, "Chronicon", in Brian Croke (ed), *The Chronicle of Marcellinus: A Translation and Commentary*, Byzantina Australiensia 7 (Leiden: Brill, 1995).

Oribasios, "Collectiones medicae (coll. med.)", in Johannes Raeder (ed), *Oribasii collectionum medicarum reliquiae*, vol. 1, books 1–8, CMG 6.1, 1 (Leipzig: Teubner, 1928).

Paul of Aegina, "Epitome Medicinae (Epit. Med.)", in I.L. Heiberg (ed), *Paulus Aegineta*, vol. 1, books 1–4, CMG 9.1 (Leipzig: Teubner, 1921).

Theophanes Nonnus Chrysobalantes, "Epitome de curatione morborum", in I.O. Steph. Barnard (ed), *Theophanis Nonni Epitome de curatione morborum graece ac latine*, vol. 2 (Gotha: C.W. Ettinger, 1795).

Modern Sources

Bouras-Vallianatos, Petros, "Clinical Experience in Late Antiquity: Alexander of Tralles and the Therapy of Epilepsy", *Medical History* 58 (2014), 337–53.

Brunet, Félix, "Le médecin byzantin du VIe siècle Alexandre de Tralles, sa personne, son œuvre: Influence historique de ses écrits", *Comptes rendus des séances de l'Académie des Inscriptions et Belles-Lettres* 78 (1934), 87–8.

Duffy, John, "Byzantine Medicine in the Sixth and Seventh Centuries: Aspects of Teaching and Practice", *Dumbarton Oaks Papers* 38 (1984), 21–7.

Fabricius, Johannes, *Bibliotheca Graeca* (Hamburg: Theodorus Christophorus Felgerinus, 1724).

Fleming, Rebecca, *Medicine and the Making of Roman Women: Gender, Nature, and Authority from Celsus to Galen* (Oxford: Oxford University Press, 2000).

Galassi, Francesco M., Frank Rühli, and Gutan Ashrafian, "Alexander of Tralles and the First Portrayal of a Placebo by Illusion in the 6th Century AD", *Clinical Trials* 13 (2016), 450.

Good, Byron J., *Medicine, Rationality, and Experience: An Anthropological Perspective*, The Lewis Henry Morgan Lectures 1990 (Cambridge: Cambridge University Press, 1994).

Guardasole, Alessia, "L'heritage de Galien dans l'oeuvre d'Alexandre de Tralles", in *La médecine grecque antique: Actes du 14ème colloque de la Villa Kérylos à Beaulieu-sur-Mer les 10 & 11 octobre 2003* (Paris: Académie des Inscriptions et Belles Lettres, 2004), 219–34.

———, "Alexandre de Tralles et les remèdes naturels", in Franck Collard and Évelyne Samama (eds), *Mires physiciens, barbiers et charlatans: Les marges de la médecine de l'Antiquité au XVIe siècle* (Paris: Dominique Guéniot, 2005), 81–99.

Korsvoll, Nils Hallvard, "Official Teaching and Popular Practice: Are Church Opinions on Magic Reflected in the Surviving Amulets Form the Early Middle Ages?" in Sarah Kiyanrad, Christoffer Theis, and Laura Willer (eds), *Bild und Schrift auf 'magischen' Artefakten* (Berlin: De Gruyter, 2018), 149–63.

Kudlien, Fridolf, "Alexander of Tralles", in Charles Gillespie and Noretta Koertge (eds), *Complete Dictionary of Scientific Biography*, vol. 27, rev. ed. (Detroit: Charles Scribner's Sons, 2008), 1:121.

Langslow, D.R., *The Latin Alexander Trallianus: The Text and Transmission of a Late Latin Medical Book* (London: Society for the Promotion of Roman Studies, 2006).

Marx, Heidi [Marx-Wolf], "Religion, Medicine, and Health", in Josef Lössl and Nicolas J. Baker-Brian (eds), *Blackwell Companion to Religion in Late Antiquity* (Oxford: Blackwell, 2018), 511–28.

Milnard, Edward, *A Letter to the Honourable Sir Hans Sloane, Bart. President of the College of Physicians, and President of the Royal Society. In Vindication of the Character of Those Greek Writers in Physick That Flourished After Galen, but Particularly That of Alexander Trallian . . .* (London: Blackwell, 1733).

———, *Trallianus Reviviscens: Or, an Account of Alexander Trallian: One of the Greek Writers That Flourished After Galen: Shewing That These Authors Are Far from Deserving the Imputation of Meer Compilers . . .* (London: F. Gyles, 1734).

Muncie, W. S., "The Psychobiological Approach", in S. Arieti (ed), *American Handbook of Psychiatry*, vol. 1 (New York: Basic Books, 1974).

Nutton, Vivian, "From Galen to Alexander: Aspects of Medicine and Medical Practice in Late Antiquity", *Dumbarton Oaks Papers* 38 (1984), 1–14.

———, "Healers in the Medical Marketplace: Towards a Social History of Graeco-Roman Medicine", in Andrew Wear (ed), *Medicine in Society: Historical Essays* (Cambridge: Cambridge University Press, 1992), 15–58.

Puschmann, Theodor, *Handbuch der Geschichte der Medizin* (Jena: Fischer, 1903).

Scarborough, John, "The Life and Times of Alexander of Tralles", *Expedition Magazine* 39 (1997), 51–60.

van der Eijk, Philip J., "Principles and Practices of Compilation and Abbreviation in the Medical 'Encyclopaedias' of Late Antiquity", in Marietta Horster and Christiane Reitz (eds), *Condensing Texts—Condensed Texts*, Palingensia 98 (Stuttgart: Franz Steiner Verlag, 2010), 519–54.

———, "Galen and the Early Christians on the Role of the Divine in the Causation and Treatment of Health and Disease", *Early Christianity* 5 (2014), 337–70.

van Nuffelen, Peter, "Galen, Divination, and the Status of Medicine", *Classical Quarterly* 64 (2014): 337–52.

von Staden, Heinrich, "Galen's Daimon: Reflections on 'Irrational' and 'Rational'", in Nicoletta Palmieri (ed), *Rationnel et irrationnel dans la médecine ancienne et médiévale: Aspects historiques, scientifiques et culturels* (Saint-Étienne: Publications de l'Université de Saint-Étienne, 2003), 15–43.

Zellmann-Rohrer, Michael, "Tantalaus and Hemorrhage: An Inscribed Hematite Gem and Its Tradition", in Emily Mackil and Nikolaos Papazarkadas (eds), *Greek Epigraphy and Religion: Papers in Memory of Sara B. Aleshire from the Second North American Congress of Greek and Latin Epigraphy*, Brill Studies in Greek and Roman Epigraphy 16 (Leiden: Brill, 2021), 310–34.

Zipser, Barbara, "Die *Therapeutica* des Alexander Trallianus: Ein medizinisches Handbuch und seine Überlieferung", in Rosa Maria Piccione and Matthias Perkams (eds), *Selecta Colligere. II. Beiträge zur Methodik des Sammelns von Texten in der Spätantike und in Byzana (Collana Hellenika)* (Alessandria: Edizioni dell'Orso, 2005), 211–34.

7 Medical Discourse, Identity Formation, and Otherness in Early Eastern Christianity

Chris L. de Wet

Introduction

The publication of Martha Nussbaum's *Therapy of Desire*, 25 years ago, had a major impact on how ancient "moral therapies" functioned in the Hellenistic world.[1] Nussbaum's work was also very important for early Christian studies, since it gave scholars of early Christianity a critical–theoretical framework with which to approach Christian sources.[2] Nussbaum herself had less to say about early Christianity. The major shift in the field, currently, is to examine how late ancient Christianity transformed Greco-Roman medical discourse.[3] Rather than viewing late antiquity as a sterile period for the development of medical knowledge, we now know that medical knowledge was discursively and practically transformed, as the Christian Empire matured. We could rightly refer to this development as the "medical turn" in early Christian studies.

The use of medical discourse is never neutral or innocent. During late antiquity, medical knowledge was disseminated through various alternative literary genres, such as homilies, hagiographies, and theological treatises. The social effects of this epistemological shift in medical discourse, however, requires further examination. The purpose of this chapter is to ask, first, how medical discourse shaped the formation of late antique Eastern Christian identities and, second, how medical discourse was utilized in the fashioning of alterities (i.e. formations of otherness).[4] What I hope to achieve with this study is a better and more nuanced understanding of the power dynamics of medical discourse when utilized in contexts that are not conventionally associated with medicine and healthcare, and how medicalized Christian discourse functions as a part of what Averil Cameron has called, the totalizing discourse of imperial Christianity.[5] I should state at the outset that I do not propose that every early Christian discourse is medical or medically structured. Rather, it seems that medical discourse functions in rather pervasive, often "invisible" or unexpected ways, as I will demonstrate in this chapter. Not all early Christian discourse is therefore medical, but the medical sphere occupies an important structuring role in early Christian discursive formations. This analysis is an exploration, therefore, into the medically constructed self and other, in terms of both individual and social bodies. To this end, I will propose four theses on how the transformation of late antique medical knowledge impacted early Christian

DOI: 10.4324/9781003080534-9

conceptualizations of identity and otherness, specifically in the East. My focus on Eastern Christianity is not simply to delimit the source material and to make the analysis more manageable, but it is also based on developing work already done on the early Christian use of medical discourse in the East, particularly by scholars such as Crislip, Schulze, Samellas, Merideth, Zecher, and Mayer, among many others.[6] This being said, I do acknowledge that there is considerable variety and complexity among Eastern Christian authors, and I hope this complexity and variety within a particular discursive unity will be showcased in this chapter.

Christian Medical Discourse and the Individual Soul and Body

Let us begin with how medical discourse shaped early Christian understandings of subjectivity. Take the following words of the fourth-century author, Theodoret of Cyrus, from his aptly titled *Curatio affectionum Graecorum*:

> If a medical treatment ['Ιατρικὴ θεραπεία] exists for the body, one should also exist for the soul. For while it is true that frequent ailments beset both body and soul, bodily ailments are for the most part involuntary, while spiritual ailments are voluntary.[7]

Here we see the most crucial move in early Christian medical discursive strategies, namely the inclusion of the entire human subject into the realm and grip of the medical. This was, of course, not a novel move. Scholars like Samellas[8] and White,[9] and more recently in the past few years, Mayer,[10] Leyerle,[11] and Papadogiannakis,[12] to name but a few, have shown how early Christian thought was shaped by ancient Greek philosophical thought about moral pathology and progress, and so-called emotional therapies. The body and the material soul[13] become subject to medical technologies aimed at restoring or improving the individual.

In Christian thought, particularly, the cure of the soul receives a position of primacy over the health of the body, although these two states of health are often related. Some bodily ailments might even be symptomatic of various psychic disorders. An excellent example of this is that of what I call "Cain's disease." In late antiquity, there was a tradition that Cain, the man who killed his brother Abel, from Genesis 4, had a soul that was so diseased by sin that it spilled over onto his body, and so Cain became cursed with a "trembling" disease. This is based on Gen. 4:12b LXX, in which God's curse says: "you will be groaning and trembling on the earth." The tradition is found in several Greek and Syriac authors of the East, including John Chrysostom, Basil of Caesarea, Basil of Seleucia, and Jacob of Serug.[14] All say that Cain had a psychic ulcer (i.e. intention to commit fratricide) that he hid from the divine Physician, which burst and spread to his body as a physical disease and curse. Cain then got a disabling disease in which he could not control his limbs from trembling. Basil of Caesarea describes it thus:

> [C]ontinual groaning, and trembling of the body, since his limbs had not the support that comes from strength. For since he had used the power of his

body wickedly, his vigour was taken away, so that he tottered and shook, being unable easily either to bring bread to the mouth or to fetch water to it, his wicked hand not being permitted after the unholy deed even to administer to the private and necessary needs of the body.[15]

John Chrysostom specifically states:

[D]isease beset the body of Cain as the result of sin. For after the murder of his brother, after that act of wickedness, his body was paralysed. For trembling is the same as palsy. For when the power which controls a living being becomes weak, being no longer able to support all the limbs, it deprives them of their natural power of direction, and then having become slack, they tremble and stagger.[16]

The disease is described by all of the authors as being a sign, being pedagogical, warning others of the dangers of ignoring psychic disease. These views link up with what Galen states in his work, *De tremore*, that the soul is responsible for motion, and that trembling could have a psychic cause.[17]

In other cases, psychic and bodily health stand in contrast to one another. In some schools of early Christian ascetic thought, disease even functions as a form of ascesis in itself, since it breaks down and weakens the body, similar to other rigorous ascetic disciplines. Andrew Crislip speaks of "illness as an ascetic practice"[7]—rightly, in my opinion.

The Christian monastic handbooks of the late antique East often function as moral–pathological maps of the body and the soul, in which every aspect of the individual subject is catalogued and discussed within some broad scope of medical discourse. For instance, the fifth-century Syriac writer, Philoxenus of Mabbug's *Memrē* (or *Discourses*) to monks start with treatments related to strengthening one's faith, down to issues of what to eat and how to control and manage bodily processes from sexual desire to physical and psychic ageing.[8] Philoxenus even applies the common medical principle of opposites to the healing dynamics of the entire individual. He writes:

Similar to how medicines are mixed and prepared by physicians for physical illnesses, medicines against the passions of sins are prepared and made ready by the Spirit of God, in order that whoever is aware of an illness may find the medicine for it at his side and from close by bring aid to himself. Everything for the most part is healed by its opposite, because the opposition of the medicine will fight with the harm of the disease. . . . Therefore, take an example from here, O discerning one who wishes to heal the ailments of the soul, and provide for your soul something that performs the art of healing to the body. On account of this, the work of external things is placed before our eyes so that it might be an example of instruction for those things that are internal, and we might heal the soul from the diseases of evil things similar to [the way] the body is healed. Let us prepare against each of the passions of sin the antidote that is the opposite of the disease.[18]

Such handbooks, like those of Philoxenus, and John the Solitary,[19] for instance, function as apparatuses that enable the individual subject to examine his or her own soul and body, whether it be a thought that might kindle the flame of lust or a pang of hunger that might lead to gluttony, and then resort to the necessary medical treatment of a particular ailment. The identity of the individual subject is therefore firstly shaped by the simultaneous dichotomization and unification of body and soul, and the meticulous and exhaustive cataloguing of the individual parts of the subject as a whole. Many monastic handbooks rely on Platonic or Aristotelian divisions of the human subject,[20] and structure their advice according to these schemes. Thus, my first thesis is as follows: *early Christian medical discourse was a major part of the totalizing discourse that encompassed the entire individual subject, in body and soul, and fixed the individual body and soul, with meticulous, exhaustive, and often paradoxical detail, by means of apparatuses like monastic handbooks, within the realm and grip of the medical.*

Christian Medical Discourse and the Social Body

The totalizing arrogation of the individual body and soul by early Christian medical discourse is also mirrored by a similar arrogation of the social body. The notion of "encyclopaedism" has often been used to describe many of the medical–literary outputs of late antiquity.[21] In this regard, we have the major collections of authors like Oribasius of Pergamum, Aetius of Amida, and Paul of Aegina, who appropriated earlier sources like Galen and others quite extensively in the creation of medical quasi-encyclopaedias. Some Christian authors like Nemesius of Emesa and John the Solitary followed suit, imbuing their maps of the individual subject with the authority of Aristotle or Galen. In this way, these authors actually claim epistemological capital, and an author like Galen is practically Christianized.

But there is no such a thing as "mere" encyclopaedism. The very act of compiling such mammoth tomes of knowledge is both a totalizing and an imperializing act. These "encyclopaedias" are not simply manuals or digests, but represent attempts at rationalizing, ordering, and institutionalizing knowledge under the precepts of Empire. In fact, Rebecca Flemming has shown that Galen's very own ordering of knowledge was essentially imperial: "So, Galen's writing, the various systematisations he proposes and enacts within, and of, his huge literary output, works for the Empire as much as the Empire works for him."[22] It stands to reason that the appropriation of Galen's works within these early Christian "encyclopaedic" trends would not diminish the inherent imperiality of Galen's works and thought.

Moreover, in this case, encyclopaedism is also an epistemological deconstruction and reconstruction. Thus, we have the extensive mapping and construction of the individual subject in the monastic handbooks and also, I argue, in these medical encyclopaedias, the social body is mapped, ordered, and constructed in a similar medically discursive way with the rise of the great heresiological and polemical treatises of late antiquity.

Such extensive heresiologies and polemical treatises represent what we might understand as "medical" (in the ancient broad sense of the term) encyclopaedias of social pathology. Todd Berzon's excellent work on the classification of late ancient heresiology demonstrates clearly how heresiology functions as an imperial form of knowledge, not very different from other forms of collections like the medical encyclopaedias and even the legal digests.[23] A heresiology like that of Epiphanius provides an excellent example of the type of encyclopaedizing tendencies we have in Christian imperial forms of medicalized knowledge. The *Panarion* represents a type of medicine chest against the psychic poisons of heresy. Heretical knowledge is here likened to snake bites. This type of discourse subtly animalizes heretical groups, and in this case, draws a long continuous line that links heretics back to the primordial serpent of Eden, and all evil forces in between. The use of medical metaphors in Epiphanius's *Panarion* is extensive, and Richard Flower has argued that Epiphanius may have directly relied on earlier medical authors, specifically Nicander of Colophon.[24] Flowers's other, more significant, conclusion support my aforementioned point, namely Epiphanius aimed to construct his own authorial persona as an expert in the field of heretical poison, not very different from Galen:

> Epiphanius presented himself as the man who could cure all heresies and, perhaps even more importantly, reliably distinguish the false teachers from the true, regardless of their status in social and ecclesiastical hierarchies. In doing so, he followed in the footsteps of Nicander and Galen and claimed to be a true doctor of the church.[25]

Thus, just as the individual subject, in body and soul, is mapped out, ordered, and organized in the monastic handbooks, so too is the social body mapped out and ordered so as to protect "orthodox" or "Nicene" Christians against heresy. The various heresies are given names—some of which the "heretical" groups, in fact, may have never called themselves—and then classified according to the danger they pose to the communal body and soul of the church. Theodoret's polemical treatise, the *Curatio*, aims to correct, by means of medical discourse, not heresy but rather "Greek" philosophy and religious practices. But the discursive operations and aims of Epiphanius's *Panarion* and Theodoret's *Curatio* are the same. We have similar attacks against Jewish identity, as seen in disturbing texts like Chrysostom's *Adversus Judaeos*. This type of thinking was not only prevalent in the East. Like the *Panarion*, Tertullian's work from the early third century, *Scorpiace*, or the "Antidote for the Scorpion's Sting", also constructs "Gnostic" heresy medically as a type of poison. Such texts classify pathological ideologies, and aim to correct or anathematize the groups associated with the ideologies. Heresiology also becomes an act of containment, or quarantine, in which socially and spiritually dangerous heresies are set apart and marked as being dangerous.

My second thesis is therefore as follows: *early Christian medical discourse was also part of a totalizing and imperial discourse that mapped out, classified, rationalized, ordered, and institutionalized the social body, especially in emergent literary genres that exhibit encyclopaedizing tendencies.*

Alterity and the Personification of Moral Pathology and Health

The result of these totalizing and imperializing tendencies in early Christian medical discourse is the personification of moral pathology and health. In late antiquity, we see the development of numerous "figures" or *exempla* within early Christian medical discourse. Certain figures function as strategies of cohesion within a group, while other figures have alterizing or "othering" functions. Some of these figures are directly borrowed from Greek and Roman moral philosophy, such as the figure of the "slave of the passions." Pathic excess becomes the major cause of various psychic and physical ailments.[26] The notion of the slave of the passions is very common in polemical treatises, and it is probably the closest ancient equivalent of what we understand today as the "addict" or the "obsessive" individual.

Addiction and obsession are important, yet highly neglected, medical discourses in late antiquity. Although he was not a Christian, when one reads, for instance, Libanius's 25th oration, entitled *On Slavery (De douleia)*, one might be surprised to read that his oration says practically nothing about the institution of late antique slavery.[27] The oration is all about the enslavement to the passions, and the title might be translated more appropriately as *On Addiction and Obsession*. But the addiction cannot be separated from the addict, the excessive indulgence in various passions is personified in the figure of the slave of passions. Libanius may have been the teacher of some influential Christian authors, such as John Chrysostom. Christian discourse inherited this type of pathological doulology[28] from Greek and Roman moral discourse.

Perhaps one of the most telling examples is Theodoret's construction of the death of the arch-heretic Arius in his *Historia religiosa* (or *The History of the Monks of Syria*).[29] Theodoret tells us that the Council of Nicaea, and the Bishop Alexander in particular, was not sure how to deal with Arius after his excommunication. Should he receive mercy or not? Then, the Syrian Monk James of Nisibis urged the Council to take seven days of fasting and prayer in order to gain the wisdom to make the right decision. After this time, Theodoret explains, in graphic and disturbing detail, what happened to Arius:

> When the appointed day arrived on which the majority anticipated the reconciliation of the miscreant, and the time had come for the divine liturgy and everyone expected to see the enemy of God receive pardon, at this very moment there occurred a truly divine and extraordinary miracle. While in a disgusting and noisome place that wretch was evacuating the refuse from his gluttony, he evacuated its receptacle as well; so with his inwards dissolved and ejected along with his excrement, the miserable creature instantly breathed his last and underwent this most shameful death, called to answer for his noisome blasphemy in a noisome place and slain by the tongue of the great James.[30]

It was therefore Arius's gluttony, his excessive passion for food and drink, that killed him. Firstly, the account tells us that Arius's did not fast when he was supposed to fast, but rather ate gluttonously, like a typical slave of the belly. Secondly, the rhetoric of filth and excrement frames the narrative persona of Arius, who is basically washed away *in toto* with the rest of his filth. Arius becomes the filth, and so, every heretic after him is also associated with filth, excrement, and impurity.[31] Finally, he is slain by the tongue or word of James, the Syrian monk. It is therefore the righteous word of the monk that cut out, as it were, the festering filth of heresy.[32] In the next point of the chapter, I will elaborate on the importance of the word in early Christian medical discourse. John Chrysostom believed that the slavery to the stomach was the primeval sin that led to the fall of Adam and Eve—Adam and Eve had to fast from the tree of knowledge of good and evil, an act in which they failed.[33] Like Adam and Eve, then, Arius ate when he should have fasted. For the Syriac context, Robert Kitchen has shown how central the idea of the slavery to the stomach is in Philoxenus's moral discourse.[34]

So it often happens that opponents of Christian authors, whether they are heretics or "Greeks" or whatever other appellation, are described as slaves of passions. Some are slaves of the stomach, others are slaves of lust or greed, and some are even described as being enslaved to demonic teachings. But this act of discursive enslavement is yet another imperializing tendency of early Christian medical discourse. Empires make slaves—this is what they do.

Empires also make war. The presence of the rhetoric of warfare in early Christian medical discourse further affirms this point. Theodoret writes:

> God . . . has assigned appropriate remedies to the two parts of our nature, [and] has even instituted specialized medicines of one kind for the body and of another for the soul, and has given them as prescriptions in the war against diseases in order to overcome them.[35]

The response against moral pathology is an imperial response of coercion, of warfare.

In addition to slavery, we often find that individuals are othered by discourses of madness.[36] Heretics are often described as being insane and frenzied, a danger to society. In some cases, the notion of the brain fever, or phrenitis, is used to classify the heretic.[37] Similar discursive strategies function in the construction of the figure of the "Greek," as we see with Theodoret's *Curatio*. So while the heresiological treatises aim to classify and discern the various forms of heresy in the minutest of details, there is also a parallel strategy at play in which persons suffering from any of these moral and spiritual pathologies are grouped in broad and almost indiscernible categories, like the pathic "slave," the "heretic," or the "Greek"—they are all, in any case, the dangerous Other, in need of medical correction. So we have, on the one hand, the categorization of heretics in the encyclopaedic heresiologies, where the heretics are discerned and differentiated, and on the other hand, the generalization of all moral–theological delinquents. Categorization and generalization, in this case, work in tandem.

As a correlate to the development of these figures of "otherness," we also have *exempla* of health being constructed. The figure of the preacher as a doctor of the soul is a good example of this. Monks are often described as being exemplary of psychic health, even when their physical health is compromised. Historical figures like Paul and the martyrs are often hailed as surgeons of the soul, who are able to extract and cure even the most serious psychic and moral pathologies through their words.[38] In the case of Cain's disease, mentioned earlier, God is seen as the great physician of the soul.

My third thesis is therefore as follows: *moral and psychic pathologies become personified, and from early Christian medical discourse, we see the development of figures like the pathic slave, the frenzied heretic, and the ironically foolish and ethnically stereotyped "Greek" or "Jew." The assault against moral pathology is therefore also an assault against the pathologically personified Other, as is evident in the language of war, enslavement, madness, and so on.*

Early Christian Medical Discourse as a Popular Discourse

Finally, early Christian medical discourse was also a popular (and perhaps even a populist) discourse. This facet is evident in the fact that many late ancient Christian homilies are permeated with medical discourse. Through popular preaching, Christian medical discourse was disseminated to not only the literate and wealthy elite, but even to the masses. Even if all did not necessarily have the means to take care of the health of the soul—which requires the luxury of free time or leisure (*otium*, in Latin) and discipline—the presence of the discourse itself was enough to fix it in the early Christian popular imagination. We should also remember that the *paterfamilias*, and not the professional physician, was usually the first port of call when medical issues are concerned. Few Christian authors are as exemplary, in this regard, as John Chrysostom. As Wendy Mayer has shown,[12] one of the primary ways in which Chrysostom fashioned his own identity was in the shape of the therapist of the soul. In his treatise, *On the Providence of God*, Chrysostom states:

> When doctors intend to treat those with a fever or those sick with some other illness, they first seek to see the afflicted ones themselves, since from far away they are unable to provide an opinion. Such is the art of medicine, and such is the nature of these illnesses. But we, who are earnest to treat not one or two but all in the world who have been scandalized, do not require anything like that. . . . By preparing the medicine of the word [τὸ τοῦ λόγου . . . φάρμακον], which for the sick becomes all these things and better than all we have mentioned. . . . Thus, having prepared this medicine, we are sending it on to everyone, and I know that everyone will benefit from the treatment, provided they pay heed with exactitude [ἀκρίβεια] and right-mindedness to what it said.[39]

Christian medical discourse was affirmed through its enunciation. Not only was Christian imperial rhetoric a medical discourse per se, but also the actual medicine, the very healing process, was one in which words were central. Here in this passage, Chrysostom seems to hint that the medicine of preaching the word acts like mass medical treatment. The medicine of the word or *logos* is not subject to the limitations of conventional medical treatment. Most of all, Chrysostom states: "And it does this without causing any money to be spent and without increasing poverty."[40] The medicine of the word is free, and available to all.

This positioning of the *logos* as medicine developed from the earliest strands of Christian discourse, most notably with the understanding of the *logos* as spiritual food or nourishment. In 1 Cor. 3:2 and Heb. 5:12, Paul and the anonymous author of Hebrews likens the teaching of the word to milk and solid foods. With reference to John 6:53—that is, eating the "flesh and blood" of the Son of Man—Clement of Alexandria argues that the blood of Christ is the main nourishment for the Christian soul.[41] John Penniman's important work on this topic has demonstrated, convincingly, that the discourse of (the *logos*-) milk as nourishment and medicine persisted well into late antiquity,[42] while Dana Robinson has analysed the curative nature of food, more generally, and not only milk, in Christian thought.[43] Fernando Soler, moreover, has demonstrated how the notion of food and spiritual nourishment was one of the main foundations of Origen's complex teaching about the *logos*.[44] We should remember that breast milk was basically considered blood in a different, more "concocted" form. Moreover, an enlightening study by Tara Mulder suggests that breast milk was possibly not only consumed by infants in ancient Rome.[45] She argues that the nutritional and, especially, curative value of breast milk could have led to its distribution and consumption by and for adults. Thus, when early Christian authors spoke about the *logos* as milk, in both the nutritional and curative sense, the discourse might not have been so bizarre as it may seem to modern readers today. My final thesis therefore is as follows: *early Christian medical discourse was a popular discourse which was perpetuated through its very annunciation. Christian medical discourse was not only about healing for the individual, the discourse itself was the medicine, and it was available to the masses.*

Conclusion

In conclusion, not all the discourse of late ancient Christianity had a medical foundation. Not everything was medical. But we must account for the fact that medical discourse keeps surfacing in numerous contexts that appear, initially, to be not medically related. What I have argued in this chapter is that one way in which late ancient Christian identity and otherness were constructed was by means of medical discourse that permeated the seemingly non-medical literature of the times. The Christian self was both deconstructed and reconstructed through meticulous and exhaustive technologies and practices of mapping and ordering the individual subject in body and soul. A similar type of mapping was also applied to the social body with the heresiological treatises. More than anything, this transformed medical discourse was a major aspect of the totalizing and imperial(-izing) discourse of late antique Christianity. By understanding this aspect of late antique Christian medical discourse, we have been able to examine the dynamics of the discourse from a bird's-eye view, thereby making connections between genres of late antique literature that seem, at first, rather unrelated. Despite the important differences between the various genres of literary outputs mentioned in this chapter, the aims of genres like medical encyclopaedias, heresiologies, apologetic and polemic treatises, monastic handbooks, and homilies might not have been all that different.

Notes

1 Martha C. Nussbaum, *The Therapy of Desire: Theory and Practice in Hellenistic Ethics* (Princeton, NJ: Princeton University Press, 2013).
2 A handful examples are illustrative in this regard; see, for example, Blake Leyerle, *The Narrative Shape of Emotion in the Preaching of John Chrysostom* (Oakland: University of California Press, 2020); Mark J. Boone, *The Conversion and Therapy of Desire: Augustine's Theology of Desire in the Cassiciacum Dialogues* (Eugene, OR: Pickwick, 2016); Kathy L. Gaca, *The Making of Fornication: Eros, Ethics, and Political Reform in Greek Philosophy and Early Christianity* (Berkeley: University of California Press, 2003).
3 This is especially evident in the work of scholars affiliated to the Religion, Medicine, Disability, and Health in Late Antiquity (ReMeDHe) working group. Andrew Crislip had already explored how healthcare, generally, was transformed in late antiquity with the rise of monasticism; Andrew T. Crislip, *From Monastery to Hospital: Christian Monasticism and the Transformation of Health Care in Late Antiquity* (Ann Arbor: University of Michigan Press, 2005); see also Andrew T. Crislip, *Thorns in the Flesh: Illness and Sanctity in Late Ancient Christianity*, Divinations: Rereading Late Ancient Religion (Philadelphia: University of Pennsylvania Press, 2012).
4 I have explored the concepts of early Christian identity and alterity, in John Chrysostom's thought specifically, previously here: Chris L. de Wet, "Paul, Identity-Formation and the Problem of Alterity in John Chrysostom's Homilies *In Epistulam ad Galatas Commentarius*," *Acta Theologica Supplementum* 19 (2014): 18–41; "Paul and Christian Identity-Formation in John Chrysostom's Homilies *De laudibus Sancti Pauli Apostoli*," *Journal of Early Christian History* 3.2 (2013): 34–47; "The Priestly Body: Power-Discourse and Identity in John Chrysostom's *De sacerdotio*," *Religion and Theology* 18.3–4 (2011): 351–79. This analysis brings focus to the problem by examining medical aspects of early Christian identity and alterity.
5 Averil Cameron, *Christianity and the Rhetoric of Empire: The Development of Christian Discourse* (Berkeley: University of California Press, 1994), esp. 87, 123.
6 Crislip, *From Monastery to Hospital*; Crislip, *Thorns in the Flesh*; Christian Schulze, *Medizin und Christentum in Spätantike und frühem Mittelalter: Christliche Ärzte und ihr Wirken*, Studien und Texte zu Antike und Christentum 27 (Tübingen: Mohr Siebeck, 2005); Antigone Samellas, *Death in the Eastern Mediterranean (50–600 A.D.): The Christianization of the East: An Interpretation*, Studien und Texte zu Antike und Christentum 12 (Tübingen: Mohr Siebeck, 2002); "Public Aspects of Pain in Late Antiquity: The Testimony of Chrysostom and the Cappadocians in Their Graeco-Roman Context," *Zeitschrift für Antikes Christentum* 19.2 (2015): 260–96; Anne E. Merideth, "Illness and Healing in the Early Christian East" (PhD dissertation, Princeton University, Princeton, 1999); Jonathan L. Zecher, *The Role of Death in the Ladder of Divine Ascent and the Greek Ascetic Tradition*, Oxford Early Christian Studies (Oxford: Oxford University Press, 2015); "Medical Art in Spiritual Direction: Basil, Barsanuphios, and John on Diagnosis and Meaning in Illness," *Journal of Early Christian Studies* 28.4 (2020): 591–623; Susan R. Holman, *Beholden: Religion, Global Health, and Human Rights* (Oxford: Oxford University Press, 2015); Wendy Mayer, "The Persistence in Late Antiquity of Medico-Philosophical Psychic Therapy," *Journal of Late Antiquity* 8.2 (2015): 337–51; "Medicine in Transition: Christian Adaptation in the Later Fourth-Century East," in

Shifting Genres in Late Antiquity, eds. Geoffrey Greatrex and Hugh Elton (Farnham: Ashgate, 2015), 11–26; Dana Robinson, *Food, Virtue, and the Shaping of Early Christianity* (Cambridge: Cambridge University Press, 2020); Junghun Bae, *John Chrysostom: On Almsgiving and the Therapy of the Soul*, John Chrysostom, Patristic Studies in Global Perspective 1 (Paderborn: Schöningh, 2020); See also this earlier excursus of my own: Chris L. de Wet, "The Preacher's Diet: Gluttony, Regimen, and Psycho-Somatic Health in the Thought of John Chrysostom," in *Revisioning John Chrysostom: New Approaches, New Perspectives*, eds. Chris L. de Wet and Wendy Mayer, Critical Approaches to Early Christianity 1 (Leiden: Brill, 2019), 410–63. Other recent works have followed a similar trajectory; see, for example, Leyerle, *Narrative Shape of Emotion*; Bae, *John Chrysostom*; Fernando Soler, *Orígenes y los alimentos espirituales: el uso teológico de metáforas de comer y beber*, Patristic Studies in Global Perspective 2 (Paderborn: Schöningh, 2021); Courtney Wilson Van Veller, "Paul's Therapy of the Soul: A New Approach to John Chrysostom and Anti-Judaism" (PhD dissertation, Boston University, Boston, 2015); "John Chrysostom and the Troubling Jewishness of Paul," in *Revisioning John Chrysostom: New Approaches, New Perspectives*, eds. Chris L. de Wet and Wendy Mayer, Critical Approaches to Early Christianity 1 (Leiden: Brill, 2019), 32–57.

7   Theodoret, *Cur. aff. Graec.* 1.1 (SC 57.104); Thomas P. Halton, trans., *Theodoret of Cyrus: A Cure for Pagan Maladies*, Ancient Christian Writers 67 (New York: Newman, 2013), 20.

8   Samellas, *Death in the Eastern Mediterranean*.

9   L. Michael White, "Moral Pathology: Passions, Progress, and Protreptic in Clement of Alexandria," in *Passions and Moral Progress in Greco-Roman Thought*, ed. John T. Fitzgerald, Routledge Monographs in Classical Studies (London: Routledge, 2008), 284–321.

10 Mayer, "The Persistence in Late Antiquity of Medico-Philosophical Psychic Therapy."

11 Blake Leyerle, "The Etiology of Sorrow and Its Therapeutic Benefits in the Preaching of John Chrysostom," *Journal of Late Antiquity* 8.2 (2015): 368–85; *Narrative Shape of Emotion*.

12 Ioannis Papadogiannakis, "Homiletics and the History of Emotions: The Case of John Chrysostom," in *Revisioning John Chrysostom: New Approaches, New Perspectives*, eds. Chris L. de Wet and Wendy Mayer, Critical Approaches to Early Christianity 1 (Leiden: Brill, 2019), 300–33.

13 On the materiality of the soul and spiritual beings, see especially Gregory A. Smith, "How Thin Is a Demon?," *Journal of Early Christian Studies* 16.4 (2008): 479–512.

14 Johannes B. Glenthøj, *Cain and Abel in Syriac and Greek Writers (4th–6th Centuries)*, Corpus Scriptorum Christianorum Orientalium 567: Subsidia 95 (Louvain: Peeters, 1997), 29.

15 Basil of Caesarea, *Ep.* 260; in Roy J. Deferrari, ed. and trans., *Basil: The Letters*, vol. 4, LCL (Cambridge, MA: Harvard University Press, 1926), 60–3.

16 John Chrysostom, *In paralyt.* 5 (PG 51.58.8–17); author's translation. On Chrysostom's views on Cain disease, see De Wet, Chris L., "Cain's Disease: Murder, Medicine, and Pedagogy in John Chrysostom's Reading of the Cain and Abel Story," in *Dealing with Difference: Patterns of Response to Religious Rivalry in Late Antiquity*, eds. Geoffrey Dunn and Christine Shepardson (Tübingen: Mohr Siebeck, 2021), 131–53 forthcoming.

17 David Sider and Michael McVaugh, "Galen on Tremor, Palpitation, Spasm, and Rigor," *Transactions & Studies of the College of Physicians of Philadelphia* 1.3 (1979): 183–210.

18 Philoxenus, *Mem.* 1.13 (Budge 21–2); in Robert A. Kitchen, trans., *The Discourses of Philoxenos of Mabbug: A New Translation and Introduction*, Cistercian Studies 235 (Collegeville, MN: Liturgical Press, 2013), 14–15.

19 Mary Hansbury, trans., *John the Solitary on the Soul*, Texts from Christian Late Antiquity 32 (Piscataway, NJ: Gorgias, 2013).

20 Mayer, "Medicine in Transition," 11–19.
21 On encyclopaedism more generally, see Jason König and Greg Woolf, eds., *Encyclopaedism from Antiquity to the Renaissance* (Cambridge: Cambridge University Press, 2013). The editors' introduction in this volume is particularly relevant, especially on the notion of ancient encyclopaedism (p. 1): "What does it mean to talk of 'encyclopaedism' before the Enlightenment? We should make it clear right from the start that this volume does not attempt to trace a systematic genealogy of the 'encyclopaedia' as a genre. It is would be hard, in any case, to find anything quite like a modern 'encyclopaedia' before the eighteenth century. Instead we are concerned with the much broader phenomenon we refer to as encyclopaedism. We are interested, in other words, in the ways in which a series of different authors (primarily located within western, European culture) made use of a range of shared rhetorical and compilatory techniques to create knowledge-ordering works of different kinds, works that often claimed some kind of comprehensive and definitive status. And we think in terms of an encyclopaedic spectrum, with different texts drawing on shared encyclopaedic markers to different degrees and for very different purposes." On the ordering of medical knowledge in the Roman world with special reference to medical works, see Rebecca Flemming, "Galen's Imperial Order of Knowledge," in *Ordering Knowledge in the Roman Empire*, eds. Jason König and Tim Whitmarsh (Cambridge: Cambridge University Press, 2007), 241–77; John Wilkins, "Galen and Athenaeus in the Hellenistic Library," in *Ordering Knowledge in the Roman Empire*, eds. Jason König and Tim Whitmarsh (Cambridge: Cambridge University Press, 2007), 69–87.
22 Flemming, "Galen's Imperial Order of Knowledge," 277.
23 Todd S. Berzon, *Classifying Christians: Ethnography, Heresiology, and the Limits of Knowledge in Late Antiquity* (Oakland: University of California Press, 2016).
24 Richard Flower, "Medicalizing Heresy: Doctors and Patients in Epiphanius of Salamis," *Journal of Late Antiquity* 11,2 (2018): 251–73.
25 Flower, "Medicalizing Heresy," 270.
26 This is a point I have explored previously in the works of John Chrysostom and Theodoret: de Wet, "Preacher's Diet"; "The Discipline of Domination: Asceticism, Violence, and Monastic Curses in Theodoret's *Historia Religiosa*," in *Religious Violence in the Ancient World: From Classical Athens to Late Antiquity*, eds. Jitse H. F. Dijkstra and Christian R. Raschle (Cambridge: Cambridge University Press, 2020), 323–44.
27 Bernard Schouler, *Libanios: Discours moraux* (Paris: Les Belles Lettres, 1973), 172–221.
28 Doulology refers to discursive slavery; see Chris L. de Wet, *Preaching Bondage: John Chrysostom and the Discourse of Slavery in Early Christianity* (Oakland: University of California Press, 2015), 1–39.
29 On the death of Arius more generally, see Rowan Williams, *Arius: Heresy and Tradition* (London: SCM, 2001), 65–81; Timothy Barnes, "The Exile and Recalls of Arius," *Journal of Theological Studies* 60.1 (2009): 109–29; Ellen Muehlberger, "The Legend of Arius' Death: Imagination, Space and Filth in Late Ancient Historiography," *Past & Present* 227.1 (2015): 3–29.
30 Theodoret, *Hist. rel.* 1.10 (SC 234.182); Richard M. Price, trans., *A History of the Monks of Syria by Theodoret*, Cistercian Studies 88 (Trappist, KY: Cistercian Publications, 1985), 17–18.
31 For more on this point, see especially Muehlberger, "Arius' Death." Helpful also are the remarks of Blake Leyerle, "Refuse, Filth, and Excrement in the Homilies of John Chrysostom," *Journal of Late Antiquity* 2.2 (2009): 337–56, in the context of John Chrysostom.
32 For a more detailed discussion of this point, see de Wet, "Discipline of Domination," 338–43.
33 de Wet, "Preacher's Diet"; more generally, see Teresa M. Shaw, *The Burden of the Flesh: Fasting and Sexuality in Early Christianity* (Minneapolis, MN: Fortress, 1998);

Veronika E. Grimm, *From Feasting to Fasting: The Evolution of a Sin: Attitudes to Food in Late Antiquity* (London: Routledge, 1996).
34 Robert A. Kitchen, "The Lust of the Belly Is the Beginning of All Sin: A Practical Theology of Asceticism in the *Discourses* of Philoxenos of Mabbug," *Hugoye: Journal of Syriac Studies* 13.1 (2010): 49–63.
35 Theodoret, *Cur. aff. Graec.* 1.2 (SC 57.104); Halton, *Cure for Pagan Maladies*, 20.
36 Wendy Mayer, "Madness in the Works of John Chrysostom: A Snapshot from Late Antiquity," in *The Concept of Madness from Homer to Byzantium: History and Aspects*, ed. Hélène Perdicoyianni-Paleologou (Amsterdam: A.M. Hakkert, 2016), 349–79.
37 Jessica Wright, "Preaching Phrenitis: Augustine's Medicalization of Religious Difference," *Journal of Early Christian Studies* 28.4 (2020): 525–53.
38 Crislip, *Thorns in the Flesh*, 36–80; Wilson Van Veller, "Paul's Therapy of the Soul."
39 John Chrysostom, *Prov.* Preface (SC 79.52), slightly adapted Monk Moses, trans., *St. John Chrysostom: On the Providence of God* (Platina, CA: St. Herman of Alaska Brotherhood, 2015), 31–2.
40 Moses, *St. John Chrysostom.*
41 This is the main line of argumentation in Clement of Alexandria, *Paed.* 1.42–3, as extrapolated in much detail in Denise Kimber Buell, *Making Christians: Clement of Alexandria and the Rhetoric of Legitimacy* (Princeton, NJ: Princeton University Press, 1999), 131–79.
42 John David Penniman, *Raised on Christian Milk: Food and the Formation of the Soul in Early Christianity* (New Haven, CT: Yale University Press, 2018).
43 Robinson, *Food, Virtue, and the Shaping of Early Christianity*, 22–68; see also de Wet, "Preacher's Diet"; Shaw, *Burden of the Flesh*; Aline Rousselle, *Porneia: On Desire and the Body in Antiquity*, trans. Felicia Pheasant (New York: Barnes & Noble, 1996), 160–94. Of course, Galen himself relied on the notion of food as being essentially curative when used and consumed correctly; see Owen Powell, trans., *Galen: On the Properties of Foodstuffs* (Cambridge: Cambridge University Press, 2007); Mark Grant, *Galen on Food and Diet* (London: Routledge, 2002).
44 Soler, *Orígenes y los alimentos espirituales*, 97–222.
45 Tara Mulder, "Adult Breastfeeding in Ancient Rome," *Illinois Classical Studies* 42.1 (2017): 227–43.

Bibliography

Ancient Texts

Basil of Caesarea, *Epistulae*, in Deferrari, Roy J., ed. and trans. *Basil: The Letters*. Vol. 4. LCL 270. Cambridge, MA: Harvard University Press, 1926.
Grant, Mark. *Galen on Food and Diet*. London: Routledge, 2002.
John Chrysostom, *De providentia Dei*, in Malingrey, Anne-Marie, ed. *Jean Chrysostome: Sur la providence de Dieu*. SC 79. Paris: Cerf, 1961. English translation in Monk Moses, trans. *St. John Chrysostom: On the Providence of God*. Platina, CA: St. Herman of Alaska Brotherhood, 2015.
———, *In paralyticum demissum per tectum* (*In paralyt.*), PG 51:47–64.
John of Lycopolis, *De anima*, in Hansbury, Mary, trans. *John the Solitary on the Soul*. Texts from Christian Late Antiquity 32. Piscataway, NJ: Gorgias, 2013.
Philoxenus of Mabbug, *Discourses*, in Budge, E. A. Wallis, ed. *The Discourses of Philoxenus, Bishop of Mabbôgh, A.D. 485–519, Volume 1: The Syriac Text*. London: Asher & Co., 1893. English translation in Kitchen, Robert A., trans. *The Discourses of Philoxenos of Mabbug: A New Translation and Introduction*. Cistercian Studies 235. Collegeville, MN: Liturgical Press, 2013.

Powell, Owen, trans. *Galen: On the Properties of Foodstuffs*. Cambridge: Cambridge University Press, 2007.

Theodoret of Cyrus, *Curatio malorum Hellenicorum*, Canivet, Pierre, ed. *Théodoret de Cyr: Thérapeutique des maladies helléniques*. SC 57. Paris: Cerf, 1958. English translation in Halton, Thomas P., trans. *Theodoret of Cyrus: A Cure for Pagan Maladies*. Ancient Christian Writers 67. New York: Newman, 2013.

———, *Historia religiosa*, in Canivet, Pierre, and Alice Leroy-Molinghen, eds. *Théodoret de Cyr: Histoire des moines de Syrie*. Vol. 1. SC 234. Paris: Cerf, 1977. English translation in Price, Richard M., trans. *A History of the Monks of Syria by Theodoret*. Cistercian Studies 88. Trappist, KY: Cistercian Publications, 1985.

Modern Texts

Bae, Junghun. *John Chrysostom: On Almsgiving and the Therapy of the Soul*. John Chrysostom. Patristic Studies in Global Perspective 1. Paderborn: Schöningh, 2020.

Barnes, Timothy. "The Exile and Recalls of Arius." *Journal of Theological Studies* 60.1 (2009): 109–29.

Berzon, Todd S. *Classifying Christians: Ethnography, Heresiology, and the Limits of Knowledge in Late Antiquity*. Oakland: University of California Press, 2016.

Boone, Mark J. *The Conversion and Therapy of Desire: Augustine's Theology of Desire in the Cassiciacum Dialogues*. Eugene, OR: Pickwick, 2016.

Buell, Denise Kimber. *Making Christians: Clement of Alexandria and the Rhetoric of Legitimacy*. Princeton, NJ: Princeton University Press, 1999.

Cameron, Averil. *Christianity and the Rhetoric of Empire: The Development of Christian Discourse*. Berkeley: University of California Press, 1994.

Crislip, Andrew T. *From Monastery to Hospital: Christian Monasticism and the Transformation of Health Care in Late Antiquity*. Ann Arbor: University of Michigan Press, 2005.

———. *Thorns in the Flesh: Illness and Sanctity in Late Ancient Christianity*. Divinations: Rereading Late Ancient Religion. Philadelphia: University of Pennsylvania Press, 2012.

de Wet, Chris L. "The Priestly Body: Power-Discourse and Identity in John Chrysostom's *De sacerdotio*." *Religion and Theology* 18.3–4 (2011): 351–79.

———. "Paul and Christian Identity-Formation in John Chrysostom's Homilies *De laudibus Sancti Pauli Apostoli*." *Journal of Early Christian History* 3.2 (2013): 34–47.

———. "Paul, Identity-Formation and the Problem of Alterity in John Chrysostom's Homilies *In Epistulam ad Galatas Commentarius*." *Acta Theologica Supplementum* 19 (2014): 18–41.

———. *Preaching Bondage: John Chrysostom and the Discourse of Slavery in Early Christianity*. Oakland: University of California Press, 2015.

———. "The Preacher's Diet: Gluttony, Regimen, and Psycho-Somatic Health in the Thought of John Chrysostom." Pages 410–63 in *Revisioning John Chrysostom: New Approaches, New Perspectives*. Edited by Chris L. de Wet and Wendy Mayer. Critical Approaches to Early Christianity 1. Leiden: Brill, 2019.

———. "The Discipline of Domination: Asceticism, Violence, and Monastic Curses in Theodoret's *Historia Religiosa*." Pages 323–44 in *Religious Violence in the Ancient World: From Classical Athens to Late Antiquity*. Edited by Jitse H. F. Dijkstra and Christian R. Raschle. Cambridge: Cambridge University Press, 2020.

———. "Cain's Disease: Murder, Medicine, and Pedagogy in John Chrysostom's Reading of the Cain and Abel Story." Pages 131–53 in *Dealing with Difference: Patterns of Response to Religious Rivalry in Late Antiquity*. Edited by Geoffrey Dunn and Christine Shepardson. Tübingen: Mohr Siebeck, 2021.

Flemming, Rebecca. "Galen's Imperial Order of Knowledge." Pages 241–77 in *Ordering Knowledge in the Roman Empire*. Edited by Jason König and Tim Whitmarsh. Cambridge: Cambridge University Press, 2007.

Flower, Richard. "Medicalizing Heresy: Doctors and Patients in Epiphanius of Salamis." *Journal of Late Antiquity* 11.2 (2018): 251–73.

Gaca, Kathy L. *The Making of Fornication: Eros, Ethics, and Political Reform in Greek Philosophy and Early Christianity*. Berkeley: University of California Press, 2003.

Glenthøj, Johannes B. *Cain and Abel in Syriac and Greek Writers (4th–6th Centuries)*. Corpus Scriptorum Christianorum Orientalium 567: Subsidia 95. Louvain: Peeters, 1997.

Grimm, Veronika E. *From Feasting to Fasting: The Evolution of a Sin: Attitudes to Food in Late Antiquity*. London: Routledge, 1996.

Holman, Susan R. *Beholden: Religion, Global Health, and Human Rights*. Oxford: Oxford University Press, 2015.

Kitchen, Robert A. "The Lust of the Belly Is the Beginning of All Sin: A Practical Theology of Asceticism in the *Discourses* of Philoxenos of Mabbug." *Hugoye: Journal of Syriac Studies* 13.1 (2010): 49–63.

König, Jason, and Greg Woolf, eds. *Encyclopaedism from Antiquity to the Renaissance*. Cambridge: Cambridge University Press, 2013.

Leyerle, Blake. "Refuse, Filth, and Excrement in the Homilies of John Chrysostom." *Journal of Late Antiquity* 2.2 (2009): 337–56.

———. "The Etiology of Sorrow and Its Therapeutic Benefits in the Preaching of John Chrysostom." *Journal of Late Antiquity* 8.2 (2015): 368–85.

———. *The Narrative Shape of Emotion in the Preaching of John Chrysostom*. Oakland: University of California Press, 2020.

Mayer, Wendy. "Medicine in Transition: Christian Adaptation in the Later Fourth-Century East." Pages 11–26 in *Shifting Genres in Late Antiquity*. Edited by Geoffrey Greatrex and Hugh Elton. Farnham: Ashgate, 2015.

———. "The Persistence in Late Antiquity of Medico-Philosophical Psychic Therapy." *Journal of Late Antiquity* 8.2 (2015): 337–51.

———. "Madness in the Works of John Chrysostom: A Snapshot from Late Antiquity." Pages 349–79 in *The Concept of Madness from Homer to Byzantium: History and Aspects*. Edited by Hélène Perdicoyianni-Paleologou. Amsterdam: A.M. Hakkert, 2016.

Merideth, Anne E. "Illness and Healing in the Early Christian East." PhD Dissertation, Princeton University, Princeton, 1999.

Muehlberger, Ellen. "The Legend of Arius' Death: Imagination, Space and Filth in Late Ancient Historiography." *Past & Present* 227.1 (2015): 3–29.

Mulder, Tara. "Adult Breastfeeding in Ancient Rome." *Illinois Classical Studies* 42.1 (2017): 227–43.

Nussbaum, Martha C. *The Therapy of Desire: Theory and Practice in Hellenistic Ethics*. Princeton, NJ: Princeton University Press, 2013.

Papadogiannakis, Ioannis. "Homiletics and the History of Emotions: The Case of John Chrysostom." Pages 300–33 in *Revisioning John Chrysostom: New Approaches, New Perspectives*. Edited by Chris L. de Wet and Wendy Mayer. Critical Approaches to Early Christianity 1. Leiden: Brill, 2019.

Penniman, John David. *Raised on Christian Milk: Food and the Formation of the Soul in Early Christianity*. New Haven, CT: Yale University Press, 2018.

Robinson, Dana. *Food, Virtue, and the Shaping of Early Christianity*. Cambridge: Cambridge University Press, 2020.

Rousselle, Aline. *Porneia: On Desire and the Body in Antiquity.* Translated by Felicia Pheasant. New York: Barnes & Noble, 1996.

Samellas, Antigone. *Death in the Eastern Mediterranean (50–600 A.D.): The Christianization of the East: An Interpretation.* Studien und Texte zu Antike und Christentum 12. Tübingen: Mohr Siebeck, 2002.

———. "Public Aspects of Pain in Late Antiquity: The Testimony of Chrysostom and the Cappadocians in Their Graeco-Roman Context." *Zeitschrift für Antikes Christentum* 19.2 (2015): 260–96.

Schouler, Bernard. *Libanios: Discours moraux.* Paris: Les Belles Lettres, 1973.

Schulze, Christian. *Medizin und Christentum in Spätantike und frühem Mittelalter: christliche Ärzte und ihr Wirken.* Studien und Texte zu Antike und Christentum 27. Tübingen: Mohr Siebeck, 2005.

Shaw, Teresa M. *The Burden of the Flesh: Fasting and Sexuality in Early Christianity.* Minneapolis, MN: Fortress, 1998.

Sider, David, and Michael McVaugh. "Galen on Tremor, Palpitation, Spasm, and Rigor." *Transactions & Studies of the College of Physicians of Philadelphia* 1.3 (1979): 183–210.

Smith, Gregory A. "How Thin Is a Demon?" *Journal of Early Christian Studies* 16.4 (2008): 479–512.

Soler, Fernando. *Orígenes y los alimentos espirituales: El uso teológico de metáforas de comer y beber.* Patristic Studies in Global Perspective 2. Paderborn: Schöningh, 2021.

White, L. Michael. "Moral Pathology: Passions, Progress, and Protreptic in Clement of Alexandria." Pages 284–321 in *Passions and Moral Progress in Greco-Roman Thought.* Edited by John T. Fitzgerald. Routledge Monographs in Classical Studies. London: Routledge, 2008.

Wilkins, John. "Galen and Athenaeus In the Hellenistic Library." Pages 69–87 in *Ordering Knowledge in the Roman Empire.* Edited by Jason König and Tim Whitmarsh. Cambridge: Cambridge University Press, 2007.

Williams, Rowan. *Arius: Heresy and Tradition.* London: SCM, 2001.

Wilson Van Veller, Courtney. "Paul's Therapy of the Soul: A New Approach to John Chrysostom and Anti-Judaism." PhD Dissertation, Boston University, Boston, 2015.

———. "John Chrysostom and the Troubling Jewishness of Paul." Pages 32–57 in *Revisioning John Chrysostom: New Approaches, New Perspectives.* Edited by Chris L. de Wet and Wendy Mayer. Critical Approaches to Early Christianity 1. Leiden: Brill, 2019.

Wright, Jessica. "Preaching Phrenitis: Augustine's Medicalization of Religious Difference." *Journal of Early Christian Studies* 28.4 (2020): 525–53.

Zecher, Jonathan L. *The Role of Death in the Ladder of Divine Ascent and the Greek Ascetic Tradition.* Oxford Early Christian Studies. Oxford: Oxford University Press, 2015.

———. "Medical Art in Spiritual Direction: Basil, Barsanuphios, and John on Diagnosis and Meaning in Illness." *Journal of Early Christian Studies* 28.4 (2020): 591–623.

Part Three

Performing Health, Preserving Communities

8 Hagiography and "Mental Health" in Late Antique Monasticism

Paul Dilley

As monasticism spread throughout the late antique Mediterranean world, exerting a heavy influence on society, culture, and spirituality, the lives of many ascetic saints were committed to writing. The resulting corpus of hagiography, which was exceptionally diverse in topics, composition, and style, held a privileged if ambiguous place for the practice of individual piety. Their promotion of holy men and women as models of virtue to be imitated is well known, but this hardly exhausts their significance. Gerontius, the biographer of the aristocrat-turned-pilgrim-and-ascetic Melania the Younger, described her daily routine of reading, which began with Scripture and followed with homilies. Only after that, presumably because they were less canonical, she "would go through the Lives of the fathers as if she were eating dessert."[1] While their appeal was multifaceted and hardly universal, the lives of saints constituted an engaging means of seeing the Christian life in action, in their portrayal of virtue as well as vice, as demonstrated in explicit behaviours and motivations which were often implicit; in short, hagiography was "good to think with" for those imagining the possibilities for a life of piety.

In this chapter, I will explore the role of saints' lives for the mental health of their readers and listeners, beginning with a culturally specific definition of the term. In particular, I will highlight the importance of hagiography for developing a "theory of mind" in the Christian, especially the monastic context. By learning that one's thoughts could be influenced by external forces, and that they were also subject to monitoring by an advisor, and ultimately by God, readers learned their role within spiritual hierarchies, as well as strategies for dealing with their disappointments in the monastic life. They also learned the concept of concealed holiness, an important framework at all points in the hierarchy, but especially for those of lower status, to understand their spiritual potential apart from community recognition. In the last section, I consider two saints' lives, the *Life of Euphrosyne* and the *Life of Athanasia and Andronicus*, which offer new perspectives on the mental distress caused by the separation from family and significant others because of ascetic renunciation, to help monks and their significant others cope with the pain of not seeing one another.

DOI: 10.4324/9781003080534-11

Approaching "Mental Health" in the Context of Late Antique Monasticism

"Mental health" as a category in late antiquity is a mostly unexplored field, similarly to related concepts in contemporary personal health discourse such as "human flourishing." On the other hand, the past decade has seen an increase in studies on "mental disorders," which focus on various departures from a (often unspecified) normative mind/body condition.[2] This approach reflects the *Diagnostic and Statistical Manual of Mental Disorders*, which does not provide a definition of mental health, but instead offers an encyclopaedic discussion of "mental disorders," defined for the first time in the most recent edition, DSM-5, as "a syndrome characterized by clinically significant disturbance in an individual's cognition, emotion regulation, or behavior that reflects a dysfunction in the psychological, biological, or developmental processes underlying mental functioning."[3] But the implicit assumption of normative mental function, combined with a lack of explicitly acknowledging it, has led to criticism of the Manual and the broader project.

For a definition of mental health, one can turn to the World Health Organization, which understands it as "state of well-being in which the individual realizes his or her own abilities, can cope with the normal stresses of life, can work productively and fruitfully, and is able to make a contribution to his or her community."[4] This approach to mental health thus combines self-knowledge, competence in one's way of life, and a social component, namely contributing to one's group(s). While this is certainly a normative definition, its highly ambiguous language leaves scope for variation. Indeed, it implies that understandings of mental health are culturally specific, given that emotional, intellectual, and spiritual ideals vary widely.[5] This is in line with the developing field of neurodiversity studies, which interrogates "the epistemic and ideological rules that govern and produce 'normals' and 'others' according to scientific, cultural, and social practices."[6]

Neither the Manual nor other contemporary definitions are closely aligned with the nuances of the various understandings of mental illness and health in the ancient world.[7] Within late antique monasticism, mental health can be broadly conceived as an effective socialization into the ascetic lifestyle, including functioning within institutional expectations related to worship and work, or special conditions such as illness, and appropriate relationships with other monks, whether disciples or superiors. The mental component was intimately tied to all these aspects, as late antique monasticism placed extraordinary weight on the management of thoughts (and related emotions) in the formation of the moral subject. New disciples gradually learned a specifically monastic form of what might today be called a "theory of mind," an important concept from interdisciplinary cognitive studies defined as "the cognitive capacity to attribute mental states to self and others," with "mental states" further defined as "perceptions, bodily feelings, emotional states, and propositional attitudes (beliefs, desires, hopes, and intentions)."[8] Anthropologist Tanya Luhrmann has argued that theory of mind is culturally specific, and has advanced a typology for theory of mind based on various "dimensions of mind."[9]

The monastic theory of mind assumed that the mind/body was permeable, and especially subject to demonic influence; that thoughts were ethically significant, even if not acted upon; technologies of the imagination, such as learning how to visualize the last judgement, were key for mental regulation; audition, such as listening to scriptural readings or demonic whispers, was as crucial as visualization; and one's thoughts and feelings were transparent to God, as well as certain monastic superiors.[10] Disciples were taught to monitor, report, and regulate a disorderly stream of thoughts, usually identified as linguistic expressions of opinions, values, and desires; as well as to harness their imaginative capacities in specific ways. The strategic recitation of scripture, cultivation of the fear of God, and thankful contemplation of God's creation were all practices encouraged through spiritual direction. These cognitive disciplines promoted a particular view of mental health, in which the monk became gradually less subject to negative thoughts and their closely associated emotions, such as lust or inappropriate fear or grief. In this model, mental health does *not* include the regular experience of happiness or joy as a primary goal, though these may be part of a pious life; indeed, the practice of tearful repentance, with its remorse over individual and collective sins, was often put forward as a lifelong model for monks, even as it might alternate with feelings of joy in the divine.

Hagiography and Mental Health

The *Lives* of monastic saints often provide far more than an account of the virtuous actions on the protagonist, by consistently describing the ascetic hero's mental and emotional states.[11] This feature is present in the earliest and best-known example of monastic hagiography, the *Life of Antony*. Interpretations of this text usually focus on Antony's progressive isolation and staged withdrawal to the desert as a model for monastic regulation; but this same narrative equally describes his gradual overcoming of temptations such as fornication and avarice, a series of events which were often conflated in the later reception of the work, especially in art. This is more a discussion of Antony's experience with passion, understood to be triggered by external (demonic) agents, than an intimate account of his thoughts; but it is emblematic of the larger point I want to make, that the saint can be an exemplar not only for virtuous action but also for the affective and cognitive progress that accompanied it.

While Antony, Pachomius, and other saints could serve as models for the practice of cognitive disciplines, the monastic audience's engagement with hagiography had far broader implications for mental health as understood in their communities. The rich tapestry of explicit and implied thoughts, feelings, motivations, fantasies, and attitudes of the characters, as they played out against the background of the plot, was surely a major factor in the popularity of these texts, as documented not only by their rapid dissemination and translation into multiple languages, but also by anecdotes such as Melania the Younger's consumption of *Lives* as a kind of ascetic dessert.

As Lisa Zunshine has argued, literature, and especially the novel, is pleasurable for readers because it allows them to practice "theory of mind:"

> We may see the pleasure afforded by fictional narratives as grounded in our awareness of the successful testing of our mind-reading adaptations, in the respite that such a testing offers us from our everyday mind-reading uncertainties, or in some combination of the two.[12]

For the late antique readers, including monastics, hagiography could provoke reflection upon the inner thoughts, emotions, attitudes, and motivations of the ascetic hero, and also of the people with whom the ascetic interacted, in scenes of teaching, contest, temptation, and otherwise.[13] For disciples, texts such as the *Life of Pachomius* allowed a rare perspective into the thoughts and concerns of their monastic superiors, from correct attitudes about food, family relations, and possessions to the practice of cardiognosticism (mind-reading), through which the thoughts of others were exposed to them for correction. In short, it would have been a means for readers to explore the particularly monastic theory of mind.

Hagiography, Concealed Sanctity, and Attitudes towards Familial Renunciation

An important subset of the saint's life emerged in the fifth and sixth centuries, which did not feature "historical" figures, such as Antony or Pachomius, but invented ascetic heroes, often with a symbolic name, in which the arc of the plot, heavily dependent on the novel and mime, takes centre stage. There are multiple examples of this literary sub-genre of monastic hagiography, which seems to have been especially at home in the fifth- and sixth-century urban centres such as Antioch and Alexandria. I have identified three primary subdivisions: repentant prostitutes (*Life of Mary of Egypt, Life of Pelagia, Life of Thais*), estranged wives (*Life of Andronicus and Athanasia, Life of Matrona, Life of Theodora*), and daughters (*Life of Eugenia, Life of Euphrosyne, Life of Macrina*).[14] These heroines typically join monasteries where they live anonymously as humble disciples, though a few are later chosen as abbots. Most are examples of the hagiographic trope which Derek Krueger has described as "concealed sanctity," usually through adopting male clothing and presenting as eunuchs or men in their new communities, only to have their birth-assigned sex, and other aspects of their identity, revealed at death.[15] In the following, I examine two of them, the *Life of Euphrosyne* and the *Life of Andronica and Athanasius*, for their subtle approach to disarming grief related to separation from family as a result of monastic renunciation by the inculcation of new assumptions and attitudes related to significant others and their identities.

Joining a monastery often meant "leaving behind" family members, including parents, children, spouses, or siblings. Sometimes one or more family members might join together, with, for example, the male relatives joining the men's community, and female relatives joining an affiliate women's community.[16] In either case, the family members might cut off subsequent contact with one another, or they might maintain it, usually in a more restricted way. The relationship between a monastic's family members often involved ambiguities and conflict, as is demonstrated, for example, by the numerous regulations about them in the Rules of Pachomius and Shenoute. Opinions on best practices varied widely, and often tolerated continued interaction of some kind. Traditions about the family of Theodore, a successor to Pachomius as head of his monastic federation, the Koinonia, illustrate the tensions involved: when his mother and brother come to visit him, Pachomius at first commands him to meet them, but Theodore refuses. Pachomius relents, but asks him to treat his brother more gently, and he joins the community himself.[17] This anecdote suggests opinions could vary even among monastic leaders, and that even stricter attitudes about maintaining separation did not prohibit the presence of family members in the same community.

The *Life of Euphrosyne*

The *Life of Euphrosyne* recounts how Euphrosyne ("joy"), the young daughter of an elite Alexandrian family, escaped her planned marriage by running away from home, dressing as a man, and joining a monastery, where she presented herself as a eunuch.[18] The story begins with the efforts of Paphnutius (meaning, roughly, "godly one" in Egyptian) and his unnamed wife to conceive a child. Paphnutius frequents a monastery outside the city (which is unnamed, but could be the Ennaton), to which he donates substantial funds of money. The couple conceive because of the abbot's prayers, and give birth to a daughter, whom they name Euphrosyne. Euphrosyne's mother dies while she is still in childhood, so her father raises and educates her, "And her reputation spread throughout the city [like Theodora], both because of her wisdom and learning, and because she was very beautiful, and well put together in face and soul." (3) The *Life*'s opening section thus serves to illustrate the strong bond of the family, and the centrality of Euphrosyne as the long-hoped-for child, but also the tenuous nature of such worldly connections, given the untimely loss of her nameless mother. Instead, her ongoing bond with her father Paphnutius is emphasized.

In the next section, various suitors approach Paphnutius, requesting to marry Euphrosyne. He ultimately makes an agreement with one power family, prophetically exclaiming, "Let God's will be done." Paphnutius takes his daughter to be blessed by the abbot before the marriage, and she becomes enamoured of the monastic life during her visit. Later, when a member of the monastery visits Paphnutius's house in Alexandria to take him to the festival in honour of its founder, he speaks alone with Euphrosyne, who communicates her desire to join his community. The monk encourages her not to "defile her body" through marriage, suggesting that she instead cut her hair and join a monastery while he distracts Paphnutius. Euphrosyne sends a slave to the church of Theodosius, who finds a monk from Scetis selling his wares there, and brings him to her. She addresses him:

> My Lord, I have a father, a servant of God, who is very wealthy. He had a
> wife and from her he begot me. And he desires, on account of his possessions,

to give me over to the world of injustice. I do not want to be polluted by its filth, and I am also afraid to disobey my father. And what I will do I do not know, for I have passed the whole night without sleep, calling upon God to make known what is profitable for my wretched soul. And when dawn came it seemed like a good idea to send [my slave] to the church, and to bring back one of the fathers, and to hear a word from him. So I exhort you, as one sent from God, to teach me what is profitable for me.

The monk then responds by emphasizing the importance of rejecting one's family in the quest for holiness:

As the Lord says, "whoever does not renounce father and mother and siblings and children, and still too her own soul, is not able to be my disciple" (Luke 14). What more than these words can I say to you? So if you know that you are able to bear the temptations, leave it all behind and flee. For your father's possessions will find many heirs. Behold, churches, houses for the poor, houses for the aged, hostels, monasteries, widows, orphans, foreigners, the injured, captives. Let him leave it wherever it is pleasing to him. Only do not destroy your soul.

Euphrosyne convinces him to cut her hair and to give her the monastic schema. She realizes that her father will find out if she joins a women's monastery, so she instead dresses as a man and goes to the very monastery which her father was just visiting. Presenting herself as a eunuch from the palace of Alexandria named Smaragdus ("emerald"), she makes a donation to the monastery, and is assigned a spiritual director, Agapitus, who keeps her in a cell so that the beauty of her face does not tempt the other monks. When Paphnutius realizes that his daughter is gone, he is distraught, crying ironically: "Who has invaded my wealth? Who has scattered my possessions?" He frantically searches the city and its environs, but, as expected, does not think to look in the men's monastery. Eventually, he goes to the abbot, requesting that he and his monks pray for Euphrosyne's discovery. They are granted no revelations about her whereabouts, but the abbot reassures Paphnutius that she has not fallen into sin, and suggests that he speak to Smaragdus for consolation.

The subsequent father–daughter reunion is emotional, resulting in an instant bond that will last many more years, but only Smaragdus recognizes it as such. Although her face has changed because of ascetic practice, she covers it to ensure that her identity remains hidden. She cries instantly, which Paphnutius interprets as compunction, that is, the attitude of continuous repentance practised by some monks. The ambiguity here is one of the pleasures of reading hagiography, which leaves the mental state of Smaragdus undescribed, to be filled in by the reader or listener. She may be feeling personal guilt for disobeying her father's wish to marry, or empathetic pain at seeing him so distressed,[19] or she may simply be mourning the sinful attachment to worldly things which led to the present situation: a separation, and yet now a half-recognized reconnection, between daughter and father.

After (or through) her tears, Smaragdus consoles her father, repeating the claim of the abbot that, had Euphrosyne fallen into sin, this would have been revealed to him. She then quotes Matthew 10:37, emphasizing the need to prioritize God over love of one's parents. Finally, she prophetically asserts that God has the power to reveal his daughter to him in this world. After their conversation, Paphnutius declares to the abbot, "My soul has been edified by that brother, and thus I have been made happy in the grace of God through his consolation, as though I had found my daughter," word-play on the birth-name of his daughter, who has now been renamed Smaragdus, perhaps to signify his lost "wealth." The dramatic irony is heavy: Paphnutius is deeply hurt by the disappearance of his daughter, but has regained her without explicitly knowing it, even if he senses it through his joy. Although Smaragdus's mental state is not explicitly noted, she presumably feels comfort, obligation, or both at seeing her father, because she agrees to his request to continued meetings.

The two proceed with their new relationship over a period of 38 years. No details are given, but it is clear that their roles are reversed: Smaragdus is now the authority figure, the monastic spiritual director of a pious layman seeking consolation and advice. On her deathbed, she reveals her own identity as Euphrosyne to her astounded father Paphnutius. She requests that he give their family wealth to the monastery, and then passes away. Paphnutius is in a state of shock, feeling hurt by his daughter's decision to stay disguised, a decision which he does not understand. However, when Euphrosyne's true identity is revealed to her community, the monks celebrate and commemorate her virtuous life. Paphnutius then joins the monastery, where he lives in her cell for ten years, suggesting his continued goodwill and strong connection to his daughter, as does his donation of their family's possessions. After his death, daughter and father are buried, and commemorated, together.

Euphrosyne's decision to join a men's monastery to avoid marriage may well have served as a model for some young women. But the ongoing popularity of the *Life* into the early modern period and beyond suggests that it had significance for a wider audience than this group. What was the appeal? The *Life of Euphrosyne* would have exerted a special draw upon disciples who encountered difficult family separations as a result of joining a monastery; or their non-monastic relatives who were on the other side of such separations. The story was not necessarily a precise mirror of their circumstances, but it could offer an imaginative, consolatory, and inspirational depiction of the possibility for familial connections even in the face of renunciation. For those monks who continued to visit with their relatives (such as their parents), it might function as a justification for their ongoing relationship, perhaps with a change in dynamics, as when Smaragdus became her father's advisor. For those monks and their relatives who did cut ties, the persistent efforts of Paphnutius for spiritual advancement, despite the apparent loss of his daughter, could serve as a consolation, by demonstrating the possibility of finding replacements for significant others through new pious relationships; or even to promote the sense that one's family was closer than realized, and bound by mutual ties of faith. It might also offer a simple wish fulfilment, appealing to those who hoped for a reunion with relatives, licit or otherwise. These are just a few of the possible reader or listener responses, both monastic and secular, to the *Life of Euphrosyne*.

Whatever the particulars of the ascetic family relationship, the key message of the text is that separation from one's relatives may indeed cause pain, but this pain is insignificant next to their eventual shared glory and salvation. In short, renunciation is "worth" it, despite the potential for anguish. The proper flow of family wealth to the monastery is also emphasized: Euphrosyne/Smaragdus in effect promises it to the monks when she enters, and, when she reveals her identity to Paphnutius before dying, she requests that he keep her promise, which he does. Thus, his original goal of marrying his daughter to effect the intergenerational transfer of property, a typical concern for elites, is thwarted, but something even better is achieved: the monastery in which he and his daughter practised asceticism and were sanctified is gifted their financial legacy and is equally charged with their commemoration.

If the *Life of Euphrosyne* reflects the concern of wealthy Christian families especially, its potential role in the mental health of monastics and their relatives was broader. It did not deny the grief and tears following upon the family's separation; indeed, it suggests that these could endure in this world, as experienced by Paphnutius. At the same time, the father feels joy through his new relationship with Smaragdus, who presumably does as well. This sense of joy, suggested by the very name of the heroine, might bring temporary relief from the pain of no longer being able to see a loved one who was now a monk. Most importantly, however, the *Life* presented the correct attitude with respect to family renunciation: it was tolerable because it could lead to the spiritual advancement and salvation of the whole family, and contribute to its reputation for Christian piety.

The *Life of Athanasia and Andronicus*

Another hagiographic narrative, the *Life of Athanasia and Andronicus*, features a married couple who, like Paphnutius, his wife, and Euphrosyne, are exemplary pious Christians, who are wealthy and share that wealth with the church (1–3).[20] The couple is at first based in Antioch, but much of the later story takes place in and around Alexandria, like the *Life of Euphrosyne* and other similar works. When their two children die of a sudden illness, the mother is overcome by grief, and wishes that she too would die with them; their father, like Job, accepts the will of God and, hopeful for the salvation of their daughter and son, consoles her (4–5). After Athanasia's vision of the martyr Julian convinces her to become a monk, the couple resolve to go on a pilgrimage to the Holy Land, beginning the process of donating their wealth (6–7). They continue on to Alexandria and the nearby shrine of Saint Menas, close to Alexandria, at which point they go their separate ways: Andronicus to Scetis, where only men are accepted, under the spiritual direction of abba Daniel; and Athanasia, tonsured by her husband, goes to the confederation of Pachomian monasteries in the Thebaid (Upper/Southern Egypt), which included communities of women (8).

Twelve years later, both resolve to return to the Holy Land. On the way, they run into each other. While Athanasia recognizes Andronicus, he does not recognize her, because she has dressed as a man. They continue together in silence, and on their return to Egypt, Athanasios proposes that they stay together until death in a cell close to the monastery of Oktokaidekaton, at the 18th mile outside of Alexandria. Andronicus agrees, and returns after getting the blessing of Daniel of Scetis, who consents even though Athanasios' identity has been revealed to him by God (9–10). The couple live together in holy asceticism for 12 years, with Daniel visiting regularly, yet Andronicus remains unaware that he is once again with his wife. As Athanasios approaches death, Andronicus mourns, though he did not mourn at the death of his children and his earlier separation from his wife (11). When Athanasios is "found to be a woman by nature" at death, Daniel, and the monks of Scetis and Alexandria, gather to honour her (12). Although we are not told Andronicus's specific feelings about the revelation, there is no hint of resentment or betrayal; on the contrary, he refuses to return to Scetis, declaring, "At the place where my lady <lies>, O Father, it is necessary for me to die <there> too" (13).

The *Life of Athanasia and Andronicus*, like the *Life of Euphrosyne*, dramatizes families rent asunder by asceticism, focusing on husband–wife separation, rather than father–daughter. A number of sources suggest that husband and wife might join monasteries at the same time, especially coenobitic federations with male and female communities, and experience varying degrees of separation afterwards. Athanasia and Andronicus present an imaginary scenario of full reunion, a kind of wish fulfilment in which they can enjoy mutual support in the life of piety, apart from the previous concerns of their marriage, such as children and household management. For those married couples who maintained some form of contact after renunciation, this *Life* could be taken as offering tacit approval for such ongoing connections, albeit in a new framework. For those couples who maintained full separation, it could help them imagine a continued partnership in the common goal of salvation, even while apart; or to imagine a new significant other in the ascetic life as a replacement spouse. For elite families, it also suggested a means of shifting their status, and potentially fame, to a new ascetic context, even if the transfer of property to the monastery is not emphasized as in the case of Paphnutius. In short, *Life of Athanasia and Andronicus* are not simple models for a specific form of behaviour, they also promote a particular attitude for both monastics and their relatives: a hopeful acceptance of family renunciation, in the various forms that might take, in which the grief is acknowledged but responded to in creative ways; and the confidence in an ending marked by divine joy, in which concealed virtue will ultimately be acknowledged.

Conclusion

In conclusion, I hope to have demonstrated the complexity of defining "mental health" in a late antiquity monastic context, which espoused a complex theory of mind and earnest observation, reporting, and response to a disorderly stream of thoughts and emotions; and that hagiography, an extremely popular genre among both monks and non-monks, was a key area in which this specific approach to mental health was promoted. The two examples discussed in this chapter, the *Life of Euphrosyne* and the *Life of Athanasia and Andronicus*, specifically address the pain of family renunciation, but as a corpus monastic hagiography engages with a broad range of thoughts, emotions, and attitudes. Its popularity stems in part from being not overtly prescriptive, in contrast to monastic homilies, rules, or treatises. Moreover, different audiences could assign their own inferences about the thoughts and motivations of the characters, which no doubt contributed to hagiography's broad resonance. Within this flexibility, however, the texts offered an approach to managing suffering related to family separation, and promoted attitudes that relativized or reformulated relationships to relatives, while at the same time assuring that virtuous lives in the monastery would be rewarded, even commemorated.

Notes

1 Gerontius, *Life of Melania* 23; SC 90: 174. The same expression occurs in the Greek; see Elizabeth Clark, *Melania the Younger: From Rome to Jerusalem* (Oxford: Oxford University Press, 2021), 213.

2 Jean-Claude Larchet, *Mental Disorders & Spiritual Healing: Teachings from the Early Christian East* (Hillsdale, NY: Angelico Press, 2005); William Harris, *Mental Disorders in the Classical World* (Leiden: Brill, 2013); Youval Rotman, *Insanity and Sanctity in Byzantium: The Ambiguity of Religious Experience* (Cambridge: Harvard University Press, 2016); Peter N. Singer and Chiara Thumiger, *Mental Illness in Ancient Medicine: From Celsus to Paul of Aegina* (Leiden: Brill, 2018); Jackie Pigeaud, *La Maladie de l'âme: Étude sur la Relation de l'Âme et du Corps dans la Tradition Médico-Philosophique Antique* (Paris: Les Belles Lettres, 1981); Inbar Graiver, *Asceticism of the Mind: Forms of Attention and Self-transformation in Late Antique Monasticism* (Toronto: PIMS, 2019).

3 American Psychiatric Association, *Diagnostic and Statistical Manual of Mental Disorders*, 5th ed. (Washington, DC: American Psychiatric Association, 2013), 20. This definition is flawed, as many have pointed out. For an overview, see Bruce Thyer, "The DSM-5 Definition of Mental Disorder: Critique and Alternatives," in *Critical Thinking in Clinical Assessment and Diagnosis* (Cham: Springer, 2015).

4 World Health Organization, "Mental Health: Strengthening Our Response," www.who.int/en/news-room/fact-sheets/detail/mental-health-strengthening-our-response (accessed October 8, 2021).

5 Conversely, on the cultural constructedness of mental disorders, see, most famously, Michel Foucault, *Madness and Civilization: A History of Insanity in the Age of Reason* (New York: Vintage, 1988).

6 Hanna Bertilsdotter Rosqvist, Nick Chown, and Anna Stenning, "Introduction," in *Neurodiversity Studies: A New Cultural Paradigm* (London: Routledge, 2020), 2.

7 This chapter is related to a broader project exploring connections and divergences between ancient and modern notions of mental health and illness. There is not space here to pursue the general question, so instead I focus on one particular area, namely late antique monasticism, a particularly active locus of innovation on this topic.

8 Alvin Goldman, "Theory of Mind," in *The Oxford Handbook of Philosophy of Cognitive Science*, eds. E. Margolis, R. Samuels, and S. Stich (Oxford: Oxford University Press, 2012), 402–24, at 402.

9 Tanya Luhrmann, "Towards an Anthropological Theory of Mind," *Journal of the Finnish Anthropological Association* 36 (2011): 5–69. The dimensions of mind are mental boundedness/porosity; the significance attributed to interior thoughts and emotions; the

significance attributed to imagination; the relative emphases given to the senses; relational access to thoughts and emotions; and the ethics of acting upon such knowledge (pp. 7–8). For a more popular discussion of some of the same concepts, see Tanya Luhrmann, *When God Talks Back: Understanding the American Evangelical Relationship with God* (New York: Vintage, 2012).

10 On the monastic theory of mind, see Paul Dilley, *Monasteries and the Care of Souls in Late Antique Christianity: Cognition and Discipline* (Cambridge: Cambridge University Press, 2017).

11 For the saint as moral example more generally, see, for example, Peter Brown, "The Saint as Exemplar in Late Antiquity," *Representations* 2 (1993): 1–25.

12 Lisa Zunshine, *Why We Read Fiction: Theory of Mind and the Novel* (Columbus, OH: Ohio State University Press, 2006), 20.

13 For more on cognitive and affective responses to monastic hagiography, see Dilley, *Monasteries and the Care of Souls in Late Antique Christianity*, 233–59.

14 This corpus is the subject of my in-progress monograph.

15 Derek Krueger, *Symeon the Holy Fool: Leontius's Life and the Late Antique City* (Berkeley: University of California Press, 1996), 66–71, *passim*.

16 See Rebecca Krawiec, "'From the Womb of the Church': Monastic Families," *Journal of Early Christian Studies* 11 (2003): 283–307; and, on children, see now Caroline Schroeder, *Children and Family in Late Antique Egyptian Monasticism* (Cambridge: Cambridge University Press, 2020).

17 Bohairic Life of Pachomius 37–8, in L.T. Lefort, *S. Pachomii vita bohairice scripta*, Corpus Scriptorum Christianorum Orientalium 89 (Louvain Typographeum Reipublicae, 1925).

18 I use the Greek text in Anatole Boucherie, "Vita sanctae Euphrosynae secundum textum graecum primaevum," *Analecta Bollandiana* 2 (1883): 195–205. English translations are my own.

19 Later in the same passage it is noted: "But seeing her father in great pain, she sympathized with him."

20 See the text, translation and notes in Anne P. Alwis, *Celibate Marriages in Late Antique and Byzantine Hagiography: The Lives of Saints Julian and Basilissa, Andronikos and Athanasia, and Galaktion and Episteme* (London: Bloomsbury, 2011), 249–277. I use her chapter division and translation.

Bibliography

Ancient Sources

Bohairic Life of Pachomius, in Lefort, L.T., *S. Pachomii vita bohairice scripta*, Corpus Scriptorum Christianorum Orientalium 89 (Louvain: Typographeum Reipublicae, 1925).

Gerontius, "Life of Melania 23," in *Anonyme. Vie de sainte Mélanie*, ed. Denys Gorce, SCh 90 (Paris: Éditions du Cerf, 1962).

Life of Athanasia and Andronicus, in Anne P. Alwis, *Celibate Marriages in Late Antique and Byzantine Hagiography: The Lives of Saints Julian and Basilissa, Andronikos and Athanasia, and Galaktion and Episteme* (London: Bloomsbury, 2011).

Life of Euphrosyne, in Anatole Boucherie, "Vita sanctae Euphrosynae secundum textum graecum primaevum," *Analecta Bollandiana* 2 (1883): 195–205.

Modern Sources

American Psychiatric Association, *Diagnostic and Statistical Manual of Mental Disorders*, 5th ed. (Washington, DC: American Psychiatric Association, 2013).

Brown, Peter, "The Saint as Exemplar in Late Antiquity," *Representations* 2 (1993): 1–25.

Clark, Elizabeth, *Melania the Younger: From Rome to Jerusalem* (Oxford: Oxford University Press, 2021).

Dilley, Paul, *Monasteries and the Care of Souls in Late Antique Christianity: Cognition and Discipline* (Cambridge: Cambridge University Press, 2017).

Foucault, Michel, *Madness and Civilization: A History of Insanity in the Age of Reason* (New York: Vintage, 1988).

Goldman, Alvin, "Theory of Mind," in *The Oxford Handbook of Philosophy of Cognitive Science*, eds. E. Margolis, R. Samuels and S. Stich (Oxford: Oxford University Press, 2012), 402–24.

Graiver, Inbar, *Asceticism of the Mind: Forms of Attention and Self-Transformation in Late Antique Monasticism* (Toronto: PIMS, 2019).

Harris, William V. (ed.), *Mental Disorders in the Classical World* (Leiden: Brill, 2013).

Krawiec, Rebecca, " 'From the Womb of the Church': Monastic Families," *Journal of Early Christian Studies* 11 (2003): 283–307.

Krueger, Derek, *Symeon the Holy Fool: Leontius's Life and the Late Antique City* (Berkeley: University of California Press, 1996).

Larchet, Jean-Claude, *Mental Disorders & Spiritual Healing: Teachings from the Early Christian East* (Hillsdale, NY: Angelico Press, 2005).

Luhrmann, Tanya, "Towards an Anthropological Theory of Mind," *Journal of the Finish Anthropological Association* 36 (2011): 5–69.

——, *When God Talks Back: Understanding the American Evangelical Relationship with God* (New York: Vintage, 2012).

Pigeaud, Jackie, *La Maladie de l'âme: Étude sur la Relation de l'Âme et du Corps dans la Tradition Médico-Philosophique Antique* (Paris: Les Belles Lettres, 1981).

Rosqvist, Hanna Bertilsdotter, Nick Chown, and Anna Stenning, "Introduction," in *Neurodiversity Studies: A New Cultural Paradigm* (London: Routledge, 2020).

Rotman, Youval, *Insanity and Sanctity in Byzantium: The Ambiguity of Religious Experience* (Cambridge: Harvard University Press, 2016).

Schroeder, Caroline, *Children and Family in Late Antique Egyptian Monasticism* (Cambridge: Cambridge University Press, 2020).

Singer, Peter N., and Chiara Thumiger (eds.), *Mental Illness in Ancient Medicine: From Celsus to Paul of Aegina* (Leiden: Brill, 2018).

World Health Organization, "Mental Health: Strengthening Our Response," www.who.int/en/news-room/fact-sheets/detail/mental-health-strengthening-our-response (accessed October 8, 2021).

Zunshine, Lisa, *Why We Read Fiction: Theory of Mind and the Novel* (Columbus, OH: Ohio State University Press, 2006).

9 Shaping Water

Public Health and the "Medicine of Mortality" in Late Antiquity[1]

Susan R. Holman

Introduction

It is now more than a decade since the United Nations General Assembly passed Resolution 64/292, affirming acceptable, accessible, affordable, safe, and sufficient water as a global human right.[2] The UN Sustainable Development Goals (SDGs) further emphasize water's importance in the global political agenda, with SDG 6, a vision to "ensure availability and sustainable management of water and sanitation for all" by 2030.[3] The need for clean water goes beyond safe hydration for all living things; UN Special Rapporteur Jean Ziegler reminds us that as an essential nutrient,[4] water also "must be a component of the human right to food."[5] As a basic human need in community health, agriculture, and a sustainable global environment, water and concerns for its safe clean, adequate, and affordable access cross sectors. Water's relevance to sanitation in disease prevention during the COVID-19 pandemic prompted a 2020 "Global Acceleration Framework" to help fast-track actions to meet SDG 6 target goals, largely around issues of funding, cross-sectoral communications, and measures of accountability.[6]

Despite the inclusion of water in the last century's history of economic, social, and cultural rights,[7] the state of the world's water access has not radically improved since 2006, when the United Nations reported that one person in six lacked even the minimal health standard of 20 litres per day of clean water—about the equivalent of three toilet flushes.[8] According to a 2021 update on the state of global water and sanitation, one quarter (26%) of the world's population in 2020 still lacked access to safely managed drinking water, nearly half (46%) lacked safely managed sanitation, and almost one-third (29%) lacked basic handwashing services.[9] Even hospitals and health clinics continue to fall short; as of 2016, "one in eight health care facilities had no water service and one in five had no sanitation service."[10] Groundwater "often represents the largest share of fresh water in a country," yet in 2020 only 20–40% of bodies of water in the United States had "good ambient water quality"; this percentage is half that of both water-rich Canada and water-challenged Australia, and worse by a third compared to ambient water resources in

DOI: 10.4324/9781003080534-12

both Mexico and drought-ridden South Africa.[11] As South African theologian Steve de Gruchy put it in 2010,

> [T]he truth of the hydrological cycle is that "we all live downstream." There is only one stream of water. What passes through the bodies of animals, insects and plants . . . flushes through our sanitation systems, flows through the rivers, seeps through wetlands, rises to the heavens to become clouds and returns to nourish us and all living things. There is no life outside this cycle, and theology has to get real about it.[12]

This chapter explores what such a challenge might mean for discussions about water as a public health measure in Christian late antiquity.

Theology and Space in the Hydrological Cycle

De Gruchy translated "getting real" into a call for a five-part approach that he called "Jordan River ethics" or the "Olive Agenda," which de Gruchy envisioned as a blend of "brown" economic concerns with "green" environmentalism drawing on biblical ideals around that iconic, much-contested, and today sadly polluted river.[13] This ethical agenda, which faith communities are invited to adopt and practice, includes taking responsibility; protecting the value of the "commons"; upholding legal limitations to bind the strong and check those in power; promoting vocations in environmentally life-affirming services; and celebration of all that is good in the natural world.[14] De Gruchy's theological structuring of water equity into analogies of community embodiment continued to influence dialogue beyond the tragic irony of his death to a drowning accident in 2010. Isabel Apawo Phiri, in 2018, built on de Gruchy's legacy in her emphasis on "the wound of water stress."[15] This wound, she noted, festers in imminent water shortages, pollution, land desiccation, and waterborne diseases that most affect infants, children, and the poor who lack control over water supply and access.[16] Whether we call it hydration, osmolality, electrolyte balance, or simply a drink, de Gruchy and Phiri highlight how water maps on meaning-making of the body in particular and varying religious ways.

To "get real" about the hydrological cycle in a theological and practical way of what Denise Kimber Buell called "mediating membranes"[17] invites us to think more intentionally about how space maps on religious history and public health. "The organisation of space and its boundaries," write medical historians Patricia Baker and Han Nijdam, "form important factors in the culture of medicine today, just as it would have done in the past."[18] One aspect of such boundaries is suggested by geographer Doreen Massey's philosophy of space. In what follows here, I suggest that Massey's space mapping may offer a provocative kinetic image to help connect religious and public health history with water ethics across time, including the health-related legacies of Christian late antiquity.

Space: Articulated Story Mapping

Doreen Massey was a British geographer whose philosophy was informed by the work of Henri Lefebvre.[19] Massey understood space as "articulated moments in networks of social relations . . . constructed on a far larger scale than what we happen to define for that moment as the place itself."[20]

"Space is not just walking across a surface," she said in a 2013 Berlin lecture; "It is walking across a multitude of stories."[21] Drawing a dotted line across a blank white board, she highlighted the oft-overlooked narrative histories that inhabit the gaps between the diversity of stories shaping each of our moments and steps, the physical and conceptual places we inhabit. These gaps may be so culturally distinct from one another that, she says, "it would be entirely possible to fall through" them into the disconnects that can "trip us up" if we are not paying attention. What she calls the "constellation of ongoing trajectories" shape the ever-shifting relationships in our interconnected communities. Simply to leave home and walk across the square is likely to cross intersecting planes of different worlds and histories in those we meet and spaces we encounter. Paying attention to these kinetics, Massey says, we may—hopefully and ideally—encounter "the politics, the productivity, the questions, the expectations, the potential for surprise."

Massey was not a religious person and I apply a certain shameless instrumental syncretism in drawing on her framework here. Yet her socially tectonic kinetics of space and time bear relevance for theological ethics and history related to resource equity concerns in even something as "mundane" as water. Massey cared much about urban social justice and equity, concerns that have troubled religious communities and moral voices across history. While medical and religious texts from antiquity are unlikely to solve a global water crisis, theological history runs as a live current through the lens of Massey's subterranean narratives—unspoken assumptions that shape how people think and act, including how they use water. As Massey reminded her Berlin audience, "It matters who moves and how you move."[22]

Water, Place, and Public Health in Late Antiquity

The ancient history of public health also rested on movements of water, air, and persons across narratives of need. One of the oldest medical texts in the Hippocratic corpus, *Airs, Waters, Places*—"the most fundamental text for the study of the different categories of water and their relationship with health and disease in the history of western medicine"[23]—informed how Greek, Roman, and Christian medical writers such as Celsus, Rufus, Galen, Oribasius, Aetius, Paul of Aegina, and others categorized waters. Most water-related details in *Airs, Waters, Places* construct disease risk based on water's location, flow, appearance, weight, and climate. Marsh and lake waters, for instance, stagnant or slow moving, were said to increase risk of dysentery, diarrhoea, and quartan fevers that may (or may not) suggest malaria.[24] An early witness to how intense heat and vigorous aeration—boiling—improve water safety, *Airs, Waters, Places* recommended that even the lightest rain water "needs to be boiled and purified."[25] Later medical writers said the same. "Wholesome water ought to be very like air," said Pliny the Elder; better when boiled.[26] For Galen, the best waters were "neutral, without anything extraneous and without any taste or smell"[27]; for the best honey he advised, "mix it with a lot of water, then boil it until it stops foaming."[28] Oribasius repeated earlier advice to treat acute fever with food "boiled in water . . . for a long time."[29]

Water was life, but might also carry death, sometimes associated with faecal contamination. Galen wrote that the "worst" fish were those

> which live in rivers that flow through a big city, feeding off human sewage . . . and contain . . . an excess of excrementitious matter. It is therefore hardly surprising if bad juice collects in the bodies of those who eat them every day.[30]

As still in poor communities around the world today, diarrhoea was recognized in the Roman world as a leading cause of death for "children up to the age of ten."[31]

Even these so-called "medical" texts were grounded in a cosmology that assumed religious forces and causative meanings. Ignatius of Antioch, a martyred contemporary of Galen, may have dubbed Eucharist—the ritual wine commonly mixed with water—the "medicine of immortality,"[32] but therapeutic and religious uses of water in late antiquity could just as easily make you sick. Ingesting or applying unclean water, even to affirm God-given incarnation, might act as a mortal poison.

One of my pre-med students encountered this partnership of water as blessing and toxin during a semester abroad. Describing it later, she wrote:

> [I]n Palestine, a fellow student decided to be baptized in the Jordan River. The following Sunday, a group of students accompanied by a local pastor, traveled to the site of Jesus' baptism to witness the sacrament. Due to unusually high levels of pathogenic bacteria present in the water, the student was unable to be fully submerged and the baptism was forced to take place on the riverbank with limited amounts of water drizzled on her head. Though the sanctity of baptism was [in] no way diminished by the amount of water used, the contrast between spiritual rebirth and potentially deadly water was startling.[33]

Across time, resource disparities and perceptions relevant to water, sanitation, and hygiene (WASH) have further complicated both fundamental cultural health practices and religious practices.[34] Such tensions skyrocketed in the 2020 pandemic messaging about proper handwashing, the complex moratoria on Christian Eucharist and religious meals, and alarming public health statistics of viral loads in urban wastewater.[35] Providing the needy with a "cup of cold water" is a universal ideal in Judaism, Islam, and Christianity, associated with God-given human entitlements, "righteousness" and social justice, and (especially in Christianity) "works of mercy" based on Matthew 25:31–46. Religious history, ethics, and theology continue to shape medical and public health choices at household and community levels across the globe. So it is that stories about water ethics from the history of religious traditions remain relevant to community connections on public health and water policies. This is all part of the hydrological cycle that, de Gruchy would remind us, calls for a "get-real" theological narrative.

Water and Place as Public Health in Late Antiquity

Christian writers in the fourth and fifth centuries CE, whose works shaped many of the belief systems that fund faith-based healthcare today, did not precisely share our modern ideas about human rights, climate change, development goals, or environmentalism. They did, however, share our worries about wellness, illness, and civic justice. They also shared values resonant with aspects of de Gruchy's 5-point agenda (noted above).

Funding free public water supplies was a pious ethic across Mediterranean late antiquity. John Scarborough's hallmark 1980 survey on (pre-Christian) Roman medicine and public health is overwhelmingly about water and civic order, including (by the very rich and politically powerful) the construction and maintenance of aqueducts.[36] Championing water as part of patronage for wellness continued to define Christian civic duty following Constantine. Basil of Caesarea, for instance, spoke of a saint's fountain available within his church complex as "water for souls. . . . a prophylactic . . . and comfort for the sick."[37] He also advised drinking water as a core principle in his ideals for public welfare. In his sermons on fasting, he argued, against drunkenness, that drinking water could help effect "the orderliness of the city, the tranquility of the forum"[38] and further dispose "every city as a whole and all its people to good order."[39] His brother, Gregory of Nyssa, writing about community justice in care for diseased homeless beggars, similarly applied water ethics in condemning discrimination against the marginalized sick poor who depended for their water on the city's public fountains. While Nyssen believed that a sick person could not pollute good water, he did admit that "certain illnesses, such as the plagues, have an external cause and can be traced to pestilence in the air *or water*."[40] A similar sermon by Gregory of Nazianzus paints a scene in which the sick and disabled poor are

> driven away from cities, they are driven away from homes, from the market-place, from public gatherings, from the streets, from festivities, from drinking parties, even—how they suffer!—from water itself. They neither share the flowing springs with everyone else nor are they permitted the use of rivers to rinse away their contamination; and the strangest thing of all is that we drive them away from our midst as pariahs on one hand, and on the other bring them back to us claiming that they are really harmless, but all the while denying them shelter and failing to provide them with basic sustenance, treatment for their wounds, and dressings for their sores as best as we can.[41]

By the fifth century, both rich men and women were funding water projects in expression of Christian piety. A reused stone in a small bath complex on a steep hillside from urban Ephesus praises the woman Scholastikia, as "pious and very wise" when she funded its repair, likely after an earthquake.[42] There is no adjoining church; the cross that begins the inscription is the only hint of Scholastikia's Christian identity. Theodoret, the fifth-century bishop of Cyrrhus, defended his orthodoxy on the basis of practical water ethics: "From the revenues of my sees I . . . looked after the public baths. On finding that the city was not watered by the river . . . I built the conduit, and supplied the dry town with water."[43] The same intersection of public and private power in water narratives and patronage is evident in architectural, archaeological, and textual evidence from and concerning Byzantine Constantinople.[44] And in even a superficial reading of Procopius's *Buildings*, one is constantly tripping over water spaces that demonstrate Justinian's pious passion for construction. Indeed, this emperor's vexing penchant for levelling and wiping clean to the ground to reconstruct each early Christian holy site he "rediscovers" seems as recurrent as Procopius's emphasis on public water facilities.[45]

Episcopal power is evident in spatial archaeology down to the water pipes. The cruciform church of the martyr Babylas at Qausiyeh, in ancient Antioch, displays its water power in the dramatic intersection of a "mess of pipes buried under floors . . . cutting across disconnected pipes, and stone drains."[46] Centuries later and much farther west, episcopal power and its competition with civic water access is seen in the surviving evidence of wells, tightly documented controlled water towers, subterranean brickworks, and water pipes for the city of Exeter and its early and medieval cathedral.[47] Articulated "moments of networks in social relations" indeed.

Thus far this chapter has highlighted three ideas that connect religion and health in modern and late antique Christian ethics of water: de Gruchy's theology in the intercellular space of the hydrological cycle, Massey's space-tripping political and productive kinetics, and late antique civic–religious patronage. The following section brings these ideas together as it explores one final example to suggest this construction of conceptual space, in which one may walk across a multitude of subterranean stories about water. This example is the creation and use of a monumental well in the fifth-century Egyptian White Monastery under its founder, abbot Shenoute of Atripe.

The Shape of Water in Shenoute's "Great Well"

Shenoute (c. 347–465 CE) is best known as the energetic, even violent founder of a federation of monastic communities in Coptic Egypt that he controlled for more than 80 years, as an administrator with strong theological and disciplinary convictions, and as the author of an extensive collection of religious texts, sermons, letters, and canons.[48] The textual and architectural remains of water facilities at the White Monastery offer an unusually specific glimpse into the community's natural resources during an incident in which Shenoute and his monks reportedly provided crisis relief to help "around 20,000" desperate refugees, families fleeing raiders on their villages in the south, who crowded, with their animals and goods, into the complex for part of a year sometime after 451.[49] Scholars and archaeologists have critiqued Shenoute's claims about this event in some detail (noted later); my focus here is on what the story suggests about the place and shape of water at the nexus of religion and public health.

In his sermon, *Continuing to Glorify the Lord,*[50] Shenoute lists the community costs and actions to help the refugees.[51] Efforts, he says, included medical care, burials, midwifery, luggage and livestock management, daily cooked meals, and water. At the end of his litany of aid, he says, "And also the small spring . . . had [God] not blessed it, would not have been enough for them to drink water."

In fact, as the late Peter Grossmann and colleagues argued in 2009 on the basis of Shenoute's *Arabic Life*, this "small" spring most likely failed. Indeed, that text hints, when Shenoute saw that it was nearly dry, he "immediately started digging [a] new well to remedy the situation."[52] Both the old and the new—the "small" and the "great well"—remain today on site, with detailed notes from their twenty-first century excavations.

The larger well was indeed massive, 12.5 metres deep, with a 12-foot-wide square-shaped shaft of dressed limestone blocks, fired bricks, and high arches. A staircase leads down into an eastern niche.[53] Pots of water were raised using animals hitched to a Saqiyeh wheel gear drive, which circled above the well at ground level, emptying the water into a gravity-fed distribution system still visible, of pipelines, conduits, inspection boxes, sediment tanks, plastered cisterns, and drainage or soak-away areas. Described in detail by Louise Blanke in 2019, Shenoute's two wells were both engineering feats of evident detailed planning and "significant economic investment."[54]

In 2004, Peter Grossmann, Darlene Brooks-Hedstrom, and Mohamed Abdal-Rassul noted a curious detail in the shape of the great well that hints at potentially intentional connection to the site's religious meaning. In measuring the space, they noted:

> The general construction of the well and the proportions of the central shaft correspond exactly with the central space of the triconch in the great church, except that the dimensions are reduced by half. This unusual coincidence might point to the fact that the builders, or at least the chief engineers, were the same ones who constructed the church and that both structures are more or less contemporary.[55]

The 2009 report expands further on this spatial connection and its possible implications, with details that merit quoting at length. After discussing the well's brickwork structure, the authors write:

> A final and even more interesting observation concerns the inner spatial proportions of the well. As was observed only by chance, the rather complicated formation of the two opposite longer sides corresponds exactly with the proportions of the central square unit of the triconch in the great church of the monastery, but reduced by fifty percent. Only the transverse width of the well is enlarged by exactly ten percent in comparison with the corresponding unit in the church. Also the curious principle of the building of the well—that is, treating both its sides as two independent elements—has its model in the

church sanctuary. Since there is no technical reason for shaping the well in exactly the same way as the church sanctuary, there must have been some underlying concept, which eludes us today.

These details matter, the authors continue, because

> Shenute may have been directly engaged in the construction of the well, because no one else would have known the proportions of the center of the triconch of the church to repeat them correctly in the groundplan of the well. Shenute's own understanding of the building of the well as a very significant action in the establishment of the monastery [is suggested by the Arabic life story of] refugees . . . assembled in the monastery [when] Shenute determined that the original, small well could not supply enough water for so many people and was close to drying up.[56]

The design of the larger well, in other words, seems to have intentionally mirrored the design of the most ritually significant portion of the church and, given what is known about Shenoute's emphasis on controlling monastic detail, this was most likely intentional.

It is important to keep in mind what the archaeological report does *not* say. The authors' phrase, "shaping the well in exactly the same way as the church sanctuary," refers, they are clear, *only* to the limited area they specify as "the central square unit of the triconch in the great church." There is no suggestion here that the well copied or inverted the church's majestic triconch or any of its three apses; the ratio similarities are limited entirely to a particular rectangular dimension between floors and walls below the church's easternmost front.[57]

Even so, assuming the observations are correct, such parallels evoke what Massey might call a theological "articulated story mapping." It was, after all, precisely that area of the church floor space in Shenoute's (and indeed most similar late ancient) church structures that locates the space around the altar that is its most active and actively charged liturgical and incarnational ground. If modelled on these church dimensions, the well's floor space (however proportionally reduced) suggests at least some designed ideological connection between ordinary well water as a public good and the focal point of priestly activities in sacramental worship at the church sanctuary. While the great well was obviously built to facilitate ordinary water for ordinary purposes, it would soon take on added theological value for its role in Shenoute's ever-God-centred humanitarian aid efforts and disaster management.

One cannot, of course, "prove" that some fifth-century engineer-architects actively meditated on theology as they measured and placed the well's floor and walls. How precisely Shenoute himself was "in the weeds" of design construction remains conjecture. But texts do say that his strident control of community details included choosing and directing the monastery's construction workers.[58] Thus, given what we do know of this space, and of Shenoute himself, we may reasonably posit that the shape of the well reflected some theological message.

Caroline Schroeder has noted how "the church building functions as a potent symbol of Shenoute's theology . . . his building projects offering a moment for theological reflection on the nature of the communal . . . life"[59] And Shenoute himself said that physical church design can and should point to more "spiritual" meanings. In "God is Holy," he wrote:

> Just as it is good to decorate what is external, it is even better to decorate what is internal. I am talking about the church. . . . Every adornment . . . in the house of God . . . in every place in it . . . are good, and it is possible for us to bring them to the spiritual, since they are fleshly things, like the water that became wine in Cana of Galilee.[60]

Thus, it seems entirely possible—at this particular site, given the particular personality of this monastic leader—that we have here an example of a public water supply in Christian late antiquity built with deliberate intent to identify, indeed *shape*, religious meaning directly pertinent to healthcare. The well was, after all, not a baptistery. It served everyone—monks, guests, and outsiders. Its water not only took different literal shapes—according to container, environment, weather; it also shaped users, through the physiology of absorption, ingestion, cleansing, and excretion. By it, Shenoute's theological messaging flowed into public health and civic therapeutics. These connections might have been strengthened by, if ultimately independent of, mathematical dimensions.

We might, therefore, consider the well as one of those (in Massey's terms) "moments in networks of social relations." To walk between well, church, and amidst the imagined crowds of refugees would indeed resemble "walking across a multitude of stories" marked by a "constellation" of gaps in their diverse trajectories. Nor is this narrative journey simply an act of neatly distanced scholars carefully reading the site reports. We ourselves are a part of Massey's imagined dotted line in that we, too, bring to it our own stories. We too attempt to walk across (and sometimes fall through) the grounded differences of religious and public health meanings in such space.

Ancient medicine and healthcare took place at the intersections of such imagined spaces and stories. Shenoute's sermon, "A priest will never cease," reminds us of this in his association of spiritual health with "the blessing with which the priests bless us, as he treats us in the doctor's office, which is the church."[61] Wendy Mayer and others have noted how theological *medicine* was, for many Christian writers in late antiquity, a core theme in both homiletics and the mundane service of the body for a healthy soul.[62] Both sermon and service directly—sometimes literally—paired the late ancient "science" of medicine with construction of meaning that affirmed theological humanity.

Conclusion

In conclusion, the enduring presence of ancient narratives about water ethics, and the enduring subterranean presence of Shenoute's great well point to a spatial construction of theology that moves within and intersects with a multitude of stories, past and present. As water continues to mean life—and death—around the world today, religious meanings persist in shaping airs, waters, and places. Whether our water ethic views such concerns through what Mormon environmentalist Terry Tempest Williams calls "an ecology of awe"[63] or as what João Biehl and Peter Locke call an "unfinished anthropology of becoming," these cross-disciplinary frames, from antiquity to Sustainable Development Goal 6, suggest that theology still needs to "get real" in the hydrological cycle and spaces of civic and global wellness.

Notes

1 Early versions of this essay were delivered at the Spirituality, Theology and Health Research Seminar in the Department of Theology and Religion at the University of Durham (UK) in 2018, at the Oxford Patristics Conference, and at the New England Medieval Conference held at Brown University, both in 2019. I thank the organizers of those sessions as well as all who participated in discussion and who offered critical feedback; all errors remain my own.
2 United Nations General Assembly Resolution 64/292: The Human Right to Water and Sanitation, July 28, 2010. https://documents-dds-ny.un.org/doc/UNDOC/GEN/N09/479/35/PDF/N0947935.pdf?OpenElement. For recent updates and publications issued during 2020 as part of the Resolution's tenth anniversary, see www.ohchr.org/EN/Issues/WaterAndSanitation/SRWater/Pages/10Anniversary.aspx. For the latest on global water concerns, see UN Water, www.unwater.org. These twenty-first-century affirmations build on the 1966 International Covenant on Economic, Social and Cultural Rights (ICESCR), Article 12, which affirms the human right to "the enjoyment of the highest attainable standard of physical and mental health" and includes in that not only disease control and medical services but also "all aspects of environmental and industrial hygiene" (12.2.b). The Committee on Economic, Social and Cultural Rights (CESCR)'s General Comment 14 on ICESCR Art. 12, the right to health, Section 12, clarifies that health rights include "safe and potable drinking water and adequate sanitation facilities," and mandates that such water and facilities be *available, accessible, acceptable*, and of scientifically and medically *appropriate* good quality. A Resolution is not a law, and even international covenants must be ratified by member states; the United States, for example, never ratified the ICESCR and, as the often woeful state of its water (discussed below) demonstrates, still does not legally recognize a judiciable right to water.
3 https://sdgs.un.org/goals/goal6.
4 Water as an essential nutrient is included, for example, in the US government–supported national standards published and periodically updated since 1941, the United States Recommended Dietary Allowances, now known as Dietary Reference Intakes (https://ods.od.nih.gov/Health_Information/Dietary_Reference_Intakes.aspx). Current DRIs for water and electrolytes are summarized at www.nap.edu/read/10925/chapter/1.
5 Jean Ziegler, Christophe Golay, Claire Mahon, and Sally-Anne Way, *The Fight for the Right to Food: Lessons Learned*. International Relations and Development (Geneva: Palgrave Macmillan, 2011), 377. For more on the Special Rapporteur on the Right to Food, see www.ohchr.org/en/issues/food/pages/foodindex.aspx.
6 www.unwater.org/sdg6-action-space/.
7 The 1948 United Declaration on Human Rights (UDHR), Article 25, affirms universal human rights to "food, clothing, housing and medical care and necessary social services." Water is not mentioned but, given its identity with nutrition, sanitation, and hygiene, could be implicitly argued within several of these Article 25 rights. The 1966

International Covenant on Civil and Political Rights (ICCPR, which the United States has ratified) focuses chiefly on the court system, but includes articles that affirm, for example, every person's "inherent right to life" (Article 6), forbids torture or "cruel, inhuman or degrading treatment" (Article 7), and affirms treating persons "with humanity and with respect for the inherent dignity of the human person" (Article 10), which all might also be core in basic provision of water. Both CESCR's General Comment 12 on "the right to adequate food" (1999, Article 11) and the 1974 Declaration on the Eradication of Hunger and Malnutrition (DEH&M) focus on freedom from hunger and malnutrition without naming water per se. However, the DEH&M's focus on agriculture does affirm the need to promote "rational" use of "marine and inland water sources" (Para. 5), and internal collaboration to properly conserve "natural resources . . . to facilitate the preservation of the environment, including the marine environment" (Para. 9).

8 United Nations Development Programme, *Human Development Report 2006: Beyond Scarcity: Power, Poverty and the Global Water Crisis* (New York: United Nations Development Programme [UNDP], 2006), 1.

9 UN Water, *Summary Progress Update 2021-SDG 6: Water and Sanitation for All* (Geneva: UN Water, 2021), 5, www.unwater.org/publications/summary-progress-update-2021-sdg-6-water-and-sanitation-all.

10 As quoted in "Water and Sanitation in a Post-COVID World [Editorial]," *The Lancet Global Health* September 2020; 8: e1101, www.thelancet.com/journals/langlo/arti cle/PIIS2214-109X(20)30368-5/fulltext, citing the WHO/UNICEF Joint Monitoring Programme for Water Supply, Sanitation and Hygiene (JMP)'s *WASH in Health Care Facilities* global baseline report, available at www.who.int/water_sanitation_health/publications/wash-in-health-care-facilities-global-report/en/.

11 UN Water, *Summary Progress Update 2021*, 20.

12 Steve de Gruchy, "Water and Spirit: Theology in the Time of Cholera," *The Ecumenical Review* 2010; 62(2): 198.

13 For more on the Jordan River and environmental theology, see also Christiana Zenner, *Just Water: Theology, Ethics, and Fresh Water Crises: Revised Edition* (Maryknoll: Orbis, 2018), especially 168–90.

14 These principles are listed in "Water and Spirit," (200), and developed in more detail in Steve de Gruchy, "Dealing with Our Own Sewage: Spirituality and Ethics in the Sustainability Agenda," *Journal of Theology for Southern Africa* July 2009; 134: 53–65, originally delivered as an address to the World Conference on Theologies of Liberation, Belem, Brazil, January 2009. He also tells the story of his environmental and political action pertinent to water in " 'A Pain in the Neck to the Powers that Be:' Steve de Gruchy on the Olive Agenda," www.youtube.com/watch?v=UxeClAwvlos. The fifth ethic, celebration, resonates closely with Pope Francis' encyclical summons in 2015: "In union with all creatures, we journey through this land seeking God . . . Let us sing as we go. May our struggles and our concern for this planet never take away the joy of our hope." *Laudato Si'* section IX, chapter 244, www.vatican.va/content/francesco/en/encyclicals/documents/papa-francesco_20150524_enciclica-laudato-si.html.

15 Isabel Apawo Phiri, "God of Life Lead Us to Water Justice," the Steve de Gruchy Memorial Lecture, Rodebosch United Church, Cape Town, South Africa, April 24, 2018, www.oikoumene.org/en/resources/documents/general-secretary/steve-de-gruchy-memorial-lecture-rodebosch-united-church-cape-town-south-africa-by-prof-dr-isabel-apawo-phiri-24-april-2018.

16 For more on practical solutions, see, for example, WWAP (United Nations World Water Assessment Programme)/UN-Water, *The United Nations World Water Development Report 2018: Nature-Based Solutions for Water* (Paris: UNESCO, 2018), www.unesco.org/new/en/natural-sciences/environment/water/wwap/wwdr/2018-nature-based-solutions; *Water and Sanitation for Health: Facility Improvement Tool (WASH FIT): A Practical Guide for Improving Quality of Care through Water Sanitation and Hygiene*

in Health Care Facilities (Geneva: World Health Organization, 2017), www.who.int/ water_sanitation_health/publications/water-and-sanitation-for-health-facility-improve ment-tool/en/. For gender disparity in water access, see the work of the United Nations World Water Assessment Programme (WWAP), for example, Amber J. Fletcher and Roselie Schonewille, *Overview of Resources on Gender-sensitive Data Related to Water*, WWAP Gender Series 4 (Paris: UNESCO, 2015); Joni Seager, *Sex-Disaggregating Indicators for Water Assessment Monitoring and Reporting*, WWAP Gender Series 1 (Paris: UNESCO, 2015), www.unesco.org/new/en/natural-sciences/environment/water/wwap.

17 Denise Kimber Buell, "The Microbes and Pneuma that Therefore I am," in *Divinanimality: Animal Theory, Creaturely Theology*, ed. Stephen D. Moore (New York: Fordham University Press, 2014), 63–87, at 72.

18 Patricia Baker and Han Nijdam, "Introductions: Conceptualizing Body, Space and Borders," in *Medicine and Space: Body, Surroundings and Borders in Antiquity and the Middle Ages*, eds. Patricia A. Baker, Han Nijdam, and Karine van't Land. Visualizing the Middle Ages 4 (Leiden: Brill, 2011), 1.

19 Henri Lefebvre, *Production of Space*, first published in 1974, English trans. Donald Nicholson-Smith (New York: Oxford University Press, 1991). For Massey's legacy, see, for example, Richard Meegan, "Doreen Massey (1944–2016): A Geographer Who Really Mattered," *Regional Studies* 2017; 51(9): 1285–96; Cristina Capineri, "Kilburn High Road Revisited," *Urban Planning* 2016; 1(2): 128–40. I thank Matthew Larsen, whose presentation at Harvard Divinity School on carceral geography in late antiquity first alerted me to Massey's work and the relevance of her approach to early Christian studies.

20 Doreen Massey, "A Global Sense of Place," first published in *Marxism Today*, June 1991; 24–9, later reprinted in Doreen Massey, *Space, Place and Gender* (Minneapolis: University of Minnesota Press, 1994), 146–56; the quote here is on 155.

21 "Doreen Massey on Time, Space, and Responsibility," lecture at the Institut für Raumexperimente, UdK Berlin, April 2013, https://vimeo.com/158902032. Quotes in this paragraph are from the online lecture.

22 "Doreen Massey on Time, Space, and Responsibility."

23 Philip van der Eijk, "Water, Health and Disease in the Hippocratic Treatise *Airs, Waters, Places*," in *Greek Medicine from Hippocrates to Galen: Selected Papers*, ed. Jacques Jouanna (Leiden: Brill, 2012), 155.

24 *Airs, Waters, Places*, trans. J. Chadwick and W. N. Mann, in G. E. R. Lloyd, ed., *Hippocratic Writings* (New York: Penguin Books, 1950, repr. 1978), 152–3. For more on malaria in Graeco-Roman medicine and religion, see, for example, Robert Sallares, *Malaria and Rome: A History of Malaria in Ancient Italy* (New York: Oxford University Press, 2002); and Laura D. Lane, "Malaria: Medicine and Magic in the Roman World," in *A Roman Villa and a Late Roman Infant Cemetery: Excavation at Poggio Gramignano Lugnano in Teverina*, eds. David and Noelle Soren (Rome: L'Erma di Bretschneider, 1999), 633–51; see also now Robin Lane Fox, *The Invention of Medicine: From Homer to Hippocrates* (New York: Basic Books, 2020), 246–9.

25 *Airs, Waters, Places*, trans. J. Chadwick and W.N. Mann, in G.E.R. Lloyd, ed., *Hippocratic Writings* (New York: Penguin Books, 1950, repr. 1978), 154. Celsus too said rainwater is the lightest water.

26 Pliny, *Natural History* XXII, trans. W. H. S. Jones, vol. 8, Loeb Classical Library (Cambridge: Harvard University Press, 1963), 401.

27 Galen, "On Barley Soup," in *Galen on Food and Diet*, trans. Mark Grant (London: Routledge, 2000), 62.

28 Galen, "On the Powers of Foods Book 3," in *Galen on Food and Diet*, trans. Mark Grant (London: Routledge, 2000), 187.

29 Oribasius, *Med. Comp.* 4.9, in Mark Grant, trans., *Dieting for an Emperor: A Translation of Books 1 and 4 of Oribasius' Medical Compilations with an Introduction and Commentary*, Studies in Ancient Medicine 15 (Leiden: Brill, 1997), 251.

30 Galen, "On the Powers of Foods Book 3," 174–5. A similar claim is in the Hippocratic treatise, *Regimen* II.48, where fish that feed in muddy marshy water are "heavier (of digestion)" and so unhealthy that even "the air of which also, entering a person, hurts and oppresses him," though not in this case connected with sewage (trans. W. H. S. Jones, in *Hippocrates IV* [Loeb Classical Library; Cambridge: Harvard University Press, 1979], 321).

31 Celsus, "*De Medicina* Book II.30," in *De Medicina*, trans. W. G. Spencer (Loeb Classical Library; Cambridge: Harvard University Press, 1935, reprinted 1971), Vol. 1, p. 147.

32 Ignatius of Antioch, *Eph.* 20.

33 Taylor Justison, "Water: A Matter of Life and Death," unpublished research paper for "Studies in Theology, Health, and Healing" seminar, December 9, 2019; quoted here with permission.

34 COVID-19-related safety concerns to limit Christian eucharist are obvious examples, but confessional warnings that "wrong" participation could be deadly begin in the New Testament. Of twentieth-century concerns about bacteria, see, for example, James Pellerin and Michael B. Edmond, "Infections Associated with Religious Rituals [Review]," *International Journal of Infectious Diseases* 2013; 17: e945–8.

35 See, for example, David A. Larsen and Krista R. Wigginton, "Tracking COVID-19 with Wastewater," *Nature Biotechnology* 2020; 38: 1151–3; see also, Richard C. Larson, Oded Berman, and Mehdi Nourinejad, "Sampling Manholes to Home in on SARS-CoV-2 Infections," *PLoS One* 2020; 5: e0240007, https://doi.org/10.1371/journal.pone.0240007.

36 John Scarborough, "Roman Medicine and Public Health," in *Public Health: Proceedings of the 5th International Symposium on the Comparative History of Medicine—East and West*, ed. Teizo Ogawa (Tokyo, Japan: Division of Medical History, The Taniguchi Foundation, 1980), 33–74.

37 Basil of Caesarea, "On the Martyr Julitta," trans. Susan R. Holman, in *St Basil the Great on Fasting and Feasts*, eds. and trans. Susan R. Holman and Mark Del Cogliano, Popular Patristics Series 50 (Yonkers, NY: St. Vladimir's Seminary Press, 2013), 111.

38 Basil of Caesarea, "First Homily on Fasting," trans. Mark Del Cogliano, in *St Basil the Great on Fasting and Feasts,* 71.

39 Basil of Caesarea, "Second Homily on Fasting," trans. Mark Del Cogliano, in *St Basil the Great on Fasting and Feasts*, 77.

40 Gregory of Nyssa, *Paup.* 2, trans. Holman, in Susan R. Holman *The Hungry Are Dying: Beggars and Bishops in Roman Cappadocia* (New York: Oxford University Press, 2001), 205; my emphasis.

41 Gregory of Nazianzus, *Or.* 14.12, trans. Martha Vinson, *St. Gregory of Nazianzus: Select Orations*. The Fathers of the Church (Washington, DC: Catholic University of America Press, 2003), 47.

42 "O guest-friend [or stranger], you see here the statue of a woman who was pious and very wise, Scholastikia. She provided a great sum of gold to [construct or repair] the part of the [buildings] here that had fallen down." Trans. Mary R. Lefkowitz and Maureen B. Fant, *Women's Life in Greece & Rome: A Sourcebook in Translation,* 2nd ed. (London: Duckworth, 1992), 161. The precarious location of this bath complex on a steep hillside is obvious to the modern viewer, though the sloping may not necessarily reflect its fifth-century topography.

43 Theodoret, *Ep.* 81, to Nomus, trans. Blomfield Jackson, *Nicene and Post-Nicene Fathers (NPNF)*, series 2, vol. 3 (Grand Rapids: Wm. B. Eerdmans, 1983, 1892, reprinted), 277.

44 See, for example, James Crow, Jonathan Bardill, and Richard Bayliss, *The Water Supply of Byzantine Constantinople*, Journal of Roman Studies Monograph 11 (London: Society for the Promotion of Roman Studies, 2008).

45 Procopius, *Buildings*, trans. H. B. Dewing and Glanville Downey, Loeb Classical Library (Cambridge: Harvard University Press, 1940).

46 Wendy Mayer and Pauline Allen, *The Churches of Syrian Antioch (300–638 CE)*, Late
    Antique History and Religion (Leuven: Peeters, 2012), especially 32–49 and 292–320
    (Figs. 7–57). Figure 28 is a sketch of "Distribution of Plumbing" (p. 304) and Figs.
    28–33 (pp. 304–7) focus on the church's plumbing pipes. The pipes may lead to rooms
    "where certain of the clergy had their quarters" or rooms "being used to generate income
    through an activity that produced a quantity of waste water" (39). Mayer also notes (36)
    that "individual segments of ceramic pipes are cemented together, a technique that sug-
    gests that they were intended to carry pressurized water (that is, water into a building)
    rather than waste." See also, Wendy Mayer, "The Late Antique Church at Qausiyeh
    Reconsidered: Memory and Martyr Burial in Syrian Antioch," in *Martyrdom and Perse-
    cution in Late Antique Christianity: Festschrift Boudewijn Dehandschutter*, ed. J. Lee-
    mans (Leuven: Peeters, 2010), 161–77. This prominent church and popular veneration
    site may have been the burial site of the bishop Meletius, whose death while presiding
    over the Council of Constantinople in 381 meant so much to the subsequent career (and
    resignation) of Gregory of Nazianzus.
47 Mark Stoyle, *Water in the City: The Aqueducts and Underground Passages of Exeter*
    (Exeter: The University of Exeter Press, 2014). I remain forever grateful to the Right Rev-
    erend Robert Atwell, Bishop of Exeter, for his hospitality and trust when I crawled through
    these medieval subterranean tunnels with the Bishop's Palace house key in my pocket.
48 For a summary of the scholarship and visual imagery of the site, see, for example,
    "Yale in Egypt," https://egyptology.yale.edu/expeditions/current-expeditions/yale-
    monastic-archaeology-project-south-sohag/white-monastery. For a critical edition of
    Shenoute's writings, see Stephen Emmel, *Shenoute's Literary Corpus*, vol. 2 (Leuven:
    Peeters, 2004). My discussion here draws largely on the site reports and select transla-
    tions noted below, and on Ariel G. López, *Shenoute of Atripe and the Uses of Poverty:
    Rural Patronage, Religious Conflict, and Monasticism in Late Antique Egypt* (Berke-
    ley: University of California Press, 2013). Shenoute's church at the White Monastery
    complex was massive; López, for example (98), says that the Church of St. Catherine's
    monastery in Sinai would have fit four times over inside it. At its peak, the community
    may have contained more than 500 monks; Louise Blanke, "Life on the Edge of the
    Desert: A Late Antique Monastery and Its Water Supply," in *Water of Life: Proceedings
    of the Danish Institute in Damascus 11*, eds. John Kuhlmann Madsen, Nils Overgaard
    Anderson, and Ingolf Thuesen (Copenhagen: Danish Institute in Damascus, 2016), 131.
49 Shenoute of Atripe, *Continuing to Glorify the Lord*, trans. and discussed in detail in
    López, *Shenoute of Atripe and the Uses of Poverty*, 57–62. On the date soon after
    451, see Stephen Emmel, "The Historical Circumstances of Shenoute's Sermon 'God
    Is Blessed'," in *Themelia: Spätantike und koptologische Studien: Peter Grossmann
    zum 65 Geburtstag*, eds. Martin Krause and Sofia Schaten, Sprachen und Kulturen des
    Christlichen Orients 3 (Wiesbaden: Reichert, 1998), 81–96. Emmel notes that the places
    named suggest the barbarian invasions had affected cities and towns in a 250-km range
    south of the monastery.
50 Three surviving sermons (the last three texts in Canon 7) mention the refugee crisis:
    "God is Blessed"; "Continuing to Glorify the Lord"; and "The Rest of the Words."
    His sermon "The Rest of the Words," for instance, was preached in a time "when the
    barbarians despoiled [the land] . . . at the time also when this large crowd dwelled with
    us in their flight from those Ethiopians." For details and translations, I follow López,
    Shenoute of Atripe and the Uses of Poverty, as noted above.
51 The full passage reads: "Seven doctors healed those who were sick among them and
    those who had been wounded with arrows or spear, and we paid their salary, which
    amounted to 500,000 [myriads of] *denarii* (lit. 'money'). Fifty [men] and forty-four
    [women] who died were buried by us, *with our property. But it is [really] the property of
    the King, Christ.* For the need of those [women] who gave birth to fifty-two [babies] we
    spent sometimes 25,000, sometimes 30,000 [myriads of *denarii]* on boiled vegetables

every week, besides the vegetables that we have [in the monastery]. One hundred and fifty *sextarii* (ca. 75 litres) of oil was the daily measure used for cooking every day; of lentils, sometimes 17, sometimes 16 *artabas* (1 *artaba* = ca. 30 kg) or even more daily. Four ovens were baking bread daily, some days 18, others 19, 20, 17, or 16 palms [?], and it was [all] eaten. And we did not allow the brothers to eat from them, so that they (i.e. the refugees) would find enough. And [still] it was not enough for them. And besides we took care of all their numerous animals, camels, sheep and calves, cows, dogs, goats, and all their baggage. And also the small spring was wonderful, *for had He* (i.e. God) *not blessed it,* it would not have been enough for them to drink water" (trans. López, *Shenoute of Atripe and the Uses of Poverty*, 58).

52 Peter Grossmann, Darlene L. Brooks Hedstrom, and Said Mohamad Osman, "Second Report on the Excavation in the Monastery of Apa Shenute (Dayr Anba Shinuda) at Suhag," *Dumbarton Oaks Papers* 2009; 63: 188–9; the full report is on pp. 167–219; I focus on section 1.1.6, "Further Observations on the Great Well," pp. 186–9. The authors note that the Coptic *Life* refers to the events but only to the smaller, earlier well. On the Arabic life, cf. J. Leipoldt, "Berichte Shenutes über Einfälle der Nibier in Ägypten," *Zeitschrift für ägyptische Sprache und Altertumskunde* 1902–3; 40: 126–40.

53 "The lower end of the stairway, which is covered by water, was not excavated." Grossmann et al., "Second Report," 189. The threshold in winter is about 1.10 m above the water table (186).

54 Louise Blanke, *An Archaeology of Egyptian Monasticism: Settlement, Economy, and Daily Life at the White Monastery Federation*, Yale Egyptological Publications 2 (New Haven: Yale Egyptology, 2019), 122–33; the quote is on p. 130.

55 Peter Grossmann, Darlene Brooks-Hedstrom, Mohamed Abdal-Rassul, and Elizabeth S. Bolman, "The Excavation in the Monastery of Apa Shenute (Dayr Anba Shinuda) at Suhag, with an Appendix on Documentary Photography at the Monasteries of Anba Shinuda and Anba Bishoi, Suhag, by Elizabeth S. Bolman," *Dumbarton Oaks Papers* 2004; 58: 371–82, at 379.

56 Peter Grossmann et al., "Second Report on the Excavation in the Monastery of Apa Shenute (Dayr Anba Shinuda) at Suhag," 188. López, *Shenoute of Atripe and the Uses of Poverty* (161, n. 11) follows Grossmann in noting that the well "was built by the same architects as the great church."

57 I thank Amanda Luyster and Robin Fleming for comments and questions on this point.

58 We are told he himself "arranged for the workmen and craftsmen, the stonemasons and the carpenters," for the church building. And his sermons also speak of "The buildings that we have built" (López, *Shenoute of Atripe and the Uses of Poverty*, 47). These buildings as identified by the site excavations also included a series of latrines, basins, and washing areas, one directly adjacent to the great well.

59 These reflections may have been fresh on his mind as the refugees arrived, since the chronological nexus of sermons on the church and sermons on the crisis in the same codex (Canon 7) illustrates at least (says Schroeder) that Shenoute happened to be writing on both at the same time. See Caroline T. Schroeder, *Monastic Bodies: Discipline and Salvation in Shenoute of Atripe* (Philadelphia: University of Pennsylvania Press, 2007), 118; for further discussion, see especially her chapter 3, "The Church Building as Symbol of Ascetic Renunciation," 90–125. Schroeder also notes how both Shenoute's five sermons on church construction are contained within the same text (Canon 7) as his three that mention the refugee crisis: "The texts treating these two seemingly disparate events seem to have been collected together in one codex due to their chronology." (Schroeder, *Monastic Bodies*, 93).

60 López gives his source here as "C7.1, "God is Holy," in ShA2, pp. 144–5 and ShA2, p. 156. He also notes how Caroline Schroeder "puts Shenoute's rhetoric on the church in the context of his 'one-body ideology' (p. 68) manifest throughout the Canons" (López, *Shenoute of Atripe and the Uses of Poverty*, 161, n. 9). See discussion below.

61 Shenoute, "A Priest Will Never Cease, trans. Andrew Crislip," in *Selected Discourses of Shenoute the Great: Community, Theology, and Social Conflict in Late Antique Egypt*, eds. and trans. David Brakke and Andrew Crislip (New York: Cambridge University Press, 2015), 140. On medical imagery in Shenoute more broadly, see for example, Andrew Crislip, "Shenoute of Atripe on Christ the Physician and the Cure of Souls," *Le Muséon* 2009; 122(3–4): 247–77.
62 See, for example, Wendy Mayer, "Medicine and Metaphor in Late Antiquity." *Studies in Late Antiquity* 2018; 2(4): 440–63. See also now Jonathan L. Zecher, *Spiritual Direction as a Medical Art in Early Christian Monasticism*, Oxford Early Christian Studies (London: Oxford University Press, 2022).
63 Terry Tempest Williams, *Hour of Land: A Personal Topography of America's National Parks* (New York: Sarah Crichton Books/Farrar, Straus & Giroux, 2016), 41. An edited version of the lecture is in Terry Tempest Williams, *Erosion: Essays of Undoing* (New York: Farrar, Straus, & Giroux, 2019), 311–14. See also, João Biehl and Peter Locke, *Unfinished: The Anthropology of Becoming* (Durham: Duke University Press, 2017).

Bibliography

Ancient Sources

Basil of Caesarea. "First Homily on Fasting." In *St Basil the Great on Fasting and Feasts*, ed. and trans. Susan R. Holman and Mark Del Cogliano. Popular Patristics Series 50. Yonkers, NY: St. Vladimir's Seminary Press, 2013. Pp. 55–71.

———. "On the Martyr Julitta." In *St Basil the Great on Fasting and Feasts*, ed. and trans. Susan R. Holman and Mark Del Cogliano. Popular Patristics Series 50. Yonkers, NY: St. Vladimir's Seminary Press, 2013. Pp. 109–22.

———. "Second Homily on Fasting." In *St Basil the Great on Fasting and Feasts*, ed. and trans. Susan R. Holman and Mark Del Cogliano. Popular Patristics Series 50. Yonkers, NY: St. Vladimir's Seminary Press, 2013. Pp. 73–81.

Celsus. *De Medicina* (vol. 3). Trans. W. G. Spencer. Loeb Classical Library. Cambridge: Harvard University Press, 1935, repr. 1971.

Galen. "On the Powers of Foods." In *Galen on Food and Diet*, trans. Mark Grant. London: Routledge, 2000. Pp. 68–190.

Gregory of Nazianzus. "Oration 14: On Love for the Poor." In *St. Gregory of Nazianzus: Select Orations*, ed. Martha Vinson. The Fathers of the Church. Washington, DC: Catholic University of America Press, 2003. Pp. 39–71.

Gregory of Nyssa. "On the Love of the Poor: 2, On the Saying 'Whoever Has Done It to One of These Has Done It To Me'" [In illud: Quatenus uni ex his fecistis mihi fecistis]. In *The Hungry Are Dying: Beggars and Bishops in Roman Cappadocia*, ed. Susan R. Holman. Studies in Historical Theology. New York: Oxford University Press, 2001. Pp. 199–206.

Hippocrates. Lloyd, G. E. R., ed. *Hippocratic Writings*. New York: Penguin Books, 1950, repr. 1978.

Ignatius of Antioch. "Letter to the Ephesians." In *The Apostolic Fathers*, trans. Bart D. Ehrman, vol. 1. Loeb Classical Library. Cambridge: Harvard University Press, 2003. Pp. 218–41.

Oribasius. Mark Grant, ed. and trans. *Dieting for an Emperor: A Translation of Books 1 and 4 of Oribasius' Medical Compilations with an Introduction and Commentary*. Studies in Ancient Medicine 15. Leiden: Brill, 1997.

Pliny. *Natural History*, trans. W. H. S. Jones, vol. 8. Loeb Classical Library. Cambridge: Harvard University Press, 1963.

Procopius. *Buildings*, trans. H. B. Dewing and Glanville Downey. Loeb Classical Library. Cambridge: Harvard University Press, 1940.

Shenoute. "A Priest Will Never Cease," trans. Andrew Crislip. In *Selected Discourses of Shenoute the Great: Community, Theology, and Social Conflict in Late Antique Egypt*, ed. and trans. David Brakke and Andrew Crislip. New York: Cambridge University Press, 2015. Pp. 137–45.

Shenoute of Atripe. "Continuing to Glorify the Lord." In *Shenoute of Atripe and the Uses of Poverty: Rural Patronage, Religious Conflict, and Monasticism in Late Antique Egypt*, trans. Ariel G. López. Berkeley: University of California Press, 2013. Pp. 57–62.

Theodoret. Blomfield Jackson, trans. *Nicene and Post-Nicene Fathers (NPNF)*, Series 2, vol. 3. Grand Rapids: Wm. B. Eerdmans, 1983.

Modern Sources

Baker, Patricia, and Han Nijdam. "Introductions: Conceptualizing Body, Space and Borders." In *Medicine and Space: Body, Surroundings and Borders in Antiquity and the Middle Ages*, ed. Patricia A. Baker, Han Nijdam, and Karine van't Land. Visualizing the Middle Ages 4. Leiden: Brill, 2011.

Blanke, Louise. "Life on the Edge of the Desert: A Late Antique Monastery and Its Water Supply." In *Water of Life: Proceedings of the Danish Institute in Damascus 11*, ed. John Kuhlmann Madsen, Nils Overgaard Anderson, and Ingolf Thuesen. Copenhagen: Danish Institute in Damascus, 2016.

———. *An Archaeology of Egyptian Monasticism: Settlement, Economy, and Daily Life at the White Monastery Federation*. Yale Egyptological Publications 2. New Haven: Yale Egyptology, 2019.

Buell, Denise Kimber. "The Microbes and Pneuma That Therefore I am." In *Divinanimality: Animal Theory, Creaturely Theology*, ed. Stephen D. Moore. New York: Fordham University Press, 2014. Pp. 63–87.

Capineri, Cristina. "Kilburn High Road Revisited." *Urban Planning* 2016; 1(2): 128–40.

Crislip, Andrew. "Shenoute of Atripe on Christ the Physician and the Cure of Souls." *Le Muséon* 2009; 122(3–4): 247–77.

Crow, James, Jonathan Bardill, and Richard Bayliss. *The Water Supply of Byzantine Constantinople*. Journal of Roman Studies Monograph 11. London: Society for the Promotion of Roman Studies, 2008.

De Gruchy, Steve. "Dealing with Our Own Sewage: Spirituality and Ethics in the Sustainability Agenda." *Journal of Theology for Southern Africa* July 2009; 134: 53–65.

———. "Water and Spirit: Theology in the Time of Cholera." *The Ecumenical Review* 2010; 62(2): 188–201.

———. "'A Pain in the Neck to the Powers That Be:' Steve de Gruchy on the Olive Agenda." Interview originally filmed by John G. Clark "several weeks" prior to de Gruchy's death in February 2010; posted online and dated May 12, 2017. www.youtube.com/watch?v=UxeClAwvlos.

Emmel, Stephen. "The Historical Circumstances of Shenute's Sermon 'God Is Blessed'." In *Themelia: Spätantike und koptologische Studien: Peter Grossmann zum 65 Geburtstag*, ed. Martin Krause and Sofia Schaten. Sprachen und Kulturen des Christlichen Orients 3. Wiesbaden: Reichert, 1998. Pp. 81–96.

———. *Shenoute's Literary Corpus*, vol. 2. Corpus Scriptorum Christianorum Orientalium 599. Leuven: Peeters, 2004.

Fletcher, Amber J., and Roselie Schonewille. *Overview of Resources on Gender-Sensitive Data Related to Water*. WWAP Gender Series 4. Paris: UNESCO, 2015.

Fox, Robin Lane. *The Invention of Medicine: From Homer to Hippocrates*. New York: Basic Books, 2020.

Grossmann, Peter, Darlene Brooks-Hedstrom, Mohamed Abdal-Rassul, and Elizabeth S. Bolman. "The Excavation in the Monastery of Apa Shenute (Dayr Anba Shinuda) at Suhag, with an Appendix on Documentary Photography at the Monasteries of Anba Shinuda and Anba Bishoi, Suhag, by Elizabeth S. Bolman." *Dumbarton Oaks Papers* 2004; 58: 371–82.

Grossmann, Peter, Darlene L. Brooks Hedstrom, and Said Mohamad Osman. "Second Report on the Excavation in the Monastery of Apa Shenute (Dayr Anba Shinuda) at Suhag." *Dumbarton Oaks Papers* 2009; 63: 167–219.

Lane, Laura D. "Malaria: Medicine and Magic in the Roman World." In *A Roman Villa and a Late Roman Infant Cemetery: Excavation at Poggio Gramignano Lugnano in Teverina*, ed. David and Noelle Soren. Rome: L'Erma di Bretschneider, 1999. Pp. 633–51.

Larsen, David A., and Krista R. Wigginton. "Tracking COVID-19 with Wastewater." *Nature Biotechnology* 2020; 38: 1151–3.

Larson, Richard C., Oded Berman, and Mehdi Nourinejad. "Sampling Manholes to Home in on SARS-CoV-2 Infections." *PLoS One* 2020; 5: e0240007. https://doi.org/10.1371/journal.pone.0240007.

Lefebvre, Henri. *Production of Space*, trans. Donald Nicholson-Smith. New York: Oxford University Press, 1991.

Leipoldt, J. "Berichte Shenutes über Einfälle der Nibier in Ägypten." *Zeitschrift für ägyptische Sprache und Altertumskunde* 1902–3; 40: 126–40.

López, Ariel G. *Shenoute of Atripe and the Uses of Poverty: Rural Patronage, Religious Conflict, and Monasticism in Late Antique Egypt*. Berkeley: University of California Press, 2013.

Massey, Doreen. "A Global Sense of Place." first published in *Marxism Today*, June 1991; 24–9, reprinted in Doreen Massey, *Space, Place and Gender*. Minneapolis: University of Minnesota Press, 1994. Pp. 146–56.

———. "Doreen Massey on Time, Space, and Responsibility." Online lecture, Institut für Raumexperimente, UdK Berlin, April 2013. https://vimeo.com/158902032.

Mayer, Wendy. "The Late Antique Church at Qausiyeh Reconsidered: Memory and Martyr Burial in Syrian Antioch." In *Martyrdom and Persecution in Late Antique Christianity: Festschrift Boudewijn Dehandschutter*, ed. J. Leemans. Leuven: Peeters, 2010. Pp. 161–77.

———. "Medicine and Metaphor in Late Antiquity." *Studies in Late Antiquity* 2018; 2(4): 440–63.

Mayer, Wendy, and Pauline Allen. *The Churches of Syrian Antioch (300–638 CE)*. Late Antique History and Religion. Leuven: Peeters, 2012.

Meegan, Richard. "Doreen Massey (1944–2016): A Geographer Who Really Mattered." *Regional Studies* 2017; 51(9): 1285–96.

National Institutes of Health, Office of Dietary Supplements. "Dietary Reference Intakes." https://ods.od.nih.gov/HealthInformation/nutrientrecommendations.aspx#dri.

Pellerin, James, and Michael B. Edmond. "Infections Associated with Religious Rituals [Review]." *International Journal of Infectious Diseases* 2013; 17: e945–8.

Phiri, Isabel Apawo. "God of Life Lead Us to Water Justice." The Steve de Gruchy Memorial Lecture, Rodebosch United Church, Cape Town, South Africa, April 24, 2018. www.oikoumene.org/en/resources/documents/general-secretary/

steve-de-gruchy-memorial-lecture-rodebosch-united-church-cape-town-south-africa-by-prof-dr-isabel-apawo-phiri-24-april-2018.

Pope Francis. "*Laudato Si*'[On Care for Our Common Home] [Encyclical letter]." 2015. www.vatican.va/content/francesco/en/encyclicals/documents/papa-francesco_20150524_enciclica-laudato-si.html.

Sallares, Robert. *Malaria and Rome: A History of Malaria in Ancient Italy*. New York: Oxford University Press, 2002.

Scarborough, John. "Roman Medicine and Public Health." In *Public Health: Proceedings of the 5th International Symposium on the Comparative History of Medicine—East and West*, ed. Teizo Ogawa. Tokyo, Japan: Division of Medical History, The Taniguchi Foundation, 1980. Pp. 33–74.

Schroeder, Caroline T. *Monastic Bodies: Discipline and Salvation in Shenoute of Atripe*. Philadelphia: University of Pennsylvania Press, 2007.

Seager, Joni. *Sex-Disaggregating Indicators for Water Assessment Monitoring and Reporting*. WWAP Gender Series 1. Paris: UNESCO, 2015. www.unesco.org/new/en/natural-sciences/environment/water/wwap.

Stoyle, Mark. *Water in the City: The Aqueducts and Underground Passages of Exeter*. Exeter, UK: The University of Exeter Press, 2014.

UN Water, *Summary Progress Update 2021-SDG 6—Water and Sanitation for All*. Geneva: UN Water, 2021. www.unwater.org/publications/summary-progress-update-2021-sdg-6-water-and-sanitation-all.

United Nations. "Universal Declaration of Human Rights." United Nations General Assembly Resolution 217A, December 10, 1948. www.un.org/en/about-us/universal-declaration-of-human-rights.

———. "International Covenant on Civil and Political Rights." United Nations General Assembly Resolution 2200A (XXI), December 16, 1966. www.ohchr.org/en/instruments-mechanisms/instruments/international-covenant-civil-and-political-rights.

———. *Universal Declaration on the Eradication of Hunger and Malnutrition*. Geneva: U.N. General Assembly (28th session, 1973–1974). https://digitallibrary.un.org/record/57723?ln=en.

———. "United Nations General Assembly Resolution 64/292: The Human Right to Water and Sanitation." July 28, 2010. https://documents-dds-ny.un.org/doc/UNDOC/GEN/N09/479/35/PDF/N0947935.pdf?OpenElement.

———. "Goal 6: Ensure Availability and Sustainable Management of Water and Sanitation for All." UN Department of Economic and Social Affairs: Sustainable Development, 2022. https://sdgs.un.org/goals/goal6.

——— "Special Rapporteur on the Rights to Water and Sanitation." United Nations Office of the High Commissioner for Human Rights (OHCHR), 2022. www.ohchr.org/en/special-procedures/sr-water-and-sanitation.

United Nations Committee on Economic, Social and Cultural Rights. "CESCR General Comment No. 12: The Right to Adequate Food (Art. 11)." May 12, 1999. www.refworld.org/docid/4538838c11.html.

United Nations Development Programme. *Human Development Report 2006: Beyond Scarcity: Power, Poverty and the Global Water Crisis*. New York: United Nations Development Programme [UNDP], 2006.

Van der Eijk, Philip. "Water, Health and Disease in the Hippocratic Treatise *Airs, Waters, Places*." In *Greek Medicine from Hippocrates to Galen: Selected Papers*, ed. Jacques Jouanna. Leiden: Brill, 2012.

"Water and Sanitation in a Post-COVID World [Editorial]." *The Lancet Global Health* September 2020; 8: e1101. www.thelancet.com/journals/langlo/article/PIIS2214-109X (20)30368-5/fulltext.

WHO/UNICEF Joint Monitoring Programme for Water Supply. "WASH in Health Care Facilities." www.who.int/water_sanitation_health/publications/wash-in-health-care-faci lities-global-report/en/.

Williams, Terry Tempest. *Hour of Land: A Personal Topography of America's National Parks*. New York: Sarah Crichton Books/Farrar, Straus & Giroux, 2016.

———. "The Liturgy of Home." Ingersoll Lecture on Immortality, Harvard Divinity School, April 12, 2018, initially published in *Harvard Divinity Bulletin*, Spring/Summer 2018. https://bulletin.hds.harvard.edu/the-liturgy-of-home/. Reprinted in Terry Tempest Williams, *Erosion: Essays of Undoing*. New York: Farrar, Straus, & Giroux, 2019. Pp. 311–14.

World Health Organization. *Water and Sanitation for Health: Facility Improvement Tool (WASH FIT): A Practical Guide for Improving Quality of Care Through Water Sanitation and Hygiene in Health Care Facilities*. Geneva: World Health Organization, 2017. www.who.int/water_sanitation_health/publications/water-and-sanitation-for-health-facility-improvement-tool/en/.

WWAP (United Nations World Water Assessment Programme)/UN-Water. *The United Nations World Water Development Report 2018: Nature-Based Solutions for Water*. Paris: UNESCO, 2018. www.unesco.org/new/en/natural-sciences/environment/water/wwap/wwdr/2018-nature-based-solutions.

Zecher, Jonathan L. *Spiritual Direction as a Medical Art in Early Christian Monasticism*. Oxford Early Christian Studies. London: Oxford University Press, 2022.

Zenner, Christiana. *Just Water: Theology, Ethics, and Fresh Water Crises: Revised Edition*. Maryknoll: Orbis, 2018.

Ziegler, Jean, Christophe Golay, Claire Mahon, and Sally-Anne Way. *The Fight for the Right to Food: Lessons Learned*. International Relations and Development. Geneva: Palgrave Macmillan, 2011.

Reflections

Reflections

10 Intersecting Christian Antiquity and Modern Healthcare

Brenda Llewellyn Ihssen

Introduction

Historically, healthcare considered all aspects of a person's life: physical, spiritual, emotional, economic, linguistic, familial, and social; physicians paid attention to the patient by seeing them as they were, by listening to what they said and did not say and by asking a variety of questions.[1] This was the norm in the classical world, in late antiquity, and in high- and late-medieval centuries in Europe and the Middle East. Only in the past two centuries, with the advance of biomedical sciences and evidence-based medical practice, have many countries shifted from this model, somewhat to the peril of patients and frustration of physicians.[2] With religion and medicine on distinct paths, it is tempting and reductive to ask each to remain in their lane. But human frailty and the nuance of our existence makes it clear that this is an unproductive approach to these fields. The ongoing project of viral disease is resolutely met by an ever-growing understanding of the body and mind for the scientific community, but disease, illness, and disability impact the soul as much as the body and must be addressed as such; this is both the cultural worldview and argument of many of the early Christian texts explored by our authors. In a contemporary setting, analysis of the relationship between religion and medicine is sometimes seen as inappropriate, even self-indulgent, or dangerous,[3] with no clear consensus among medical professionals about appropriate ways to approach the juncture of religion and medicine.[4] But it is an essential crossroad, and no devil stands there.

I have interacted with three chapters in the foregoing collection as highlighting the variety of disciplinary approaches and ways that we can identify and engage "intersections" when reading texts from late antiquity for the purpose of not only better (or different) understanding of late antique narratives and approaches to medical care, but also for the purpose of engaging modern healthcare concerns and challenges. In her chapter, Susan Holman's reference of Doreen Massey reminds us that not only are there many paths to cross *within* late antique texts, *between* late antique texts and *across* the centuries between late antiquity and today, there also remain for us a "constellation of ongoing trajectories."[5] This is a hopeful location for a scholar to find herself, as it suggests that in addition to all that we know that

DOI: 10.4324/9781003080534-14

is available for us to translate, to think about, to interpret, and about which to write, there does remain a likelihood of innumerable routes forward.

There are additional reasons for engaging these intersections as well, apart from the theoretical conversation: there are numerous instabilities in higher education, and there is much suspicion about the role, import, value, and contributions of the Humanities to the sciences, even as human relationships weaken and crack at roughly the same rate that diseases strengthen their resistance to antibiotics or adapt to find ways around a vaccine. My charge as respondent to the academic contributions of Chris L. de Wet, Susan R. Holman, and Helen Rhee is to consider the intersections of these three unique studies, as well as the intersections between them; in process I will subsequently introduce some potential intersections between their work and my own thinking on these topics and suggest, at the end, some ways forward.

* * *

Susan R. Holman, Shaping Water: Public Health and the "Medicine of Mortality" in Late Antiquity

The first representative intersection between Christian antiquity and modern healthcare is provided in Susan R. Holman's analysis of the social intersection between religion and public health: "Shaping Water: Public Health and the 'Medicine of Morality'" This approach should come as no surprise; those of us who have followed Holman's work have always noted the careful balance of her vocational callings, as she marries expert translations and careful study of patristic texts with her concern for the social vulnerability of disenfranchised persons in the contemporary setting.[6] In her current work, she continues in this vein by analysing the philanthropic actions[7] of the famous Abba Shenoute (348–466) of the White Monastery in Egypt towards a refugee wave of thousands of displaced persons fleeing civil unrest, as evidence of the need for theology to "get real"[8] about the "wound of water stress."[9] Holman does so against a backdrop of models that offer multiple methods to analyse the way in which Abba Shenoute of the White Monastery approached a water shortage crisis and refugee crisis, simultaneously.

Much academic attention has been devoted in the past two decades to Abba Shenoute and his monks' (over?) zealous approach to the religious transformation of late antique Egypt as well as Abba Shenoute's contribution to the development of coenobitic monastic life.[10] In a chapter titled "Limits of Intolerance"[11] in his study of the fiery Abba, historian Ariel G. López describes Abba Shenoute as representative of the "ugliest face of the late Roman Near East."[12] It is certainly easy for Abba Shenoute's methods—and the enthusiastic rhetoric that accompany his writings and descriptions in the sources—to make us forget that there were aspects of his organization that were, in many ways, standard practice of emerging monastic philanthropy in the Christian east around food, water, and medicine.[13] When we consider the general landscape of monastic life in late antiquity, physical as well as spiritual care for the lives of those settled nearby and those unsettled by civil unrest was increasingly a feature that accompanied the angelic life of both coeno-bite monastic communities and the solitary figure working out her or his salvation in the desert arena. Darlene L. Brooks Hedstrom's notable work on the architecture of both real and imagined sacred sites and monastic settlements in Egypt reminds us that the distinctive contribution of the Egyptian monk to the architecture of the desert landscape was well known by them even if not by us, and their presence was not a secret; even one "Elias," a hermit who dwelt for 70 years in a rugged desert location was constantly approached by those willing to tread the narrow, challeng-ing, craggy, albeit well-worn path.[14] To be fair, the only solitary figures who were ever *truly successful* at being solitary were those of whom we have absolutely no knowledge or evidence. But whether the monastic figure was embedded in a fed-eration, existed as an ephemeron, or operated as a shadowy figure on the outskirts of the terrain, variables related to health were part of the balance of the ascetic life. In truth, apart from God, Christ, and the Virgin, every Christian monk required one essential item without which they could not survive: clean water.

Clean water is a non-negotiable that levels every playing field; one can live without sex and procreation, without meat, clothing, or an established address; one cannot live without clean water. And one certainly cannot build a monastic federa-tion without water, as water is the key ingredient in bricks and plaster,[15] as well as requisite components in the construction of a well.[16] With that in mind, I turn to Holman's analysis of Abba Shenoute's great well, and the theological messaging[17] embedded in his water project, the significant contribution of her paper.[18]

It would be easy to argue that the consumption of water from the great well is *de facto* an involuntary sacramental action by everyone who drinks from it, but this is not suggested in Holman's article; she is *very clear* that Abba Shenoute is pro-viding water for the "common body—monks, guests, and outsiders,"[19] as an act of charity and in the interest of public health, and I agree with her assessment. But in the practice of intersecting texts from Christian late antiquity with modern health-care, ritual studies encourage us to think a little more about the shape of the well and how individuals engage with it, and discourse theories encourage us to keep in mind that our engagements with objects and each other are informed by hierarchy and struggle.[20] Ronald L. Grimes, for example, in "Ritual Theory and the Envi-ronment" argues that people bond with inanimate objects both consciously and unconsciously as they participate through their behaviours in a specific space, and that "ritual participants believe ritual activity enables them to cultivate a bond with animals and plants, even rocks, mountains, bodies of water, and specific places."[21] This approach allows us to think differently about the "underlying concept" of the shape of the well, which, as described by Grossman, Brooks Edstrom, and Osman, was "exactly the same way as the church sanctuary."[22] Holman identifies what the authors claim "eludes"[23] them: apart from humanitarian efforts—which are real—the Abba likely intended "a deliberate theological intent,"[24] and this is supported within the Abba's general theological vision.

While it is fair to view Abba Shenoute's actions as primarily focused on the distribution of clean water, we cannot know the distinction that he or others might have been making between water from within a sanctuary and water from a well that was redolent of a sanctuary, water which would under normal circumstances be considered "mundane." The many questions that we cannot answer are quickly revealed, as we cannot know what role the shape of the well might have played either by those who distributed the water or by those who received and drank it. Further, we cannot know to what degree the recipients of the water might have been viewed by the Abba as they engaged in the act of drinking water drawn from a well that was constructed quite likely with theological intent in the shape of sanctuary.[25] If Abba Shenoute understands righteous people to be an "internal" adornment[26] of the external components of a monastery, might drinking water from this sanctuary site contribute to the most *interior*-internal adornment of an individual? Thus, while the distribution of the water might not be a formal, intentional liturgical rite, nevertheless, drinking water that has been drawn from a well that has been constructed along the same architectural model as a sanctuary could be viewed as a liturgical action (known or unknown), which is no insignificant component of the "theological messaging" of the White Monastery, as identified by Holman.[27]

In support of this theological messaging, Holman makes reference to Shenoute's homily, "A Priest will Never Cease,"[28] a central theme of which is the relationship between physical and spiritual health, clergy, and the site of the Church itself as a healing agent.[29] Charity, as well, is the central image in the piece: if healing was obtained by the person unable to walk as described in Acts 3:1–9 "because of the opportunity for charity," the Abba writes, then "how much healing and blessing and grace and all good things will we gain both bodily and spiritually, pertaining both to the healing of our visible illnesses and the healing of our sins"[30] if they emulate the charitable activity of Peter? Thus, sharing water from the great well must be understood as a charitable action with the intended reward, but neither as baptism nor as an aspect of the Eucharist, for Shenoute is specific in this homily that "each one's house is not the baptistry, nor is it the place for receiving the mystery."[31] But, he writes, water will lead people to a sanctuary that is transformed by the presence of the divine:

> Because of the manner that the Lord spoke to his disciples, "Go into the city to a certain man, and a man carrying a gallon of water will meet you. Follow him into the house that he enters and say to the master of the house . . . the place into which the Lord will go with his disciples is, rather, the church."[32]

More explicitly, Shenoute ties physical care to the locale of the church: "The place for receiving medicine and for treating us is the church and everywhere they teach truthfully."[33] With this view of the priesthood and sharing of matter and theology, it is fair to offer agreement with Holman's assessment that the construction of the well along the lines of the sanctuary does not elude us: the distribution of something that people cannot refuse without loss of life,[34] by someone committed to charity, and from a space shaped like the central site of worship makes the site, the substance, and the situation metaphorically rich for offering living sanctuary, a "type" of charity-driven salvation for thousands who arrive and drink from life-sustaining produce of that site.[35] Perhaps by modelling the well on the sanctuary

Shenoute is predicting the role that his monastery would play in the future hope for the salvation of the area, if not as a site of an immediate, physical salvation.[36]

The importance of clean water and the shape of water containers can inform ancient and modern views on theological therapeutics, spatial meaning, and ethics in late antiquity, as well as health concerns that contribute to our "constellation of ongoing trajectories"[37] in these historical moments. Holman argues that Abba Shenoute's distribution of water (along with other items central to healthcare) is an explicit and important image of how theology directly shapes public health,[38] and inspired by the direction she takes with the text and his benevolence, I would like to think more about the shape of water itself, and water agency.

Water is a hyper-object, it is neither singular nor plural, it is impossible to hold and difficult to contain, and water does not have a fixed, or precise shape; rather, water assumes the shape of any container into which it is poured, including a flexible human container, making it sentient.[39] Moreover, when water is in liquid form, it is in constant renunciation of its own shape. The scientific qualities of water's self-renunciation are so lovingly described by Theodor Schwenk, a pioneer in the study of water, that one cannot help but view water as a clear manifestation of the Christian theology of salvation, as water perpetually surrenders itself in order to sustain the life of something other than itself,[40] quite evocative of *Philippians*.[41] As a result, if Abba Shenoute's well was constructed in imitation of the sanctuary, it is not an imitation because when filled with water, it *is* a sanctuary; much like an image portrayed in an icon indicates by virtue of its energies to the divine essence that it cannot be, the water points to the sanctuary shape that the well dictates, a shape that Holman effectively argues must have been intentional in its construction.[42] The likelihood of this calculated shape in its construction is subtle, the great well does not include a transept, making it redolent of a cross; however, while a Christian approaching baptism would hardly be dissuaded from the ritual based on the shape of the container, those in desperate need of water are unlikely to care in what shape the container might be, even as the very need for water allows the Abba to avoid what hydro-archaeologist Luci Attala describes as "the usual intellectual"—and I would add, theological—"distance placed between bodies and the rest of the material world."[43] If, as Caroline Schroeder writes,[44] and as Holman notes, "the church building functions as a potent symbol of Shenoute's theology,"[45] then the great well operates in that manner as well. Taking this approach, the water, the well, and the well's shape play a significant role in the theological messaging, as do even the bricks and the earth that supports the site. And though I am not claiming that this is Abba Shenoute's view, it certainly rejects monastic exceptionalism; even as the water is put to the service of vulnerable persons, this can be interpreted as an interaction of materials which influence each other[46]—the water shapes the human by taking human form, and the human shapes the water by consuming the theology that it carries into the human body.

Finally, this leads me to think also about the role of water, or water agency, in this account. When those in need drank water from a well that was (a) composed of bricks made with water drawn from the earth of a monastery and (b) quite likely intentionally constructed in the dimensions of a sanctuary, they initiated the process of contributing to their own internal adornment of Abba Shenoute's community through the water's activity of being consumed. Again, to quote Attala, "we are the very water we so regularly claim to 'need'."[47] And this water, having first assumed the shape of the well in the form of a sanctuary now assumes the shape of the one who drinks it, a shape shared by the monks and a shape that is—if we follow the theological thread—in God's image.[48]

Abba Shenoute's care for the displaced poor through the medium of water prompts Holman to consider how we theorize space in an age of an emerging global water crisis, and the questions that she raises about how hydrological shaping informs contemporary readings of the ancient past,[49] that awareness of these texts can influence contemporary discussions in global policy and practice,[50] and how the existence of pathogenic bacteria impacts religious rituals, if in fact it does.[51] I believe that it is fair to say that Holman accurately identifies how, when faced with a crisis, Abba Shenoute's theology allows him to "get real."[52] And while I agree that although medical and religious texts from antiquity are unlikely to solve a global water crisis,[53] nevertheless, there is a simple, yet profoundly significant, conclusion we can draw from Abba Shenoute's response at the White Monastery to an influx of refugees, one which is consistent with Christian theology and one that can be read through the perspective of the New Materialities[54] approach: Abba Shenoute, when faced with a crisis, addressed the situation in its full context, rather than seeing himself, his monastery, and their water as isolated elements which must survive while others do not. In other words, the religious assumptions about the material world that Abba Shenoute carried with him resulted in his concern to provide basic care for vulnerable persons who otherwise would likely die without his help. As Holman observed, the great well is *not* the well which the author of the *Life of Shenoute* describes,[55] but according to Grossman it was constructed because the monastery well was seen as insufficient to meet the immediate needs of a large body of displaced persons.[56] By all accounts, Shenoute's monastery addressed a refugee and water crisis more effectively than the current Lebanese government, which has framed their water and refugee crises along politically driven, national security lines.[57] This supports Holman's view of the great well as yet another example of how late antique theology contributed to shaping public space, and it is a continuation of the direction in which scholarship about monasticism has been moving of late, as we slowly dismantle romantic views of monastic federations as surrogate societies, apart from (at best) or indifferent to (at worst) the trials of secular citizens. Rather, we have here additional evidence that within the monastic landscape, consistently lines between "sacred" and "profane"—if they exist at all—are hazy or are easily crossed when people need help.[58] Holmen demonstrates how Shenoute here represents the best of Massey's aforementioned "constellation of ongoing trajectories"[59] as a contemporary approach to this late antique text turns the obvious environmental message on its head: Abba Shenoute's use of water does not necessarily demonstrate how we should use water, but his use of water demonstrates to us how he believed water should be used, which provides insight about who he was. Thus, Holman's analysis offers to us a way of thinking about how our use of water shapes who we are too.

* * *

Helen Rhee, "Pain in Ancient Medicine and Literature, and Early Christianity: Paradox of In-shareability and Agency"

The second representative intersection between Christian antiquity and modern healthcare is Helen Rhee's textual intersection between ancient medical literature and patristic texts focused on patient, physician, and communal understanding of pain, the experience of pain, and pain as a shared emotion. Like Holman, Rhee's current work on communal and shared pain falls within her expertise of Christian theology as it pertains to identity, philanthropy, and care in the historic milieu of shifting and stabilizing religious identities, orthodoxies, and authorities of second-century Greco-Roman culture.[60] Her current academic project presents a difficult task, for whether dealing with the subject of pain in the historic past or the immediate present, one of the more challenging aspects of this topic is, of course, deconstructing how patients, physicians, and communities of care in the narratives, images, or texts describe, interpret, or understand genuine degrees of pain, however it is presented.

Rhee's chapter begins with a reminder of the attention given by physicians in antiquity to understand the types of pain that was experienced by their patients, to explore where and how pain originated, how pain travelled and its impact, and the way in which pain and suffering[61] linked the patient and physician together in a relationship unique to all others.[62] Rhee begins with a brief and helpful elucidation on Celsus' claims regarding pain subjectivity and the important dialogue of trust that is required between patient and physician,[63] and she carefully works through the systematic analysis of pain in select writings of Galen, whose aetiologic of pain included standard humoural explanations, presumed cause, and how interpretation of pain was impacted by patient emotions such as distress, grief, or anxiety.[64] Rhee notes that both physicians placed relationships of trust between physician and patient as a central component of communication of an experience of pain (and subsequent pain management and healthcare),[65] which highlights an important distinction in medical care between the communication of pain by the patient and the comprehension of and sensitivity to the patient's experience of pain by the physician. In short, verbal and interpretive skills are essential for both parties to arrive at anything close to understanding in pain management, which lays bare how easily disadvantaged are patients in medical settings that lack language training or resources that facilitate empathetic interpretation of medical moments.[66] Rhee introduces the narrative component of pain history, and explores the relationship between language and pain in the physician–patient relationship in *Sacred Tales* of the second-century sophist, Aelius Aristides. While his career was dependent on his ability to speak, he lacked sufficient vocabulary to describe his pain.[67] Inability to give adequate voice to his medical trials forced the sophist to explore his pain and suffering and to transform the experience for himself in relationship *not* with physicians, but with the divine being. *Sacred Tales* is thus an important link between medical documentation by physicians and Christian narratives highly dependent on a vocabulary of suffering that emerges and develops alongside transformative bodily experiences.

Rhee applies the medical and introspective heritage of these important authors to Christian texts, to explore specifically the topics of "shareability of pain"[68] and "solidarity with pain"[69] (and with the one in pain) in select writings of Augustine of Hippo[70] and *The Life of Syncletica*.[71] Rhee's analysis accurately identifies that Christianity and Christians understood pain and suffering differently from both medical predecessors and peers who mused on this fundamental aspect of human existence; for Christianity, physical and social suffering is, of course, written into its foundational narrative.[72] The Christological framework begins with a broken, despondent, and suffering body, and—very importantly—a suffering body that has made a rational decision to freely enter into relationship with pain at physical, emotional, and spiritual levels. When viewed through this lens, suffering is not passive; the Christian is an actor, an agent in their own suffering, and therefore exercises considerable control and autonomy. Additionally, both of Rhee's very divergent source choices support a singular, Christian understanding of pain as something that can be—and should be—shared because pain can be shared within an individual in the domains of the body, the emotions, and the spirit, and eventually beyond the bodily constraints of the individual. The emotive aspects of pain are significant for this history, Crislip recently argued,[73] and is, as such, uniquely linked with identity construction for Christianity. This, the sharing of bodily, spiritual, and emotional pain and suffering, is supported by Christian practice in the account of Amma Syncletica, and by Christian theology and ethics in Augustine's writings. But the degree to which the pain and suffering can—or should—be shared differs in the texts, as I will explore later.

There is, quite simply, no finer late antique text for conversations about pain and suffering, human agency, illness, and ageing than *The Life and Regimen of the Blessed and Holy Teacher Syncletica*.[74] The language of the *Life* is graphic, and though the greater portion of the text is devoted to Amma Syncletica's teachings, still, the passages that address her ascetic practices as they pertain to her struggles with several illness and ageing—especially the disease of her jaw—make up in striking detail for what they lack in length.

The role of the servants and the clear and active presence of others in the narrative of the Amma's pain and suffering is notable. In "Scenting Saintliness: The Ailing Body, Chicana Feminism, and Communal Identity in Ancient Christianity," Peter Mena writes [of Amma Syncletica] that "her sick and decaying body is the material grounds on which a communal identity is constructed"[75]; from a specific, decaying body as the foundation, Rhee builds on that which the "decaying body" experiences—the pain and suffering—as the centre around "her ascetic co-sufferers and as a means of constructing communal subjectivities."[76] This portrays pain and suffering in a distinctly "Christian" way. First, in Rhee's interpretation of pain in the *Life*, the subjective—or independence—of Amma Syncletica's suffering is intersected by a cohort of individuals who, "perceiving with their eyes the sufferings, they strengthened further the will."[77] This transforms the subjectivity of Amma Syncletica's circumstances because her pain is now carried by others—perhaps even diffused—and therefore it becomes considerably less distinct and personal. In Rhee's interpretation of pain in the *Life*, the inexpressibility of Amma

Syncletica's suffering is additionally intersected in the actual construction of her *Life*. In the Amma's account, the author drapes and adorns her ascetic feats lovingly with biblical imagery, the consequence of which allowed those with either small or great degrees of separation from the saint to grasp the evil origins of her suffering and her mortal and immortal support system. The author writes:

> When she turned eighty years old, the devil transferred to her the contexts of Job. For he made use then of the same scourges . . . Therefore on Job the devil made the beginnings of wounds on the outside; on her he added punishments from the inside. For her internal organs [entrails] having been struck by him, he assigned to her greater and more difficult sufferings.[78]

The inexpressibility of the Amma's pain is transformed as it is expressed, and in Rhee's interpretation of pain in the *Life*, the in-shareability of Syncletica's suffering is intersected by those who lived in community with her, most especially those whose task it was to serve their Amma. The author writes, regarding bone disease in her jaw: "And the bone itself was corrupted and little by little wasted away; putrefaction and the heaviest stench governed her whole body so that the ones who served her suffered more than she did."[79] The in-shareability of Amma's circumstances is transformed *and therefore shared* and no longer isolated, or in-shareable.

Of the three intersections Rhee addresses in the *Life* that support the notion of "pain as a social relationship,"[80] the modern reader would be right to question the sanctification of suffering[81] in the "shareability" of the Amma's pain. Though the author of the *Life* stresses the role of the community in her care, I am less convinced with the argument that the community willingly shares the Amma's suffering except perhaps by default, unless one is inclined to consider other options; for example, that one might share begrudgingly, unwillingly, or even share badly in someone else's suffering. And I do wonder if the author is offering a veiled critique of the servants' unwillingness to share in their Amma's suffering when the author writes of their less-than-subtle attitude towards the conflicted caregivers in the sick room:

> Most of the time they [her servants] withdrew, not bearing the inhuman odour; but when need called, the multitude approached, kindling incense, and again withdrew because of the inhuman stench. The blessed one clearly saw the adversary, and did not at all agree to have human aid brought to her, demonstrating again in this her own virility [*andreia*]. But those who came with her exhorted her to anoint the places with unguent for their own weakness, but she was not persuaded. For she believed that through external assistance they would destroy the glorious contest.[82]

Might this not be a critique of these conflicted caregivers? It would not be unheard of, for Amma Syncletica's wound and the distress that it causes is redolent of Homer's Philoctedes, who, when he sustained a painful and pongy wound on his foot,[83] was abandoned by his peers on Lemnos during the Trojan War.[84] As noted by the morally ambiguous Odysseus, "no sooner would we attend to the usual libations or sacrifices, [then] he'd fill our whole camp with his wild and far-from-good-omened cries—groaning, howling."[85] There was no theological imperative to keep Philoctedes' companions on Lemnos, and only the desire for Philoctedes' skill with archery brought his companions back to him, ten years later, and still indifferent to his physical pain and abandonment. The ageing, ailing body of the Amma impacts her servants in ways that are not fully masked by the sanctified language of the hagiography, and for future, Rhee's analysis of the co-suffering of the caregivers has prompted me to think more about the Amma's servants, and the possibility of intersections found along a theme of "Conflicted Caregiver."

Augustine would argue that there should be no conflict amongst the caregivers, not for the Christian, anyway. His language about pain and suffering in select passages analysed by Rhee is shaped by a mystical view of the body; by this I do not mean to suggest that Augustine is not impacted by the realities of human bodily pain and suffering, but that readers should keep in mind the different purposes and intent of the two texts. Through a Christological structure, Augustine seeks to cultivate an ethic that encourages compassion for and—if necessary—solidarity with those in pain; this is, as Rhee carefully explores, a departure from other philosophical views about the role of suffering in society.[86] Augustine's view of pain is certainly dependent on and rooted in the language of Paul,[87] and he presents a view of the passion and martyr narratives that reads Jesus' role as a moral exemplar rather than an object of atonement.[88] As Rhee notes, Augustine roots pain in Original Sin and the need for punishment for human transgression (not surprising),[89] and he interprets the experience of pain as evidence of a healthy body (quite surprising)[90]; this is quite distinct from the approach taken by the author of *The Life of Syncletica*, which attributes the Amma's illness and subsequent pain and suffering to the devil and the frailty of her age.[91] Also different from the author of *The Life*, Rhee notes, is Augustine's intersectional shareability of pain firstly with the suffering of Jesus (vertical), and secondly with fellow Christians (horizontal); an individual can engage as a co-sufferer with another precisely because they share in Christ's suffering and thus contribute to the construction of a community of co-sufferers.[92] Were Augustine commenting on the Amma's situation, he would likely condemn the Amma's caregivers for failing to care properly for her because they display their disgust with her ageing, ill body, they are disregarding her coping mechanism as an end-stage cancer patient,[93] and because of this they have failed to offer "fellow feeling"[94] for her misery and have violated the social contract.

Taken together, these sources outline not only *why* one is to share in another's pain (because of Jesus' death) but also *how* one is to share in another's pain. The author of the *Life of Amma Syncletica* would probably not agree that her servants are sharing in her pain and suffering; rather, the author might even agree that their view towards her body adds to her distress. Alternatively, in Augustine's view, one is encouraged to feel compassion for the wounded, care for the angry, the fearful, the sad, and the sinful; this is more than kindness, it is justice.[95] Augustine would have little patience for the Amma's servants, but Celsus would have understood that "one's 'moderate pain' will be the other's 'intolerable pain' and vice versa,"[96] and perhaps Celsus might even agree that the servants suffer independent of the

Amma, or even because of her. These are unique responses, and they raise important questions for the modern reader about the role of the ill in society, our duties to one another, and the challenges for the caregiver. It is inadequate to claim that a simple demonstration of compassion for someone whose sufferings are visceral is enough, and it is equally inadequate to suggest that compassion is not authentic unless it gets one into the room.

* * *

Chris L. de Wet, "Medical Discourse, Identity Formation, and Otherness in Early Eastern Christianity"

The third and final intersection to consider between Christin antiquity and modern healthcare is Chris L. de Wet's integration of medical discourse and Christian identities of the self and others. De Wet's typological study of Christian medical discourse within the historical context of the growth of medical encyclopaedic work *and* the unique relationship that medical discourse has with theological formation is consistent with his recently published work on religious conflict and slavery[97] within an imperial setting. This chapter reflects de Wet's focus on and attention to early Christian power discourses, especially as they impact sexuality, social identity, as well as literal and metaphorical slavery and enslavement. There are more than a few parallels between those discourses and current medical studies on gender and gender identity.

De Wet's chapter differs from the previous two by taking a larger, historiographic view of the rise of a particular method of theological construction, and his insightful analysis of the theological, medical, and philosophical thought world of antiquity affirms not only that the totality of Christian medical discourse was vast, but also that it included the individual and collective soul and body, the social body, moral pathologies, and in time, popular discourse.[98] De Wet's thesis, that medical discourse shapes or informs an early Christian identity, is displayed unambiguously in the *Life of Syncletica* as analysed by Rhee; Syncletica's identity as a wise, ascetic teacher is fashioned for posterity—in part—through (as discussed earlier) detailed, medical descriptions of her illness and elaborate organization of care by her servants in a time of her declining health and visible bodily struggles. De Wet's chapter explores the development of these types of intersections of medical and theological care, and he argues through a series of four theses that Christian medical discourse was wholistic and imperialistic in nature and, additionally, scientifically precise in situating the body and soul together within the realm of the medical. In time, this would have implications for both monastic populations and laity.

As identified by de Wet, one result for monastic practitioners was the creation of an elaborate system whereby a monastic might examine the spiritual and biological realities of their existence and seek to understand each realm alongside the other in relationship with their salvation. Though monastic in form, function, and intent, these handbooks and *rules* will in time be comparable to the *penitentials*[99] of southwest Britain and Ireland, a system of penitence that sought to "cure" rather than chastise laity, and an approach that privileged a healing of the soul rather than a punishment of the body.[100]

Analysis of one's own behaviour considering alleged social and ethical "norms" is a standard component of personal growth and human development, irrespective of the community under consideration, monastic, or lay. But, as de Wet notes, an additional consequence of a monastic medical construction within a Roman imperium[101] was that elements of health—including behaviours or beliefs—falling outside of the (imperially organized) known realm were classified as pathological by individuals who were not medical professionals though they cast themselves as such,[102] in imitation of Greek and Roman emotional therapeutics.[103]

Apart from the obvious medical benefits, taxonomies of how our bodies are "meant" to function, how people are "meant" to think, or what they are "meant" to believe are dangerous in the wrong hands, but the popular discourse of Christianity resulted in a social consumption of texts that were not necessarily intended to be read in isolation. And assumptions about the truth of such classifications have a significant—even if not openly acknowledged—impact on the social level, some of which we can see in the past century as responses to taxonomies about "proper non-negotiable" bodies are on a trajectory that spans from ongoing genocides to questions regarding bathroom use.[104] Ultimately, classification systems are all about creating, establishing, and then upholding categories of "normal" or "abnormal," with laudation and embrace of those who find themselves (or are placed) on the "normal" side of the scale, and castigation and ostracizing of those who find themselves (or are placed) on the other end of the scale.

Sometimes what was on the other end of "normal" was simply being female, and heresiologies as the encyclopaedias of belief pathologized female autonomy, ritual behaviours, and leadership as well as the theological formulations held by women, even if those formulations would become, in time, orthodox. De Wet highlights especially Epiphanius of Salamis' fourth-century contribution to this genre. Thus far, the intersections of medicine, healthcare, and theology have yielded positive results: the distribution of water, care for the ill and dying, and sharing in the pain of another. Not all intersections are beneficial, and de Wet's second and third theses on the personification of moral and psychic pathologies and totalizing of the social body[105] leads me to look more closely at one of the typologies of alleged heretical thought against which Epiphanius wrote, in order to "with God's help, be able to cure certain people of this madness"[106]: the Kollyridians.[107] The unique sect of Kollyridianism is referred to by historians as a "strange phenomenon of early Christianity"[108] and an "obscure group of women"[109] to whom there are few other links.

Epiphanius of Salamis[110] presents himself to his readers as the spiritual physician whose pedigree qualifies him to make decisions about degrees of healthy or unhealthy theologies, and Epiphanius' lineage is his evidence[111]: he was, in his own words, reared "in the faith of the fathers of Nicaea."[112] Epiphanius was educated in Alexandria and mentored by the venerable Palestinian monk Hilarion the Great, who had himself been influenced by the ascetic regime of Antony of Egypt.[113] Epiphanius was elected to the bishopric of Salamis, where he was a respected leader, much sought for opinions on doctrinal issues. As de Wet notes,[114] Epiphanius casts theology, alleged heretical sects, and religious communities in unambiguously medical terms, describing both illnesses and remedies in the preface to his *Panarion* ("Medicine Chest"):

> Since I am going to tell you the names of the sects and expose their unlawful deeds like poisons and toxic substances, and at the same time match the antidotes with them as cures for those already bitten and preventatives for those who will have this misfortune, I am drafting this Preface for the scholarly to explain the "Panarion," or chest of remedies for those whom savage beasts have bitten. It is composed in three Books containing eighty Sects, symbolically represented by wild beasts or snakes.[115]

Epiphanius was one of the first Christian theologians to address the death of Mary,[116] and he was particularly concerned with Marian veneration. The penultimate chapter of his *Panarion* is devoted to condemnation of the practices of the aforementioned Kollyridians, a group of Arabian-Christian women whose theological views rendered them in his view, "unstable, prone to error, and mean-spirited."[117] Named after the bread that they baked (κολλυρίς) and offered to Mary, little is written by Epiphanius about what, exactly, they do, other than the following description of what women have been doing centuries, which is baking[118]:

> For they say that certain Thracian women there in Arabia have introduced this nonsense, and that they bake a loaf in the name of the Ever-virgin, gather together, and < both > attempt an excess and undertake a forbidden, blasphemous act in the holy Virgin's name, and offer sacrifice in her name with woman officiants[119]

and that "certain women decorate a barber's chair or a square seat, spread a cloth on it, set out bread and offer it in Mary's name on a certain day of the year, and all partake of the bread."[120] In addition to this offence, in the remainder of the chapter Epiphanius offers a far greater percentage of outrage to the diseased behaviour of a sacrifice by female hands as he does to their veneration of Mary. In a rare display amongst patristic writings of offering kind words for the figure of Eve, Epiphanius argues that a sacrifice offered by the Kollyridians is *more* deviant than even the actions of Eve who—though she was "the cause of her spouse's death— and not only his but her children's"[121] and "by her transgression has overthrown creation,"[122] thus altering the course of human existence—"still did not undertake such a further impiety"[123] as to offer sacrifice to God, unlike the "deviation"[124] of the impious Kollyridians.

Setting aside for another time the important details about an entirely female, Arab-Christian community engaging in commonplace ritual behaviours that will later be orthodox and their very unexceptional veneration of Mary, Epiphanius carefully works through priestly typology in the Old and New Testament texts of ritual behaviour of men[125] as the established "norm" (healthy) as opposed to the "abnormal" or "deviant" (unhealthy) activity of the female Kollyridians. In comparing Epiphanius' language about the Kollyridians' alleged heresy to any other sect in his *Medicine Chest*, it is noteworthy that various communities and sects are derided for their beliefs, but not for their gender, as with the Kollyridians and other sects with women in leadership: the Montanists[126] and Quintillianists.[127]

The privileging of male ritual behaviour and theology is neither surprising nor uncommon, and neither, sadly, is the pathologizing of female ritual behaviour and theology. What is unique about Epiphanius, however, is that his heresiology adds "being female" to his list of pathological figures who pose a danger to the Christian corporate body. Epiphanius even genders all heresies as "female," claiming that "[e]very sect is a worthless woman, but this sect more so, which is composed of women and belongs to him who was the deceiver of the first woman."[128] The only cure, Epiphanius claims, is male-centric: "adopt a manly frame of mind and dispel the madness of these women. The speculation is entirely feminine, and the malady of the deluded Eve all over again."[129] De Wet is correct, Epiphanius is mapping out and ordering the individual and social subject "to protect 'orthodox' or 'Nicene' Christians against heresy;"[130] and if these sects are seen as diseases, illnesses, or psychic poisons,[131] and if "[e]very sect is a worthless woman,"[132] then women are a disease, an illness, or a psychic poison which should be confined or quarantined, "set apart and marked as being dangerous."[133] Any healer of quality, integrity, and correct theology—such as Epiphanius—can see through the deceit of these "worthless" women. The disease is femaleness, the cure is maleness.

To be clear, most often ill women were treated by themselves, female family members, or female physicians, and male physicians had little to no access to female bodies, much less a clear understanding of how those bodies functioned.[134] But deceit was a feminine concept and was considered a trait which male physicians had to carefully navigate with their female patients.[135] Just as a poor person was unworthy of credit by virtue of the fact that they had no money, an ill person's judgement was suspect because unlike the physician, they were not "with healthy mind and healthy body."[136] Seen this way, "health" was the scarce resource of a privileged few, and a resource that functioned in a similar way "alongside power, wealth and prestige."[137] Women's health was dependent on the healthy bodies and minds of physicians who were to function as a model and guide for the patient, and social membership played a significant role in their treatment.[138] As women were viewed as more innately deceptive and more ignorant of their own health, they were seen as less likely to effectively communicate their concerns about their own bodies.[139] Ill health and deceit were conflated far more often within female patients than male,[140] and because women's bodies were often viewed as "unbalanced even by definition"[141] due to the overemphasis in ancient women's health on the uterus,[142] it stands to reason that a follower of a female sect would be viewed as more poisonous and unbalanced than a follower of a male sect. This supports de Wet's thesis that the "assault against moral pathology is therefore also an assault against the pathologically personified Other, as is evident in the language of war, enslavement, madness, and so on."[143] To de Wet's list of the violent, the addicted, and the frenetic, we can add women.

De Wet's "bird's-eye view"[144] of heresiology and secular medical discourse in an imperial setting affirms that in addition to diagnoses that considered humours, invasive species, or rational versus supernational factors, medicine and medical language and ideas permeated Christian literature within multiple genres. This, in turn, resulted in a Christian medical discourse that offered distinct and problematic contributions to the aims of medical literature: the technology of heresy, the pathology of women, the creation of authority where there was none, and the conscription of future readership into that authority.[145]

* * *

Conclusion

The importance of the intersection of medicine, healthcare, and religion can be summed up by a simple question that is rarely asked by a physician of a patient: "What has this illness done to you?" A question such as this allows a patient to consider any direction that illness has impacted their life: physical, of course, but also mental, spiritual, financial, familial, or social, to name but a few. There are no rigid distinctions between the ways in which a person is impacted by illness or disease, and Holman, Rhee, and de Wet have all rightly and elegantly resisted rigid distinctions between disciplines and methods in their analyses of select texts, whose authors—a bishop, a monk, and a hagiographer—all do the following: they have demonstrated creativity and compassion as they have worked through the details and dread of medical and religious intersections by situating ascetic activity within the context of water ethics; by locating the "porous and permeable"[146] body of a dying monk within the company of her conflicted caregivers; and by identifying the dangerous implications for the female gender as it is included amongst an encyclopaedic heresiology; finally, all three have found "third space" options around which ancient texts and contemporary theology and policy can rally in support of care for (or cure of) bodily need, death, and sex: the distribution of water, the refrain from disgust, and the banishment of the female. This is not only useful in an academic sense, but it is important in the classroom, and it is essential on the ground. For example, the details related to the medical challenges of *Life of Syncletica* provide students of history and theology with the authors' interpretation about *why* she suffered; this is very distinct from what the text reveals to a medical student, which is *how* she suffered.

Taken together, these three papers address aspects of care that are fundamental to societal and individual wellness, and inspire us to meet or revisit patristic texts that we translate, analyse, study, and teach, and join our own queries to those we read in their chapters:

1. The responses of ancient faith leaders and communities towards immigration policies and immigrants, and how that might differ from—or shape—faith leaders today.

2. Theological rationale for patient care and the important role, health, and agency of the willing or conscripted caregiver.
3. The need for patient-centred studies on the idea of referred suffering and its impact on domestic and institutional abuse, self-harm, wellness, and healing. And finally,
4. The cultivation of bodies of knowledge that, rather than organize and cultivate greater understanding about and compassion for human existence, instead promote one view of body, mind, and gender at the expense of the "other."

Notes

1 Lois N. Manger, *A History of Medicine* (New York: Marcel Dekker, 1992), 43, 68–70.
2 Myrick C. Shinall Jr., ed., "The Separation of Church and Medicine," *Religion, Patients, and Medical Ethics, AMA Journal of Ethics* 11, no. 10 (2009): 745–828.
3 Christopher Hitchens, "A Note on Health, to Which Religion Can Be Dangerous," in *God Is Not Great: How Religion Poisons Everything* (New York: Hachette, 2007), 43–61.
4 Shinall Jr., "The Separation of Church and Medicine," 747–9.
5 "Doreen Massey on Time, Space and Responsibility," excerpt from a lecture at Institi-tut für Raumexperimente, UdK Berlin April 2013 (https://vimeo.com/158902032), as quoted in Susan Holman.
6 For example: Susan R. Holman, *Beholden: Religion, Global Health and Human Rights* (Oxford: Oxford University Press, 2015), 16; Susan R. Holman, *God Knows There's Need: Christian Responses to Poverty* (Oxford: Oxford University Press, 2009); Susan R. Holman, *The Hungry Are Dying: Beggars and Bishops in Roman Cappadocia* (Oxford: Oxford University Press, 2001).
7 Susan R. Holman, "Shaping Water: Public Health and the 'Medicine of Morality' in Late Antiquity," this volume, 10–16.
8 Steve de Gruchy, "Water and Spirit: Theology in the Time of Cholera," *The Ecumenical Review* 62, no. 2 (2010): 188–201, at 198; quoted in Holman, "Shaping Water," 5.
9 Isabel Apawo Phiri, "God of Life Lead Us to Water Justice," the Steve de Gruchy Memorial Lecture, Rodebosch United Church, Cape Town, South Africa, 24 April 2018, in Holman, 8.
10 A few notable publications include, in order of publication date: Rebecca Krawiec, *Shenoute and the Women of the White Monastery: Egyptian Monasticism in Late Antiquity* (Oxford: Oxford University Press 2002); Caroline Schroeder, *Monastic Bodies: Discipline and Salvation in Shenoute of Atripe* (Philadelphia, PA: University of Pennsylvania Press, 2007); Elizabeth S. Bolman et al., "Shenoute and a Recently Discovered Tomb Chapel at the White Monastery," *Journal of Early Christian Studies* 18, no. 3 (2010): 453–62; Ariel G. López, *Shenoute of Atripe and the Uses of Poverty: Rural Patronage, Religious Conflict and Monasticism in Late Antique Egypt* (Berkeley, CA: University of California Press, 2013); David Brakke and Andrew Crislip, *Selected Discourages of Shenoute the Great: Community, Theology and Social Conflict in Late Antique Egypt* (Cambridge University Press, 2015); Bentley Layton, *The Canons of Our Fathers: Monastic Rules of Shenoute* (Oxford: Oxford University Press, 2017).
11 Ariel G. López, "The Limits of Intolerance," in *Shenoute of Atripe and the Uses of Poverty*, 102–26.
12 López, *Shenoute of Atripe and the Uses of Poverty*, 102.
13 Considering specifically Besa, *The Life of Shenoute*, trans. David N. Bell (Kalamazoo, MI: Cistercian Publications, 1983): the account of the construction of the well, 24; the account of the drought in Šmin and Pšoi, 27–8; the food for the brothers in Constantinople, 76–9; the store-room of the blessing," 138–43; Psoti's generosity with vegetables, 144–50; the account of the camel and her foal, 161; the account of the gourd, 162–71.

14 Darlene L. Brooks Hedstrom, *Monastic Landscape of Late Antique Egypt: An Archaeo-logical Reconstruction* (Cambridge: Cambridge University Press, 2017), 178.
15 Brookes Hedstrom, *Monastic Landscape of Late Antique Egypt*, 87.
16 "Only the great well in the Northwestern region of the monastery dates to the lifetime of Senoute; it is constructed of fired bricks." Peter Grossmann, بيتر ،جروسمان, Darlene L. Brooks Hedstrom and Saad Mohamad Osman, "Second Report on the Excavation in the Monastery of Apa Shenute (Dayr Anba Shinuda) at Suhag," *Dumbarton Oaks Papers* 63 (2009): 167.
17 Holman, "Public Health and the 'Medicine of Morality'," 15.
18 Disclaimer: I am not a scholar of the Shenoute texts and/or the White Monastery, so my comments should be read/heard with that in mind, more as "observational" than an argument or claim.
19 Holman, "Public Health and the 'Medicine of Morality'," 15.- I have to rely on the editors here to have the correct pagination, as I do not know what it might be or how the page numbers have changed.
20 Diane Macdonell, *Theories of Discourse: An Introduction* (Oxford: Basil Blackwell, 1986), 1–23.
21 Ronald L. Grimes, "Ritual Theory and the Environment," *The Sociological Review* 51 (October 2003): 32.
22 Grossmann et al., "Second Report on the Excavation," 188.
23 Grossmann et al., "Second Report on the Excavation," 188.
24 Holman, "Public Health and the 'Medicine of Morality'," 14. I have to rely on the editors here to have the correct pagination, as I do not know what it might be or how the page numbers have changed.
25 Holman, "Public Health and the 'Medicine of Morality'," 14. I have to rely on the editors here to have the correct pagination, as I do not know what it might be or how the page numbers have changed.
26 Shenoute, "God Is Holy," in López, *Shenoute of Atripe and the Uses of Poverty,* 47; Holman, "Public Health and the 'Medicine of Morality'," 15.
27 Holman, "Public Health and the 'Medicine of Morality'," 15. I have to rely on the editors here to have the correct pagination, as I do not know what it might be or how the page numbers have changed.
28 Shenoute, "A Priest Will Never Cease," 137–46.
29 Andrew Crislip, "Shenoute of Atripe on Christ the Physician and the Cure of Souls," *Le Muséon* 122, no. 3–4 (2009): 247–77.
30 Shenoute, "A Priest Will Never Cease," 137.
31 Shenoute, "A Priest will Never Cease," 137.
32 Shenoute, "A Priest will Never Cease," 137.
33 Shenoute, "A Priest will Never Cease," 139; Crislip, "Shenoute of Atripe on Christ the Physician and the Cure of Souls," 266.
34 I am not suggesting religious blackmail.
35 Not all usage of the term "salvation" referred to *eternal* salvation, and Abba Shenoute would know that eternal salvation is not up to him anyway; the act of "being saved" was fluid in the collective mind of early Christian desert theology. John Wortley, "What the Desert Fathers Meant by 'Being Saved'," *Zeitschrift für antikes Christentum* 12, no. 2 (2008): 286–307.
36 We cannot also rule out the method that interprets water distribution as a component of colonization; because this water comes from a distinct *place* and from a container of a distinct *shape*, Shenoute has determined how the water will be distributed, whether recipients understand that or not. A special thanks to Jonathan Zecker, who pointed out this possibility, one that merits further exploration.
37 "Doreen Massey on Time, Space and Responsibility," as quoted in Susan Holman, 16.
38 Holman, "Public Health and the 'Medicine of Morality'," 15. I have to rely on the editors here to have the correct pagination, as I do not know what it might be or how the page numbers have changed.

39 Even thought we might more accurately be described as "Ugly, Ugly Giant Bags of Mostly Water," *Star Trek, The Next Generation.* Season 1, Episode 17: "Home Soil," www.imdb.com/title/tt0708730/.

40 "What is it that enables water to accomplish this? By renouncing every self-quality it becomes the creative substance for the generation of all forms. By renouncing every life of its own it becomes the primal substance for all life. By renouncing every fixed substance, it becomes the carrier of all substance transformation. By renouncing every rhythm of its own it becomes the carrier of each and every rhythm." Theodor Schwenk in Wilkens et al., *Understanding Water: Developments from the Work of Theodor Schwenk* (Edinburgh: Floris Books, 2005), 26, in Luci Attala, *How Water Makes Us Human: Engagements with the Materiality of Water*, Materialities in Anthropology and Archaeology (Cardiff: University of Wales Press, 2019), 44.

41 *Philippians* 2.8a.

42 Grossmann et al., "Second Report on the Excavation," 188.

43 Attala, *How Water Makes Us Human*, 10.

44 Caroline Schroeder, "'A Suitable Abode for Christ': The Church Building as Symbol of Ascetic Renunciation in Early Monasticism," *Church History* 73, no. 3 (2004): 472–521; Schroeder, *Monastic Bodies*, 118.

45 Holman, "Public Health and the 'Medicine of Morality'," 15. I have to rely on the editors here to have the correct pagination, as I do not know what it might be or how the page numbers have changed.

46 Attala, *How Water Makes Us Human*, 14.

47 Attala, *How Water Makes Us Human*, 16.

48 And what role does water play in God's shape?

49 Holman, "Public Health and the 'Medicine of Morality'," 5–6. I have to rely on the editors here to have the correct pagination, as I do not know what it might be or how the page numbers have changed.

50 Holman, "Public Health and the 'Medicine of Morality'," 7–8, 16. I have to rely on the editors here to have the correct pagination, as I do not know what it might be or how the page numbers have changed.

51 Holman, "Public Health and the 'Medicine of Morality'," 3. I have to rely on the editors here to have the correct pagination, as I do not know what it might be or how the page numbers have changed.

52 As Steve de Gruchy would have him do. Gruchy, "Water and Spirit," 188–201, at 198.

53 Holman, "Public Health and the 'Medicine of Morality'," 7–8. I have to rely on the editors here to have the correct pagination, as I do not know what it might be or how the page numbers have changed.

54 Inspired by the work of Judith Butler, "New Materialism" argues for a non-essentializing approach to the material world. Among the categories of a method that I do not quite yet understand, the category which would most effectively work with Abba's approach is that of "Bioethics/Biopolitics," a category that addresses questions of human/non-human justice and agency.

55 Besa, *The Life of Shenoute*, 24.

56 Continuing to Glorify the Lord—in López, *Shenoute of Atripe and the Uses of Poverty*.

57 Hussam Hussein, Alberto Natta, Abed Al Kareem Yehya, Baha Hamadna, "Syrian Refugees, Water Scarcity, and Dynamic Policies: How Do the New Refugee Discourses Impact Water Governance Debates in Lebanon and Jordan?" *Water, Selected Papers from 2019 World Water Week* 12, no. 2 (2020).

58 James E. Goehring, *Ascetics, Society, and the Desert: Studies in Early Egyptian Monasticism* (Harrisburg, PA: Trinity Press International, 1999).

59 "Doreen Massey on Time, Space and Responsibility," as quoted in Holman, "Public Health and the 'Medicine of Morality'," 7.

60 A few to note: Helen Rhee, "Portrayal of Patients in Early Christian Sources," *Studia Patristica* LXIII (2017); Helen Rhee, *Wealth and Poverty in Early Christianity*,

Ad Fontes: Early Christian Sources (Lanham: Fortress Press, 2017); Helen Rhee, "Wealth, Business Activities, and Blurring of Christian Identity," *Studia Patristica*, LXII (2013); Helen Rhee, *Loving the Poor, Saving the Rich: Wealth, Poverty, and Early Christian Formation* (Grand Rapids: Baker Academic, 2012), and the recently published *Pain, Illness, and Healthcare in Early Christianity* (Grand Rapids, MI: Eerdmans, 2022).

61 I am including both the terms "pain" and "suffering"—even though they do not mean the same thing—because Rhee notes that she uses the terms interchangeably. Rhee, "Pain in Ancient Medicine and Literature, and Early Christianity," 5. I have to rely on the editors here to have the correct pagination, as I do not know what it might be or how the page numbers have changed.

62 Rhee, "Pain in Ancient Medicine and Literature, and Early Christianity," 1–3. I have to rely on the editors here to have the correct pagination, as I do not know what it might be or how the page numbers have changed.

63 Rhee, "Pain in Ancient Medicine and Literature, and Early Christianity," 3. I have to rely on the editors here to have the correct pagination, as I do not know what it might be or how the page numbers have changed.

64 Galen, *Caus. Symp.* 1.6; Mattern, *Galen and the Rhetoric of Healing*, 123–36; Daniel King, *Experiencing Pain in Imperial Greek Culture* (Oxford: Oxford University Press, 2017), 89. Rhee, "Pain in Ancient Medicine and Literature, and Early Christianity," 2–4.

65 Rhee, "Pain in Ancient Medicine and Literature, and Early Christianity," 3. I have to rely on the editors here to have the correct pagination, as I do not know what it might be or how the page numbers have changed.

66 Clinical practices are governed and constricted by ethical and legal procedures, of which medical health professionals must be aware when attempting to communicate with a patient whose language skills are different from their own. See Tim Venkatesan, Danial Naqvi, and Rakula Patel, "Deconstructing Language Barriers in Healthcare: Where Are We Going Wrong?" *Postgraduate Medical Journal* 1157 (2021). Additionally, while machine translations are useful and transcend barriers of time and location, they lack the cultural competence that a human being might possibly provide. Rachel Showstack, "Patients Don't Have Language Barriers; the Healthcare System Does," *Emergency Medicine Journal* 36, no. 10 (2019): 580–1.

67 Rhee, "Pain in Ancient Medicine and Literature, and Early Christianity," 5–8. I have to rely on the editors here to have the correct pagination, as I do not know what it might be or how the page numbers have changed.

68 Rhee, "Pain in Ancient Medicine and Literature, and Early Christianity," 8–10. I have to rely on the editors here to have the correct pagination, as I do not know what it might be or how the page numbers have changed.

69 Rhee, "Pain in Ancient Medicine and Literature, and Early Christianity," 10–13. I have to rely on the editors here to have the correct pagination, as I do not know what it might be or how the page numbers have changed.

70 Augustine, *City of God, Expositions on the Psalms*, 30, 62.

71 Pseudo-Athanasius, "The Life and Activity of the Holy and Blessed Teacher Syncletica, trans. Elizabeth A. Castelli," in Vincent L. Wimbush (ed.) *Ascetic Behavior in Greco-Roman Antiquity: A Sourcebook*, Studies in Antiquity and Christianity (Minneapolis: Fortress Press, 1990).

72 This is too vast a subject to fill a footnote with titles. Suffice it to say, in addition to all four canonical gospels ending in the public death of Jesus of Nazareth, the suffering Christ and suffering *with* and *in* Christ is a central theme in Pauline and early Christian literature.

73 "While pain is not universally treated as emotion in clinical medicine, a burgeoning body of clinical research suggests that what might be distinguished as pain of mind and pain of body (e.g. 'social rejection' and 'physical pain') share neurological markers, activating common brain regions." Andrew Crislip, "Pain, Emotion, and Identity in Early Christianity," *Journal of Early Christian History* 12, no. 1 (2022): 27–51.

74 *The Life of the Holy Teacher Syncletica* is one of my favourite texts to assign to pre-med and nursing students, mostly because they are appalled by it and never hesitate to make known their feelings about what *they* consider to be some deeply problematic, rhetorical glorification of a very ill woman.

75 Peter A. Mena, "Scenting Saintliness: The Ailing Body, Chicana Feminism, and Communal Identity in Ancient Christianity," *Journal of Feminist Studies in Religion* 33, no. 2 (2017): 6.

76 Rhee, "Pain in Ancient Medicine and Literature, and Early Christianity," 8. I have to rely on the editors here to have the correct pagination, as I do not know what it might be or how the page numbers have changed.

77 Pseudo-Athanasius, *Life of Syncletica*, 110, 309.

78 Pseudo-Athanasius, *Life of Syncletica*, in Wimbush, *Ascetic Behavior*, 106, 308.

79 In full: "Therefore the enemy made this excuse for this blow against her: for having caused pain in one tooth, he made her gums putrid in like manner. And the bone fell out; the spreading passed into her whole jaw, and became decay of the body pressing on the neighbouring parts; and in forty dans the bone was worm-eaten. And within the space of two months' time there was a hole. The surrounding spaces were all becoming black. And the bone itself was corrupted and little by little wasted away; putrefaction and the heaviest stench governed her whole body so that the ones who served her suffered more than she did." Pseudo-Athanasius, *Life of Syncletica*, in Wimbush, *Ascetic Behavior*, 111, 309–10.

80 Rhee, "Pain in Ancient Medicine and Literature, and Early Christianity," 8, in Talal Asad, *Formations of the Secular: Christianity, Islam, Modernity* (Stanford, CA: Stanford University Press, 2003), 85.

81 This is not a discussion about religion, vaccine refusal, and COVID-19; apart from that, physicians face ethical issues about compassionate clinical care when ill individual's religious beliefs support suffering to atone for alleged sinful actions or thoughts. Benjamin W. Frush, John Brewer Eberly Jr, and Farr A. Curlin, "What Should Physicians and Chaplains Do When a Patient Believes God Wants Him to Suffer?" *AMA Journal of Ethics* 20, no. 7 (2018): e613–20.

82 Pseudo-Athanasius, *Life of Syncletica*, in Wimbush, *Ascetic Behavior*, 111, 309–10.

83 Sophocles, *Philoctetes*, trans. Carl Phillips (Oxford: Oxford University Press, 2003). A marginal figure, the different accounts include a snake bite, a wound from a poisoned arrow, and punishment for trespassing on a sacred site.

84 Homer, *Iliad*, trans. Richard Lattimore (Chicago: University of Chicago Press, 2011), 2.716–20.

85 Sophocles, *Philoctetes*, 33.

86 Rhee, "Pain in Ancient Medicine and Literature, and Early Christianity," 10–13; I have to rely on the editors here to have the correct pagination, as I do not know what it might be or how the page numbers have changed; Augustine, *Civ. dei.*, 9.5.

87 See, for example, Matthew O'Reilly, "Paul, Apostle of Pain: 'One of Us-Ness' and the Question of Suffering in 2 Corinthians," *Journal of Early Christian History* 12, no. 1 (2022): 80–95. See also Crislip, "Pain, Emotion, and Identity," 37–40.

88 Anselm versus Abelard—of course, this is all coming later.

89 Augustine, *Civ. dei.*, 21.3.

90 Augustine, *Civ. dei.*, 21.3. This raises some questions for me regarding what—if anything—Augustine had to say about Jesus' physical, emotional, and spiritual health, or if Augustine is working solely from an abstract, theological view of Jesus' body.

91 Pseudo-Athanasius, *Life of Syncletica*, in Wimbush, *Ascetic Behavior*, 106, p. 308.

92 Antigone Samellas, "Public Aspects of Pain in Late Antiquity: The Testimony of Chrysostom and the Cappadocians in Their Graeco-Roman Context," *Zeitschrift für Antikes Christentum* 19, no. 2 (2015): 263.

93 Paul K. Maciejewski et al., "Religious Coping and Behavioral Disengagement: Opposing Influences on Advance Care Planning and Receipt of Intensive Care Near Death," *Psycho-Oncology* 21 (2012): 714–23.
94 Augustine, *Civ. dei*, 9.5.
95 Augustine, *Civ. dei*, 9.5.
96 Rhee, "Pain in Ancient Medicine and Literature, and Early Christianity," 2. I have to rely on the editors here to have the correct pagination, as I do not know what it might be or how the page numbers have changed.
97 Chris L. de Wet, "'The Barbarians Themselves Are Offended by Our Vices': Slavery, Sexual Vice and Shame in Salvian of Marseilles' *De gubernatione Dei*," *Theological Studies* V, 75, no. 3 (April 2019); Chris L. de Wet, "Religious Conflict, Radicalism and Sexual Exceptionalism in John Chrysostom," in Wendy Mayer and Chris L. de Wet, eds., *Reconceiving Religious Conflict: New Views from the Formative Centuries of Christianity* (Abingdon: Routledge, 2018), 70–85; Chris L. de Wet, *The Unbound God: Slavery and the Formation of Early Christian Thought* (Routledge Studies in the Early Christian World) (Abingdon: Routledge, 2017); Chris L. de Wet, "Paul and Christian Identity-Formation in John Chrysostom's Homilies De laudibus sancti Pauli apostoli," *Journal of Early Christian History* V, 3, no. 2 (2013): 34–46.
98 de Wet, "Medical Discourse, Identity Formation, and Otherness in Late Ancient Christianity," 1. I have to rely on the editors here to have the correct pagination, as I do not know what it might be or how the page numbers have changed.
99 Though monastic in nature, the *Penitentials* are an important apothecary of sins and "cures" for laity, intended for the healing of human relationships. See, for example, the *Penitential* of Saint Columban in Terrence G. Kardong, *Saint Columban: His Life, Rule, and Legacy* (Collegeville, MN: Liturgical Press, 2017), 129–48.
100 For an extensive study of the tradition, see Wilhelm Kursawa, *Healing Not Punishment. Historical and Pastoral Networking of the Penitentials between the Sixth and Eighth Centuries* (Turnhout, Belgium: Brepols, 2017).
101 The "very act of compiling such mammoth tomes of knowledge is both totalising and an imperialising act." de Wet, "Medical Discourse, Identity Formation, and Otherness in Late Ancient Christianity, 3. I have to rely on the editors here to have the correct pagination, as I do not know what it might be or how the page numbers have changed.
102 "It is necessary that the specialists come to the aid of those in difficulties, the ones who endure those who offer them insults, even if they box or kick them." Theodoret of Cyrus, "Discourse I, On Faith," in Thomas Halton (trans.) *Theodoret of Cyrus: A Cure for Pagan Maladies* (New York: The Newman Press, 2013), 20.
103 John T. Fitzgerald, *Passions and Moral Progress in Greco-Roman Thought* (London: Routledge, 2007); Martha C. Nussbaum, "Aristotle on Emotions and Ethical Health," *The Therapy of Desire: Theory and Practice in Hellenistic Ethics* (Princeton: Princeton University Press, 2009), 78–101.
104 Amy N. Farley and Bethy Leonardi, "Beyond Bathroom Bills and the Gender Identity Debate: Complicating the Policy Conversation about Supporting Trans Students in Schools," *Educational Policy* (Los Altos, CA) 35, no. 2 (2021): 274–303.
105 de Wet, "Medical Discourse, Identity Formation, and Otherness in Late Ancient Christianity," 6, 9. I have to rely on the editors here to have the correct pagination, as I do not know what it might be or how the page numbers have changed.
106 Einar Thomassen and Johannes van Oort, eds., *The Panarion of Epiphanius of Salamis: Book I (Sects 1–46)*, trans. Frank Williams (Leiden: Brill, 2009), xiii; Francis Young, "Did Epiphanius Know What He Meant by Heresy?" in *Exegesis and Theology in Early Christianity* (London: Routledge, 2012), 199–205.
107 Some have questioned their existence, but what is not in doubt is existence of their theology and ritual practices. It is fair to say that *if* this group did exist, there is no

reason to view their veneration of Mary or rituals as a "strange phenomenon of early Christianity." Stephen Benko, *The Virgin Goddess: Studies in the Pagan and Christian Roots of Mariology* (Leiden: BRILL, 2003), 170; Brenda Llewellyn Ihssen, "Christian Thought in Political, Social and Institutional Contexts: From Μαρία to Maryam," in Lewis Ayres (ed.) *Cambridge History of Early Christian Theology* (Cambridge, forthcoming). More than one scholar has suggested that their female leadership suggests links with Montanism. Benko, *The Virgin Goddess*, 192. Carroll connects Kollyridians with Montanists and Pepuzians, a term used sometimes to refer to Montanists, and other times to designate a distinct Christian group. Michael P. Carroll, *The Cult of the Virgin Mary: Psychological Origins* (Princeton: Princeton University Press, 1986), 41–8. Shoemaker draws attention to studies that do not sufficiently connect the Montanists with the Kollyridians, including Franz J. Dölger, "Die eigenartige Marienverehrung der Philomarianiten oder Kollyridianer in Arabia," *Antike und Christentum* 1 (1929): 1–46. Shoemaker, "Epiphanius of Salamis," 373, note 3.

108 Benko, *The Virgin Goddess*, 170.
109 Averil Cameron, "The Cult of the Virgin in Late Antiquity: Religious Development and Myth-Making," *Studies in Church History* 39, no. 1–21 (2004): 6.
110 A portion of this section on Epiphanius of Salamis is drawn from the forthcoming Llewellyn Ihssen, "From Μαρία to Maryam," see note 107.
111 Richard Flower, "Medicalizing Heresy: Doctors and Patients in Epiphanius of Salamis," *Journal of Late Antiquity* 11, no. 2 (2018): 270; de Wet, "Medical Discourse, Identity Formation, and Otherness," 5–6. I have to rely on the editors here to have the correct pagination, as I do not know what it might be or how the page numbers have changed.
112 Cited in Nicephorus *Adversus Epiphanium* XIV, 61, Pitra, Spicilegium Solesmense, 340,8–10, in Epiphanius and Frank Williams, *The Panarion of Epiphanius of Salamis. Book I (Sects 1–46) I*, trans. Frank Williams, second edition, revised and expanded (Atlanta: SBL Press, 2017), xiii.
113 Williams, *The Panarion*, xiii.
114 de Wet, "Medical Discourse, Identity Formation, and Otherness," 5. I have to rely on the editors here to have the correct pagination, as I do not know what it might be or how the page numbers have changed.
115 Williams, *The Panarion*, Proem I, 3.
116 After presenting some possibilities, he concludes: "[I] am not saying that she remained immortal. But neither am I affirming that she died." Williams, *The Panarion*, 78.11.3–5 (624–5). For an empathetic and fair treatment of the Kollyridians and Epiphanius, see Stephen Shoemaker, "Epiphanius of Salamis, the Kollyridians, and the Early Dormition Narratives: The Cult of the Virgin in the Fourth Century," *Journal of Early Christian Studies* 16, no. 3 (2008): 371–401. See also Llewellyn Ihssen, "From Μαρία to Maryam," note 107.
117 Williams, *The Panarion*, 79.637.
118 Bread as an Element of Sacrifices, in Benko, *The Virgin Goddess*, 173–86.
119 Williams, *The Panarion*, 78.635.
120 Williams, *The Panarion*, 79.637. Benko puts it quite plainly that "What the Kollyridians did came quite naturally to women in the ancient world." Benko, *The Virgin Goddess*, 191.
121 Williams, *The Panarion*, 79.644.
122 Williams, *The Panarion*, 79.644.
123 Williams, *The Panarion*, 79.638.
124 Williams, *The Panarion*, 79.638.
125 From Abel to the son of Zacharias, Epiphanius gleans male figures in the Hebrew Bible and the New Testament who offer sacrifices and function in priestly authority.

Williams, *The Panarion*, 79 (638–9). Additionally, he explores leadership in early Christian communities, emphasizing that the function of the deaconess was only for the sake of women's modesty.

126 Frank Williams, "Against Those Who Are Called Phrygians or Montanists," *The Panarion* 48 (2017): 6–21.
127 Frank Williams, "Against Quintillianists or Pepuzians," *The Panarion* 49 (2017): 22–3.
128 Williams, *The Panarion*, 79.644.
129 Williams, *The Panarion*, 79.637.
130 de Wet, "Medical Discourse, Identity Formation, and Otherness," 6.
131 That is just a brilliant description of heresy, a "psychic poison," in de Wet, "Medical Discourse, Identity Formation, and Otherness," 5. I have to rely on the editors here to have the correct pagination, as I do not know what it might be or how the page numbers have changed.
132 Williams, *The Panarion*, 79.644.
133 de Wet, "Medical Discourse, Identity Formation, and Otherness," 6. I have to rely on the editors here to have the correct pagination, as I do not know what it might be or how the page numbers have changed.
134 Aline Rousselle, *Porneia: On Desire and the Body in Antiquity* (Eugene, OR: Wipf and Stock, 2013), 24–46. Rebecca Flemming, *Medicine and the Making of Roman Women: Gender, Nature, and Authority from Celsus to Galen* (Oxford: Oxford University Press, 2000), 357–61.
135 Helen King, *Hippocrates' Woman: Reading the Female Body in Ancient Greece* (London: Routledge, 1998), 44.
136 W. H. S. Jones, trans., "The Art," in *Hippocrates II* (Cambridge: Harvard University Press, 1959), 201.
137 Bryan S. Turner, *Medical Power and Social Knowledge* (London: Sage, 1995), 84.
138 Turner, *Medical Power and Social Knowledge*, 84.
139 King, *Hippocrates' Woman*, 47.
140 For example: "She said (that she had lost) another, a male, towards the twentieth day. I do not know if whether that was true" *Ep.* 4.6; "The woman from Tenedos aborted on the fourth day, so she said, a thirty-day-old male fetus" *Ep.* 4.20; "The wife of Apemantus' brother on the seventh day aborted a female fetus of sixty days, she said" *Ep.* 4.22. Wesley D. Smith, trans., "Epidemics," in *Hippocrates VII* (Cambridge: Harvard University Press, 1994), 95, 113, 115, respectively.
141 Helen King, "Women's Health in the Hippocratic Corpus," in Helen King (ed.), *Health in Antiquity* (London: Routledge, 2005), 159.
142 Rousselle, *Porneia*, 24; see also Aline Rousselle, "Observation féminine et idéologie masculine: Le corps de la femme d'après les médecins grecs," *Annales. Histoire, Sciences Sociales*, no. 5 (1980): 1089–115.
143 de Wet, "Medical Discourse, Identity Formation, and Otherness," 9. I have to rely on the editors here to have the correct pagination, as I do not know what it might be or how the page numbers have changed.
144 de Wet, "Medical Discourse, Identity Formation, and Otherness," 11. I have to rely on the editors here to have the correct pagination, as I do not know what it might be or how the page numbers have changed.
145 "The readers were, metaphorically, invited into the consulting room, ostensibly to learn from the master physician, but, perhaps more importantly, to applaud and approve his superiority over his rivals." Flower, "Medicalizing Heresy," 252.
146 Rhee, "Pain in Ancient Medicine and Literature, and Early Christianity," 8. I have to rely on the editors here to have the correct pagination, as I do not know what it might be or how the page numbers have changed.

Bibliography

Ancient Sources

Augustine, and Maria Boulding. *The Works of Saint Augustine: A Translation for the 21st Century. Vol. III/15, Expositions of the Psalms 1–32*. Hyde Park, NY: New City Press, 2002.
————. *The Works of Saint Augustine: A Translation for the 21st Century. Vol. III/17, Expositions of the Psalms 51–72*. Hyde Park, NY: New City Press, 2002.
Augustine, and G. R. Evans. *City of God*. S.I: Penguin Books Ltd., 2003.
Besa, and David N. Bell. *The Life of Shenoute*. Kalamazoo, MI: Cistercian Publications, 1983.
Crislip, Andrew, and David Brakke. *Selected Discourses of Shenoute the Great: Community, Theology, and Social Conflict in Late Antique Egypt*. Cambridge: Cambridge University Press, 2015.
Epiphanius, and Frank Williams. *The Panarion of Epiphanius of Salamis. Book I (Sects 1–46) I*. Translated by Frank Williams. Second edition, revised and expanded. Atlanta: SBL Press, 2017.
Hippocrates, and W.H.S. (William Henry Samuel) Jones. *Hippocrates Vol. II with an English Translation by W.H.S. Jones*. Repr. London: Heinemann, 1943.
Hippocrates, and Wesley D. Smith. *Hippocrates. Vol. VII*. Edited by Wesley D. Smith. Translated by Wesley D. Smith. Cambridge, MA: Harvard University Press, 1994.
Lattimore, Richard. *The Iliad of Homer*. Chicago, IL: University of Chicago Press, 2011.
Layton, Bentley. *The Canons of Our Fathers: Monastic Rules of Shenoute*. Oxford: Oxford University Press, 2014.
Phillips, Carl, and Diskin Clay. *Philoctetes: The Greek Tragedy in New Translations*. Oxford: Oxford University Press, 2003.
Pseudo-Athanasius, and Elizabeth Castelli. "The Life and Activity of the Holy and Blessed Teacher Syncletica." In Wimbush, Vincent L. (ed.) *Ascetic Behavior in Greco-Roman Antiquity: A Sourcebook*. Minneapolis: Fortress Press, 1990.
Terrence Kardong, Columban, and Columban Waldebert. *Saint Columban: His Life, Rule, and Legacy*. Athens, OH: Cistercian Publications, 2017.
Theodoretus, and Thomas P. Halton. *Theodoret of Cyrus: A Cure for Pagan Maladies*. New York: The Newman Press, 2013.

Modern Sources

Asad, Talal. *Formations of the Secular: Christianity, Islam, Modernity*. Stanford, CA: Stanford University Press, 2003.
Attala, Luci. *How Water Makes Us Human: Engagements with the Materiality of Water*. Cardiff: University of Wales Press, 2019.
Benko, Stephen. *The Virgin Goddess: Studies in the Pagan and Christian Roots of Mariology*. Leiden: Brill, 2003.
Bolman, Elizabeth S., Stephen J. Davis, Gillian Pyke, Mohammed Abdel Rahim, Louise Blanke, Darlene L. Brooks Hedstrom, Wendy Dolling, et al. "Shenoute and a Recently Discovered Tomb Chapel at the White Monastery." *Journal of Early Christian Studies* 18, no. 3 (2010): 453–62.
Brooks Hedstrom, Darlene L. *Monastic Landscape of Late Antique Egypt: An Archaeological Reconstruction*. Cambridge: Cambridge University Press, 2021.
Cameron, Averil. "The Cult of the Virgin in Late Antiquity: Religious Development and Myth-Making." *Studies in Church History* 39 (2004): 1–21.

Carroll, Michael P. *The Cult of the Virgin Mary: Psychological Origins*. Princeton, NJ: Princeton University Press, 1986.

Crislip, Andrew. "Shenoute of Atripe on Christ the Physician and the Cure of Souls." *Le Muséon* 122, no. 3 (2009): 247–77.

———. "Pain, Emotion, and Identity in Early Christianity." *Journal of Early Christian History* 12, no. 1 (2022): 27–51.

De Gruchy, Steve. "Water and Spirit: Theology in the Time of Cholera." *The Ecumenical Review* 62, no. 2 (2010): 188–201.

de Wet, Chris L. "Paul and Christian Identity-Formation in John Chrysostom's Homilies *De Laudibus Sancti Pauli Apostoli*." *Journal of Early Christian History* 3, no. 2 (2013): 34–46.

———. "Of Monsters and Men: Religious Conflict, Radicalism, and Sexual Exceptionalism in the Works of John Chrysostom." *Journal of Early Christian History* 6, no. 2 (2016): 1–17.

———. *The Unbound God: Slavery and the Formation of Early Christian Thought*. London: Routledge, 2018.

———. "'The Barbarians Themselves Are Offended by Our Vices': Slavery, Sexual Vice and Shame in Salvian of Marseilles' De Gubernatione Dei." *HTS Teologiese Studies/ Theological Studies* 75, no. 3 (2019): 1–8.

———. "Medical Discourse, Identity Formation, and Otherness in Early Eastern Christianity." In this volume.

Dölger, Franz J. "Die eigenartige Marienverehrung der Philomarianiten oder Kollyridianer in Arabia." *Antike und Christentum* 1 (1929): 1–46.

"Doreen Massey on Time, Space and Responsibility," excerpt from a lecture at Institut für Raumexperimente, UdK Berlin April 2013. Last accessed on 8 October 2022.

Farley, Amy N., and Bethy Leonardi. "Beyond Bathroom Bills and the Gender Identity Debate: Complicating the Policy Conversation About Supporting Trans Students in Schools." *Educational Policy* (Los Altos, CA) 35, no. 2 (2021): 274–303.

Fitzgerald, John T. *Passions and Moral Progress in Greco-Roman Thought*. London: Routledge, 2007.

Flemming, Rebecca. *Medicine and the Making of Roman Women: Gender, Nature, and Authority from Celsus to Galen*. Oxford: Oxford University Press, 2001.

Flower, Richard. "Medicalizing Heresy: Doctors and Patients in Epiphanius of Salamis." *Journal of Late Antiquity* 11, no. 2 (2018): 251–73.

Frush, Benjamin W., Jr Eberly, and Farr A. Curlin. "What Should Physicians and Chaplains Do When a Patient Believes God Wants Him to Suffer?" *AMA Journal of Ethics* 20, no. 7 (2018): e613–20.

Geurs, Karl, Ralph Sanchez, and Robert Sabaroff. "Home Soil." *Star Trek, the Next Generation*. Season 1, Episode 17. 1988. Last accessed on 8 October 2022.

Goehring, James E. *Ascetics, Society, and the Desert: Studies in Early Egyptian Monasticism*. Harrisburg, PA: Trinity Press International, 1999.

Grimes, Ronald L. "Ritual Theory and the Environment." *The Sociological Review* (Keele) 51, no. s2 (2003): 31–45.

Grossmann, Peter, بيتر، جروسمان, Darlene L. Brooks Hedstrom, and Saad Mohamad Mohamad Osman. "Second Report on the Excavation in the Monastery of Apa Shenute (Dayr Anba Shinuda) at Suhag." *Dumbarton Oaks Papers* 63 (2009): 167–219.

Hitchens, Christopher. *God Is Not Great: How Religion Poisons Everything*. New York: Grand Central Publishing, 2007.

Holman, Susan R. *The Hungry Are Dying: Beggars and Bishops in Roman Cappadocia*. New York: Oxford University Press, 2001.

————. *God Knows There's Need: Christian Responses to Poverty.* New York: Oxford University Press, 2009.

————. *Beholden: Religion, Global Health, and Human Rights.* New York, NY: Oxford University Press, 2015.

————. "Shaping Water: Public Health and the 'Medicine of Morality' in Late Antiquity." In this volume.

Hussein, Hussam, Alberto Natta, Abed Al Kareem Yehya, and Baha Hamadna. "Syrian Refugees, Water Scarcity, and Dynamic Policies: How Do the New Refugee Discourses Impact Water Governance Debates in Lebanon and Jordan?" *Water* 12, no. 2 (2020): 325.

King, Daniel. *Experiencing Pain in Imperial Greek Culture.* Oxford: Oxford University Press, 2017.

King, Helen. *Hippocrates' Woman: Reading the Female Body in Ancient Greece.* London: Routledge, 1998.

————. *Health in Antiquity.* London: Routledge, 2005.

Krawiec, Rebecca. *Shenoute & the Women of the White Monastery: Egyptian Monasticism in Late Antiquity.* New York: Oxford University Press, 2002.

Kursawa, Wilhelm. *Healing Not Punishment: Historical and Pastoral Networking of the Penitentials Between the Sixth and Eighth Centuries.* Turnhout, Belgium: Brepols Publishers, 2017.

Layton, Bentley. *The Canons of Our Fathers: Monastic Rules of Shenoute.* 1st ed. Oxford: Oxford University Press, 2014.

Llewellyn Ihssen, Brenda. "Christian Thought in Political, Social and Institutional Contexts: From Μαρία to Maryam." In Ayres, Lewis (ed.) *Cambridge History of Early Christian Theology* (Cambridge: Cambridge University Press, forthcoming).

López, Ariel G. *Shenoute of Atripe and the Uses of Poverty: Rural Patronage, Religious Conflict and Monasticism in Late Antique Egypt.* Berkeley, CA: University of California Press, 2013.

Macdonell, Diane. *Theories of Discourse: An Introduction.* Oxford: Blackwell, 1986.

Maciejewski, Paul K., Andrea C. Phelps, Elizabeth L. Kacel, Tracy A. Balboni, Michael Balboni, Alexi A. Wright, William Pirl, and Holly G. Prigerson. "Religious Coping and Behavioral Disengagement: Opposing Influences on Advance Care Planning and Receipt of Intensive Care Near Death." *Psycho-oncology* (Chichester, England) 21, no. 7 (2012): 714–23.

Manger, Lois N. *A History of Medicine.* New York: Marcel Dekker, Inc., 1992.

Mattern, Susan P. *Galen and the Rhetoric of Healing.* Baltimore, MD: Johns Hopkins University Press, 2008.

Mena, Peter Anthony. "Scenting Saintliness: The Ailing Body, Chicana Feminism, and Communal Identity in Ancient Christianity." *Journal of Feminist Studies in Religion* 33, no. 2 (2017): 5–20.

Nussbaum, Martha C. "Chapter 3: Aristotle on Emotions and Ethical Health." In *The Therapy of Desire.* Vol. 98. Princeton: Princeton University Press, 2009.

O'Reilly, Matt. "Paul, Apostle of Pain: 'One of Us-Ness' and the Question of Suffering in 2 Corinthians." *Journal of Early Christian History* 12, no. 1 (2022): 80–95.

Phiri, Isabel Apawo. "God of Life Lead Us to Water Justice," the Steve de Gruchy Memorial Lecture, Rodebosch United Church, Cape Town, South Africa, 24 April 2018. Last accessed on 8 October 2022.

Rhee, Helen. *Loving the Poor, Saving the Rich: Wealth, Poverty, and Early Christian Formation.* Grand Rapids: Baker Academic, 2012.

————. "Wealth, Business Activities, and Blurring of Christian Identity." *Studia Patristica* LXII, Papers presented at the Sixteenth International Conference on Patristic Studies held in Oxford 2011. Edited by Markus Vincent. Studia Patristica. Leuven: Peeters, 2013, 245–57.

———. "Portrayal of Patients in Early Christian Sources." *Studia Patristica* LXXXI, Papers Presented at the Seventeenth International Conference on Patristic Studies Held in Oxford 2015. Vol. 7, Health, Medicine And Christianity in Late Antiquity. Edited by Jared Secord, Heidi Marx-Wolf, Christoph Markschies, and Markus Vincent. *Studia Patristica*. Leuven: Peeters, 2017, 127–38.

———. *Wealth and Poverty in Early Christianity*. Lanham: Fortress Press, 2017.

———. *Pain, Illness, and Healthcare in Early Christianity*. Grand Rapids, MI: Eerdmans, 2022.

———. "Pain in Ancient Medicine and Literature, and Early Christianity: Paradox of Inshareability and Agency." In this volume.

Rousselle, Aline. "Observation féminine et idéologie masculine: Le corps de la femme d'après les médecins grecs." *Annales: Histoire, Sciences Sociales* 35, no. 5 (1980): 1089–115.

———. *Porneia: On Desire and the Body in Antiquity*. Eugene, OR: Wipf and Stock, 2013.

Samellas, Antigone. "Public Aspects of Pain in Late Antiquity: The Testimony of Chrysostom and the Cappadocians in Their Graeco-Roman Context." *Zeitschrift für antikes Christentum* 19, no. 2 (2015): 260–96.

Schroeder, Caroline T. "'A Suitable Abode for Christ': The Church Building as Symbol of Ascetic Renunciation in Early Monasticism." *Church History* 73, no. 3 (2004): 472–521.

———. *Monastic Bodies: Discipline and Salvation in Shenoute of Atripe*. Philadelphia: University of Pennsylvania Press, 2011.

Shinall Jr., Myrick C. "The Separation of Church and Medicine." *Religion, Patients, and Medical Ethics, AMA Journal of Ethics* 11, no. 10 (2009): 745–9.

Shoemaker, Stephen J. "Epiphanius of Salamis, the Kollyridians, and the Early Dormition Narratives: The Cult of the Virgin in the Fourth Century." *Journal of Early Christian Studies* 16, no. 3 (2008): 371–401.

Showstack, Rachel. "Patients Don't Have Language Barriers; the Healthcare System Does." *Emergency Medicine Journal: EMJ* 36, no. 10 (2019): 580–1.

Turner, Bryan S. *Medical Power and Social Knowledge: Medical Power and Social Knowledge*. 2nd ed. London: Sage Publications Ltd., 2007.

Venkatesan, Tim, Danial Naqvi, and Bakula Patel. "Deconstructing Language Barriers in Healthcare: Where Are We Going Wrong?" *Postgraduate Medical Journal* 98, no. 1157 (2021): 157–8.

Wortley, John. "What the Desert Fathers Meant by Being Saved." *Zeitschrift für antikes Christentum* 12, no. 2 (2008): 286–307.

Young, Frances. "Did Epiphanius Know What He Meant by Heresy?" In *Exegesis and Theology in Early Christianity*. 1st ed. London: Routledge, 2012, 199–205.

Index